KABIR
THE APOSTLE OF HINDU-MUSLIM UNITY

GREAT SAINTS OF INDIA SERIES

KABIR

The Apostle of Hindu-Muslim Unity

By

O.P. Ralhan

ANMOL PUBLICATIONS PVT. LTD.
NEW DELHI - 110 002 (INDIA)

ANMOL PUBLICATIONS PVT. LTD.
4374/4B, Ansari Road, Daryaganj
New Delhi - 110 002
Ph.: 23261597, 23278000
Visit us at: www.anmolpublications.com

Kabir: The Apostle of Hindu-Muslim Unity

First Published, 2004

ISBN 81-261-1826-1

PRINTED IN INDIA

Published by J.L. Kumar for Anmol Publications Pvt. Ltd., New Delhi - 110 002 and Printed at Mehra Offset Press, Delhi.

Dedicated to

The Sweet and Everlasting Memory

of

My Beloved Father

(LATE) FAQIR CHAND RALHAN

Contents

Preface ix

1. Kabir Sahib (1398-1518 A.D.) (As an Avtar of Shuk Deva) 1
2. Birth of Kabir Sahib 3
3. Controversy of Kabir's Date of Birth 11
4. Kabirs' Place of Birth 15
5. Early Life of Kabir 21
6. Spiritual Guru of Kabir 28
7. Domestic Life of Kabir 31
8. Birth of Kamal and Kamali 39
9. The Happy Home of Kabir 42
10. Kabir and Kamal as Robbers 44
11. Banaras Traditions and Kabir 49
12. Atrocities of Sikandar Lodhi on Kabir 52
13. Death of Kabir Sahib 59
14. Kabir Panth 62
15. Teaching of Kabir Sahib 73
16. Kabir and Guru Nanak 92
17. Works of Kabir Sahib 97
18. Kabir Hymns 119

Index 286

Preface

Kabir lived on the threshold of a momentous period in Indian history. The most probable year of Kabir's birth, 1398 A.D., coincides with Timur's invasion. Describing his attack on the fort of Hanumangarh Timur wrote in his Memoirs that the heads of ten thousand infidels (Kaffirs) were cut off. The sword of Islam was washed in the blood of the infidels (Kaffirs). Thereafter Timur turned his attention to the city of Sarsuti because the people of the place were strangers to the religion of Islam. In his sack of Delhi, Timur got all the Hindus killed while sparing the Muslims. Next day he issued orders that the Muslim prisoners should be separated and saved and the Kaffirs should be despatched to hell. He also instructed to spare the houses of the Sayyids, Sheikhs and learned Muslims and the houses of Hindus should be plundered and the fort be destroyed. It is said that there were one lakh Hindu prisoners in the camp of Timur. He got all those innocent and helpless prisoners slain in a blood bath unparalleled in the history of the world. Timur further recorded in his Memoirs that Maulana Nasir-ud-din Umar, a counsellor and a man of learning who throughout of his life had never killed a sparrow, now in execution of my orders, slew with his own sword, fifteen idolater Hindus who were his captives. Thus Islamization by the persisted throughout the rule of the Muslims in India. Timur further recorded that my main object in coming to Hindustan had been to accomplish two things. The first was to wage war with the Kaffirs and to acquire some claims to reward in the life to come. The other was to give a chance to the army of Islam to gain something by plundering the wealth and valuables of the infidels (Kaffirs); plunder in war is as lawful as their mothers milk to the Muhammadans.

Before Timur's invasion the Sultanate of Delhi had been a strong government and had exercised great power. But the most disastrous reign of Muhammad bin Tughlaq (1325-1351 A.D.) initiated its decline and though his successor, Firoz Shah Tughlaq (1351-1388 A.D.) was a little bit better ruler he did little to prevent the disintegration of the Sultanate. The process was speeded by Firoz Shah's death, after which a civil war broke out between his son and grandson. Local Hindu chiefs renounced their allegiance and the governors of the provinces became more or less independent. This weakness of the kingdom invited foreign invasion and Timur, the Mongol from Samarqand, came as had the Muslim invanders four centuries earlier looking for slaves and booty. After terrible destruction, including the sacking of Delhi Timur returned back having dealt a fatal blow to the Delhi Sultanate. Possibly it could not have survived long in any case, but certainly Timur's raid effectively prevented the Tughlaqs from regaining their control. Indeed, the familiar story of dynastic decay repeated itself as in the decade following Firoz's death. Six Sultans briefly occupied the throne. The last of the Tughlaq Line, Mahmud Shah, fled Delhi during Timur's invasion but although he returned to the capital city and managed to stay on the throne until 1413 A.D., he was not able to ensure the succession to a member of his house. The various provinces which had been under the control of the Tughlaqs now became independent and remained so even after the Sayyids finally came to power in Delhi and a small adjoining area.

By the beginning of the fifteenth century the Tughlaq dynasty had ended and that of the Sayyids and the Lodhis begun with the installation Khizar Khan as emperor (1414). He was followed by Mubarak Shah (22 May 1421) and his successors Sultan Mohammad Shah and Ala-ud-din, and on 19 April 1453 Bahlol Lodhi, the first of the Lodhis ascended the throne. After Bahlol came Sikandar Lodhi whose name was Nizam Khan.

About Sikandar Lodhi, Elliot and Dowson had recorded, he was so zealous a Musalman that he utterly destroyed diverse places of worship of the infidels (Kaffirs) and left not a vestige remaining of them. He entirely ruined the shrines of Mathura, the mine of heathenism and turned their Hindu places of worship into caravan, serais and colleges. Their stone images were given to the butchers to serve them as meat, weights and all the Hindus in Mathura were strictly prohibited from shaving their heads and beards and performing their ablutions.

Krishna P. Bahadur in his book entitled 'A New Look at Kabir' has written that Sikandar Lodhi's reigned from 1448 to 1517. He visited Banaras is historically confirmed. According to John Briggs the Shah's army crossed the Ganga river in the Moslem year Hijri 900, i.e. 1494 A.D. in order to fight with Hussain Shah Sharqi and the two armies faced each other about 27 miles off Banaras. In his commentary on the Bhaktamal, Priyadas also mentions about the ill treatment of Kabir by Sikandar Lodi, and in confirmation of the many ways in which the king tried to get rid of the poet it is mentioned in these verses that elephants were brought out so that they would trample on Kabir and he was bound in chains and cast into the Ganga river, but was miraculously saved.

Thus, it is clear beyond doubt that Sikandar Lodhi visited Banaras and perpetrated many tortures on Kabir (In 1494 Sikandar Lodhi captured Banaras as a part of his campaign against the Sharqi Hussain Shah of Jaunpur and it continued under Lodhi control until after their defeat of Panipat in 1526. Kabir's Mythology by David (Scott).... Such was the miserable political condition during Kabir Sahib's times.

About the social conditions in one of his Dohas Kabir said, that prostitutes used to wandered in the streets at night seeking clients, and thieves roamed nightlnog. People were characterless. The Hindu society was caste ridden, abuse of child marriage, cruelty towards widows lack of education, superstition and untouchability. The caste divide was so great that higher caste Hindus would not let even the shadow of an untouchable touch them ! Hindu society was in bad shape. People mistrusted each other, as Kabir noticed—selfishness, mine and thine and vanity swayed people. The

Muslim rulers added to the ills of Hindu society by forcing Hindu girls to marry Muslim boys, and very often royal princesses of Hindu kingdoms were carried off by victorious Muslim kings as prizes for their harems. That was the reason for the mass immolations (Jauhars) of Hindu queens and women of the royal household, such as the one which occurred at Chittor when Padmini and the other queens numbering several thousands burnt themselves after Ala-ud-din's sack of Mewar. The Muslim conquest had a great impact on Hindu society. The view that many low caste Hindus embraced Islam willingly because of their ill-treatment by those of the upper caste, is quite mistaken. The fact is that the condition imposed by Muslim rulers or the sword was very terrifying, and many, irrespective of caste, could not face death. With the Muslim rulers a difference cropped up inasmuch as after, every victory Hindu girls were carried off as slaves, and they made no distinction between a common girl and one of a high family, for them all of them were infidels (Kaffir's). Even princesses were carried off to swell Muslim harems. Mohammed bin Tughlaq sent to Chinese emperor, 'one hundred men as slaves and one hundred slave songstresses dancers from among the Indian infidels.. There was a great disparity in the society. The Jungle Raj was prevailing everywhere. The poor and weaker section of society was being exploited by the rich and the ruling class. The women were the worst effected. Might is the Right was the rule of the day. Grave injustices were done to the oppressed and the depressed class of the society.

Having briefly described the essential elements of the political and social conditions of that period during which Kabir Sahib lived, lets have a galance of the religious setting in Northern India at that time. Budhism had completely disappeared and Jainism was confined to a certain portion in the west. Complete control of Brahamanism was supreme over the entire sub-continent. Society was divided among castes and sub-castes. Marathi Poet Namdev, Punjabi Poet Nanak, Telgu Poet Vemana, Kannada Poet Basaveshwar and Gujarati Poet Akho share with Kabir a rare kind of catholicity and humanism which broke all connections of caste, creed or cult.

This was all the more difficult in that age when orthodoxy had a firm hold over the minds of the people. Kabir is being re-evaluated as the first rebel poet and the earliest modernist in Hindu criticism. Kabir was a dominant force in shunning caste system, the most poisonous ulcer in Indian social order. He struck the death-knell to the existing system of caste according to birth and preached unity of man in all his thousands of his songs which are on the lips of the rich and the poor even today.

The long life span of Kabir Sahib is a story of great struggle. He had struggled at home, struggle on streets and struggle in the royal court. Kabir's entire life is full of controversies. About the place of Kabir's birth there are three opinions : Magahar, Kashi and Belahara village. About Kabir's parents and his caste, too, there are several versions ruling out the miracles that he was born of divine light, or found on a full blooming lotus in the Lahartara, the two plausible versions are that he was born a discarded child. Three theories are current about his caste. He called himself in his writings a jolaha and a kori. Jolaha means a weaver, and most of the weavers in Varanasi are Muslims. Kori is a kind of weaver and in Uttar Pradesh they are considered a lower caste. According to Dr. Hazari Prasad Dwivedi, Kabir belonged to a caste named Jogi. Kabir refers to his father as Gosain, who were weavers converted to Islam. Kabir has always called himself a Jolaha, but has never referred to himself as a Muslim but has never reffered to himself 'neither Hindu nor Muslim'. Two names—Ramanand and Sheikh Taqqi have been attached with Kabir as his gurus. About his date of birth different scholars have given different date—1398, 1440... 1380, etc. etc. The question of Kabir's dates has been the subject of endless controversies. About the education discipleship, too, there are several inferences.

Kabir's family life does not seem to have been happy. Though a relentless seeker, he did not despise earthy ties but raised a family and laboured to feed it. Several legends name Loi as his wife, whose parentage is, however, unknown. How and where they were married is also shrouded in mystery. Dr. Ram Kumar Verma has advanced a theory based, according to him, on internal evidence in Kabir's writings, that Kabir had two wives, one homely, the other pretty. The second wife was called Dhania or Ramjaniya. As the latter name is also used for dancing girls, Dr. Verma suggests that this second consort was probably a courtesan. Needless to say this thesis is not accepted by the followers of the Kabir sect, and indeed resented by them. It is however, generally accepted that Kabir had a son named Kamal and a daughter named Kamali. This is amplyy evident in Kabir's writings where he has used almost harsh words in describing his wife—'bad looking, low-caste, ill mannered'. (Kurupi, Kujati, Kulasshmi).

About the year of his death, there are four different views: some place it is 1447; some in 1511; some in 1517. Anantdas maintains that Kabir lived a long life of 120 years. Shyam Sundar Das believes that Kabir died in 1517. Sir W.W. Hunter gave Kabir's date in his Indian Empire as 1380 to 1420. Harprasad Shastri put it as 1398-1518.

Kabir was a widely travelled holyman. Acharya Kshiti Mohan Sen has referred to Kabir's journey to Gujarat. Khulasatuttavarikh says that he had been to Ratnapur. In a verse included in the Adi Granth, Kabir refers to his pilgrimage to Gomati river bank, where lived a Muslim holyman whom he calls Pitambar Pir.

Haj hamari Gomati tir,
Jahan basai Pitambar Pir!

(My Haj is on the banks of Gomati, where resides the Pitambar Pir—yellow robed Pir). *Ain-e-Akbari* mentions that Kabir had been at Jagannath Puri in Orissa and *A History of Maratha People* records his travel up to Pandharpur in south Maharashtra. Kabir Mansur a work popular among the devotees of the sect, relates that Kabir went to Baghdad, Samarkand and Bokhara. But this again appears to be more of a mental projection than a historical fact. As these places were historically famous and associated with celebrated Persian Sufis, it seemed appropriate that Kabir should have visited them.

The plain speaking of Kabir and his general disregard for the connections of society raised up enemies on every side. According to Kabir Panthi tradition it was Shaikh Taqqi who voiced the feelings of Muhammedans. The famous Pir came before the Emperor Sikandar Lodi and accused Kabir of laying claim to Divine attributes. He urged that such conduct merited the penality of death. The orthodox Brahmins called him irreligious and carried tales of his intimacy with a woman of ill fame. The Emperor ordered that Kabir should be put to death. He was accordingly put to chains and placed on a boat which was filled with stones. The boat sunk but Kabir reappeared. Second time he was captured and an attempt was made to burn him alive, this attempt too did not succeed. Again he was put before a infuriated elephant but survived.

Kabir was not only a religious but a great social reformer who tried to bring in his life and literature, the followers of Hinduism and Islam nearer. He strongly condmned the caste system in the society. His writings are rich with the religious tolerance, sense of fraternity and suggestions of social reform. Kabir was a social reformer who was fully conscious of the shortcomings and ills of the society and wanted to remedy them. He was much pained to see the miserable condition of the society. He said that the Brahmins did not study the Vedas and become devoid of Vedic knowledge, and Shudras had taken their place. The cheats lived comfortably and the honest starved. Chaste women were without clothes, while the prostitites had plenty money to waste. The people had to respect for the learned persons, whereas the hypocrites became the heads of the society. The milkman vends from house to house in the lanes and by-lanes to sell milk, but the wine-dealer sells wine from his counter easily.

He was the man who's thousands of songs and couprets full of with spiritual message and worldly wisdom, and who professed oneness of the entire humanity and well being of all his fellow men on earth. Kabir Sahib wept bitterly and said in a complet:

All the people are living happily

Eating and sleeping soundly
Das Kabir alone is sorrowing
Awake and weeping profusely

Kabir Sahib was much pained due to the desparately and exploitation of the weaker section in the society when the Hindu society was being depressed by the cruel and ruthlers torture by the Muslim rulers six-seven hundred years ago. No doubt there is a lot of change due to changed circumstances. Politically we are free. There is a over all awakening in the society. A certain class of people have been priviliged by all types of comforts and they are enjoying life. But due to irony of fate, the poorer and weaker sections of society till now have only been rewarded with a right of vote and nothing else. This class is still being exploited ruthly; they are half starved, half naked, no employment opportunity, dying without medicines. Though India has been declared as a warfare state; there is nobody to safeguard the interests of this class. The country is being ruled by most corrupt politicians, most corrupt beaurucracy and most corrupt police force. There is not a single person in politics, in religious, in social and cultural field to whom one could name. People who are supposed to shape the destiny of the Nations changed their loyality overnight. By doing so they are not only deceiving themselves but also deceiving the most innocent and loyal class of Indian who are dedicated and could safeguard the interests of the Nation. Caste based reservation has proved a miserably failure and proved only a vote catching source for the corrupt forces in the country. Those who can manage money and muscle power can grap power and rule the country of their will and fancy. The poorer, weaker and loyal section of the society and the intellectuals of this country have no role to play... as they are a neglect lot.... there is no reservation for this class anywhere...

The religious position in the country is more pathetic. As one can see over crowded religious places day and night. The country has been flooded with living goods every where... Their followers are in lakhs of numbers. But in practical life the religion is not visible anywhere. Can anybody imagine a country like ours which is known world over as most religious country wherein people like Lord Ram, Lord Krishan, Mahavir, Buddha, Tulsi Dasji and Kabir Sahib, Guru Nanak and numerous sufi saints and sages born.... is full of corruption, what happened to those dreams of our beloved leader who dreamt to set up a society and government in an independent India where only intellectuals will rule the country and money and muscle power won't effect the functioning of the government.

Anmol Publications Pvt. Ltd. deserve appreciation who has taken the decision to publish biographies of Indian saints because Goswami Tulsidasji and Kabir Sahib's writings are more relevant today in the materialistic period where poorer and weaker section of society is being deprived by their legitimate demands. Present day India's political, social and religious conditions required immediate and revolutionary changes in the set up. Kabir Sahib stood for such people, fought for them and was desirious for the set up of such a society where humanity should get upper hand not the corruption, money and muscle power. This book must reach to the maximum readers to enable and empower them to fight against the present system.

I am grateful my all colleagues who have helped me to complete this book.

O.P. Ralhan
New Delhi

1

Kabir Sahib
(1398 - 1518 A.D.)
(As an Avatar of Shuk Deva)

Background

Valmiki, the well known writer of the great epic *Ramayana* while going to practise austerities he was abandoned by his parents in a forest. *Kiratas* (forest hunters) took him and brought him up as a robber. He became clever at archery and once when going to kill a sage he asked him to go and ask his wife and children if they would share his nefarious deeds. Being convinced that they would not, he repented and practise severe austerities by repeating the two letters in the word 'Rama' (रा+म) in the reverse order until he was enveloped by Valmik (an ant-hill) and therefore he was called Valmiki. Once moved through pity he cursed a hunter who had killed a pair of *Kraunch* birds. The curse was in the form of a couplet which came naturally from his lips. Brahmadeva asked him to compose the *Ramayana*. When Shri Ram abandoned Sita in the forest he took care of her when Kusha and Lava were born he educated them and sent them to Shri Ram.[1]

While Narayan was reclining on the serpent Shesh in the sea of milk, some of his bhakats arrived. Udhav[2], Akrur[3], Valmiki, Dhruva[4], Prahlada[5] and Shuka coming near him paid their reverence to the Yadavas. The saviour of the world said to Valmiki, 'In the Kali Yuga sins have become intolerable. I wish you to become an avatar among mortals and bring about the salvation of men. The Ramayana which you composed, in which you sang my name, goodness and good deeds was in the Sanskrit language which the ignorant people of the Kali Yuga did not understand. So becoming an avatar among mortals, set them to worshipping me. Valmiki hearing him say this made obeisance to him. In the northern part of the country, in the city of Hastanapur (Delhi) in the house of a Kanoja Brahman, the Rishi Valmiki became a voluntary avatar. The Brahman bore the name of Atma Ram. He became a man devoted to religion and of perfect good deeds. Mughal Emperor Akbar was king of the country at that time, and he was in the service of Akbar. Atma Ram was a wise Brahman and he enjoyed the king's favour. It was in his family that Valmiki became an avatar. The good Brahman Atma Ram, performed rituals of birth and naming of his son. He was named as Tulsidas[6].

Notes and References

1. Mahipatis Bhakatvijaya, translation, p. 413-414.
2. Udhava - The nephew of Vasudeva, a great devotee of Shri Krishna and always accompanied him. They loved each other very much. When Shri Krishna departed from Gokul to Mathura he sent Udhava to console the Gopis and Nanda and Yashoda. Shri Krishna explained to him the knowledge of the soul as he (Shri Krishna) passed away from this world. Then he went to Badrikashram in accordance with Krishna's command.
3. Akrur - one of the Yadavas, the son of Shavaphalka and Gandini, and always taking Shri Krishna's side. Considering him to be a faithful messanger, Kansa sent him to fetch Shri Krishna to Mathura from Gokul and kill him. But he explained all Kansa's plans to Shri Krishna. By many stratagems he had obtained the possession of the Syamantal jewel.
4. Dhruva - The son of king Uttanapad and Suniti. His step mother insulted him in his childhood and through anger he left his father, went into the jungle and performed severe austerities. Vishnu was pleased with these and so He gave him an sternal place.
5. Pralhad - The eldest of the four sons of Hiranya Kashipubozn from Kayadhu. While he was in his mother's womb he became a devotee of God by hearing the discourses of Narad. As he was a born bhakta of Vishnu his fther persecuted him very much. At last Vishnu assumed the avtar of Narasinha and killed his father, and thus protected him.
6. Mahipatis' Bhakatvijyas translation - p. 32-33.

2

Birth of Kabir Sahib

About the birth of Kabir Mahipati in his book entitled Bhaktavijaya has recorded the following story:-

Listen now, my hearers, to a story that is very interesting and very purifying. In thinking of its sweetness it is sweeter than nectar. This comparison even seems inadequate. I undertake to describe its purity. It seems to be superior to the river Gangas. If I look at the great extent of its influence, I have nothing with which to compare it. If I look to its depths of meaning, it looks deeper than the sea. It is more generous than the generous wish-tree to whom a prince and a pauper are alike. If I think of how it brings coolness, a comparison of it with the moon is inadequate. Although the lustre of a diamond is most precious, still the light of this story would dim it. If I look to the honour paid to it, it is sung by the five-faced god (Shiva). An equal would be impossible to find, so Indra and other gods search for it. Such being the holy story of a saint, listen, you pious folks, with reverence.... That a shell came floating down the river Bhima, and from it Gonai received the bhakta Nama. The shell fell into the Bhagirathi river, and was floating down exceedingly fast. This very obstinate avatar of Shuka was not born in the natural way, and floating down the river Ganges landed at the Manikarnika Ghat of Banares. Becoming one with human attributes, through his unnatural form of birth, he continued repeating the name of God with his lips. From the shell a sound was continually coming out. It was of 'Ram, Ram'. Just then Kamal the Muhammadan weaver came down to wash his thread. As he looked down he happened to see the shell. He waded in the water, opened the shell and looked in. There his eyes beheld a baby, and his heart was full of joy. It was as if a man without making any efforts finds a hidden store of wealth; or as if one hunting for a pool of water should suddenly see the ocean of milk; or as if one stringing glass beads, one should find them to be pearls; or as when picking up shells, one should find there a jewel; or as when hunting for the city of Yama (god of death), one should find the city of Vishnu; or as when hunting for a hut habitable to live in, one should find himself entering a golden palace, or as when seeking to hear some obscene music, one should hear a service of praise of God; or as when one might go to watch a quarrel, it should turn out to be a song from the Sama Veda; or as when spending one's energy on the shindi palm (wine yielding) tree, he should come across a wish-tree in his compound; or as when beginning to associate with a thief or immoral person, suddenly one's religious teacher should come to visit him; so, while merely carrying on his daily business, Kamal found this baby in the river Ganges. This child was the avatar of Shri Shuka[1] in this Kali Yuga, the universal saviour, a world-Guru. He wrapped the baby up in his garment, and hastened to his home. With heart over flowing with joy he said to his wife, 'I have found a baby in the Ganges, of perfect beauty, endowed with thirty two qualities. My dear wife, take care of it'. Hearing this, his wife's breasts swelled with milk. She nursed the child and her joy overflowed. A great Vaishnava was born in a Muhammadan family, therefore the name of Kabir was given to him. His father and mother loved him intensely. Even while a baby it repeated God's name, and listening to it every one was astonished. 'We wonder what good deeds this orthodox Muhammadan named Kamal performed in his former birth. How is that this Vishnu-bhakta, already distinguished by his religious characteristics, should be born to this Muhammadan? One replied, 'It was because fate was favourable to him. If fate is favourable to anyone, why does one need the power of knowledge? Madmen, born in a low caste, are often praised by all men, through the power of fate. So this man's good fortune is extra ordinary. A bhakta of Vishnu has come to birth through him'. Such the talk amongst all the people of that sacred city[2].

M.A. Macauliff has recorded the following story in the history of the Sikhs (Kabir - Bhagats of the Granth Sahib):

There was a certain Brahman in Banaras, who remained continuously in attendance on Rama Nand. The Brahman had a daughter, a virgin widow, who desired to behold the object of her father's reverence and attentions. Her father took her one day to see the holy man. She was allowed to prostrate herself before him and touch his feet with her forehead. He in ignorance of her status prayed that she might be blessed with a son. When her father replied that she was a widow, Rama Nand said that his words could not be recalled and she should have a son; but no one should see any signs of her pregnancy, and no stigma should attach to her reputation. Her son should reform religion and save the world. She consequently conceived, and in due time a son was born to her on Monday, the day of the full moon, in the month of Jeth, Samvat 1455, of the Vikramadittya era, corresponding to A.D. 1398. She exposed her child on a lake called Lahar Talao, a short distance from Banaras. He was found by a Musalman weaver, called Ali who from living beside the water (nir) was popularly known by the name of Niru when he was taking home his wife from her parents house.

He saw the boy lying in the lake, it is said, on a blossoming water-lily. The child had obviously been abandoned by an unmarried woman. Niru hastened to inform his wife Nima. They had no son of their own, and it was in their power to adopt him. Nima represented the gossip that would result and the danger to their reputation and that of the whole tribe. On looking into the child's face however, her determination gave way. He was fair to look on, and did not scream like other children but on the contrary looked bright and cheerful. They took him up and bore him home.

The Lahar Talao is a lake about a mile and a quarater long, and an eighth of a mile broad. At the time of the author's (Macauliff) visit in December, it was except for some rushes here and there, covered with a russet weed on which aquate birds alighted and sported. On the margin of the lake is a small temple sacred to Kabir. It is kept by some monks, who pride themselves on their knowledge of Sanskrit literature. Hard by is the tomb of Niru, Kabir's foster-father.

After the discovery of the child a Qazi was in due time called to give him a name. The Quran was opened, and a lot was cast The word Kabir which means great in the Arabic language, was the first that presented itself. This name was accordingly given to the child. When Kabir arrived at an age to understand the nature of the doubts cast on his birth he composed the following poem:

I have just come from God.

Mammon hath led the world astray;

it had not found the secret of my birth.

I was not born, nor did I dwell in a womb;

I have appeared a child as I am.

A weaver found me near his hut in a lake at Banaras.

I was not in heaven, or in earth, or in any country; my divine knowledge is endless.

The spirit which is manifested in His own world is my name.

I have no bones, no blood, no skin; I have been manifested by the world.

I am beyond all body and endless, a superior being whom men call the immortal Kabir.

It would appear that, though the boy was adopted by Musalmans, he was subjected to Hindu influences from his earliest years. Banaras was and is the stronghold of Hinduism, and even its Muhammadan inhabitants are often strongly tinctured with the ancient religion of India.

Moreover, it is said that Gosain Ashtanand, a Hindu saint of the period, said to have been a disciple of Rama Nand, saw the child at the time of his exposure in the tank; and it is most probable that he subsequently followed his fate and gave him religious instruction as opportunities offered.[3]

The same story has been narrated by David C. Scott in his book Kabirs Mythology as under:

According to the simplest story of the birth of Kabir, it seems that a certain brahman took his daughter, a virgin widow, to pay homage to Swami Ramananda. Ignorant of her widowhood, the man of God wished her blessing of a son. As the words of a saint do not go unfulfilled, in the due course the young woman gave birth to a son, whom, for fear of scandal, she abandoned on a lotus leaf in the pond at Lahartala. Adding a further miraculous element another tradition has it that when the Swami discovered the woman to be a widow, he promised that she would not suffer any embarrassment and that the boy would grow up to be a great saint. The woman is then said to have developed a blister on her hand. This grew rapidly and burst, yielding a lump of line flesh, which immediately took the form of a human infant. According to this story the child's name was 'Karavira' or hero of the hand.[4]

A more elaborate story relates that once when Visnu was consorting with Lakshmi he left her abruptly and without explanation. When he returned he told his offended spouse that one of his devotees had called and he had to go to the saints rescue. Lakshmi objected that there was no greater devotee than she, only to be rebuked and told that there were a number of worshippers whose demands took precedence over hers. The angry Lakshmi decided to test the devotee who had thus offended her, and taking the form of a gardener's woman she created the illusion of a beautiful garden along the way Rama Nand was detined to pass. The Swami had hardly entered the garden and picked several flowers for his puja, when Lakshmi accosted him. Being thus surprised, Rama Nanda plung the flowers at her and departed Lakshmi was extremely pleased that she had caught Vishnus devotee in the act of stealing and returned to Vaikuntha to relate the incident. To substantiate her story she began searching the folds of her sari for the flowers. But to and behold, there were no flowers, only a handsome baby boy. Vishnu feigned surprise and anger but on seeing the embarrassed confusion of his spouse he was overcome with pity. Reassuring her, Vishnu instructed Lakshmi to take the child back to earth and promised that the boy would become a great devotee of his. Accepting her defeat, Lakshmi returned the baby to earth and left him floating on a lotus leaf in the Lahartala pond. This baby, of course, was Kabir.

According to another tradition Kabir was the incarnation of the sage Sukhdev. On instructions from Siva to appear in the world for the good of mankind, the sage, who was not keen on suffering the pain of a fetal existence, enclosed himself in a shell which was thrown into the Ganga. The current soon swept the shell into the Lahartala pond, where it opened on a lotus leaf, exposing a beautiful baby boy; Kabir.

However, even these fancifully miraculous stories seem not cosmic enough to satisfy many Kabir-Panthis who believe that Kabir, being a manifestination of the Sat Purusha or "True Being" is not subject to birth and death, but incarnates himself whenever there is need to protect the well being of earthings. They believe that there had already been thirteen incarnations of Kabir in the preceding three yugs. For the fourteenth time, in the Kali Yuga the Divine Light of Sat Purusa descended on the full moon day of Jyestha in the year 1455 of the Vikarmi Samvat, at the Lahartala pond. On that auspicious occasion a certain Vaishnava, Gosain Ashtanand, was present in the gentle drizzle from a dark sky. He is reported to have described to Swami Rama Nand "intermittent flushes illumined the dark scence, revealing an abundance of beautifully blooming flowers over which beetles droned". In one of these flashes Ashtanand saw the Sat Purusa, of whom Rama Nand predicted that the Vaishnava would bear a great deal in the years to come. The Divine Light turned itself into an infant and a lotus leaf arose out of the pond to cradle it.

Related to all of these accounts is the story of how Niru, a Muslim weaver from Kashi, passed by the Lahartala pond on evening with his newly wedded wife, Nima. Floating peacefully along the edge of the pond Nima spotted a large and handsome child to whom she was immediately drawn. There was much discussion as to what they should do the child and how they would explain it to their friends and neighbours, but eventually they could not resist and decide to take the child home and adopt it as their own.

When the time came to name the child, Niru, a devout Muslim, called the Qazi, a Muslim religious functionary, who came and opened Quran in search of an auspicious name. His efforts yielded only the names Akbar and Kabir. As these both are divine epithets, two of the ninety-nine "most excellent" names of Allah, they were obviously in appropriate for a child of such a humble family. The astonished Qazi was perplexed as he continued the search without finding other names. Indeed, it seemed that the entire Quran was filled with these two names. Other Qazis were also summoned, but to of no avail, and finally they advised that the obviously cursed, child be put to death. Repeated efforts to terminate the young life before some great disaster befell to family failed, seemingly thwarted by the child's miraculous powers.

Finally the child spoke:

Now I have descended, but this maya filled world does not understand my mystery.

I was neither born, nor did I become a child in the womb.

The Julaha discovered me in a forest dwelling near Kashi.

I have not returned to these skies or this earth because of any fault or special knowledge.

I have revealed myself in the form of Supreme Spirit, hence this name of mine.

Without bone or blood, I am the revelation of eternal, cosmic sound (Shabad).

I am the embodiment of the infinite purusottama, says the immortal Kabir.

In the end the name Kabir was given to the child.[5]

There seems to be no unanimity of opinion on the historical data relating of Kabir. Historians and literary scholars as well as the followers of Kabir seat are at variance and the internal evidence in Kabir's writings about himself is very little. Nevertheless an attempt needs to be made to present a tentative biographical sketch, on the basis of such sources as are available, including legends.

In one of Kabir's lines there is a veiled reference to two saint-poets, Jaydev and Namdev, as gurus of Kabir. Jaydev lived in the twelfth century and Namdev in the thirteenth century. There is a reference to Kabir's name in the Ain-e-Akbari, written in 1596, as one of the holy men no longer living. On the other hand Maulvi Ghulam Sarwar gives 1594 as the year of Kabir's birth in his Khajinat-ul-Asafiya which seems to be incorrect. Kabir Chaint Bodh a work held in esteem by the Kabir seat, gives 1398 A.D. as the year of birth.

Notes and References

1. Shuka - Son of Vyasa. He was a born philosopher and a calibate till death. Rambha a heavenly damsel was frustrated in her attempt to seduce him. Vyasa taught him the Bhagvata, and he read it to king Parikshit.

2. Mahipatis Bhakatvijaya stories of Indian Saints translated by Abott and Godbois, pp. 78-80.

3. M.A. Macauliff - The History of the Sikhs (Kabir - The Bhagats of the Granth Sahib, pp. 123-124.

4. David C. Scott - Kabir's Mythology - Bhartiya Vidya Prakashan, 1985, pp. 102-103.

5. David C. Scott, Kabir's Mythology. Bharatiya Vidya Prakashan, Delhi 1985.

3

Controversy of Kabir's Date of Birth

Kabir is commonly believed to have been the disciple of Ramanand, though Doctor Bhandarkar and Doctor Mohan Singh do not subscribe to this belief. Grierson gives the date of Ramanand's birth as 1298. Farquhar and Keay, on the other hand, place it anywhere between 1400 and 1470. Doctor Govind Trigunayal has reached the conclusion, after sifting all the available material that Kabir was born in 1398 A.D. All these conflicting views shows how unwise it is to be dogmatic on this point.

Kabir was the name given by a Kazi who on opening the Quran came upon the Arabic word which means 'great'. Kabir has said in one of his dohas or couplets:

Kabira tu hi Kabiru tu tore nam Kabir

Ram ratan tab paiye jab pahila tajai sarir

(कबीरा! तू ही कबीरू तू ही तोरे नाम कबीर।

राम रतन तब पयिए जब पहले तजिए शरीर।।)

(Thou art great, you are the same, your name is Kabir. The Jewel Ram is found only when bodily attachment is renounced.)

About the year of his death, there are four different views; some place it in 1447; some in 1511; some in 1517. Anantdas maintains that Kabir lived a long life of 120 years. Dharamdas had started collecting Kabir's works in his lifetime; the date of this first collection is presumed to be 1463. Dr. Shyamsundar Das believes that Kabir died in 1517. Sir W.W. Hunter gave Kabir's dates in his Indian Empire (1892) as 1380 to 1420. Dr. Harprasad Shastri put it as 1398-1518.[1]

The question of Kabir's dates has been the subject of endless controversies, which have produced a bewildering variety of arguments in support of many different and often extravagant claims. In a nutshell, the entire controversy appears to involve the conviction of Kabir's Hindu biographers that he was Ramanand's (1300-1400 A.D.) actual disciple and that he was persecuted by Sikandar Lodi in person. Some authors, influenced by Sikh popular beliefs, also wanted to make him Guru Nanak's contemporary. But as we have seen this encounter is utterly improbable. By way of general observation it may be noted that western scholars have tended to doubt the Kabir-Ramanand relationship, while generally accepting Kabir as a contemporary of Sikandar Lodi (1489-1517 A.D.). For our present purpose it seems best to begin by trying to establish a probable date for Kabir's death, as there is more evidence with which to work than we shall find when we come to a discussion of a birth date.

Two dates are the main contenders in the controversy over the year of Kabir's death, Samwat 1505 (A.D. 1448) and Samwat 1575 (A.D. 1518) and the following two Sakhis are generally cited as the basis for these dates.

In the year (Vikrami Samwat) fifteen hundred and five, he (Kabir) went to Maghar.

On the light *ekadasi* of Agahan, breath mingled with breath.

In the year (Vikrami Samwat) fifteen hundred and seventy five, he (Kabir) went to Magahar.

On the light ekadasi of Magh, breath mingled with breath.

On these two dates the vast number of Indian scholars decided in favour of Samwat 1505 (A.D. 1458) as the most likely date of the sants death. The principal reason cited in favour of this conclusion is a centaoph at Magahar said to have been created by Nawab Bijli Khan in A.D. 1450. Further, Nawab Fidai

Khan is supposed to have repaired the monument in A.D. 1567. If this information, based on the Archaeological Survey of India's publication dealing with the "Monumental Antiquities and inscriptions in North-Western Provinces of Oudh, is accurate, the year A.D. 1450 would be the terminus ad quem for Kabir's death.

The followers of Kabirpanth tend to give more credence to the second sakhi, supporting the popular tradition amongst the Kabirpanth which claims the year Samwat 1575 (A.D. 1518) as the year of Kabir's death. However, there is no more than traditional claim to support this date. Indeed, it can be argued that this date has been maintained in order to make it possible for Kabir to have been prosecuted by Sikandar Lodi (1489-1517 A.D.) as well as to be a contemporary of Guru Nanak (1469-1539 A.D.) thereby giving the saint an opportunity to demonstrate his supposed supernatural powers and claim influence of the Nanak panthis. Such a demonstration would be of considerable importance to Kabir panthis.

When it comes to the matter of discovering a probable date for Kabir's birth, we are completely in the dark as far as any historical evidence is concerned. It is true that very strong tradition puts his birth in the year Samwat 1455 (A.D. 1398) and without any compelling arguments to the contrary there seems to be no reason not to accept this date. Indeed, with no other major alternatives in this matter it seems justifiable to join both Pandit Chaturvedi and Dr. Vaudevilla, among the foremost Kabirian scholars, East and West, in concluding that the available evidence does not allow one to draw definite conclusions about Kabir's dates. They both are of the opinion, however, that there is relatively greater probability that Kabir was born in Vikrami Samwat 1455 (A.D. 1398) and died in Vikram Samwat 1505, (A.D. 1448)[2].

According to Muhammad Hedayetullah to one school of Kabirpanthis, Kabir was present in the world three hundred years, or from 1149-1499. According to another tradition, Kabir was born when the year 1455 of the Vikrami era (corresponding to 1398 A.D.) was past, on Monday, full moon day of Jyeshtha, on which date also fell the Vata Savitri festival. Some followers of Kabir, according to Dr. Tiwari still continue to celebrate Kabir's birthday on the Vata-Savitri day every year. But some people think, Tiwari tells us, that Kabir was born 25 or 30 years earlier. Those who maintain that Kabir was born at Belhara do not mention any specific date. Maulvi Ghulam Sarwar gives 1594 as the year of Kabir's death, but does not give the year of his birth. Abul Fazal in his *Ain-e-Akbari*, written in 1596 makes reference to Kabir as one of the holy men but no longer living. The Kabirpanthi School which holds that Kabir was born in 1398 also maintains that he died in 1518 A.D. The former is rejected by all on the ground that dates has been given in order to make Kabir contemproray of Ramanand (b. 1299?) who is supposed to have lived in the fourteenth century. The former is commonly believed to have been the disciple of the latter, whose dates, however, have been tentatively fixed by Farquhar and others as 1400-1470. And according to them, Ramananda came to Banaras as a religious reformer in 1430. If therefore, Kabir was born in 1440, as has been suggested by many scholars and became the disciple of Ramanand about 1455, this ift in well with the circumstances of his life. Kabir is also believed to have been a contemporary of Guru Nanak, who lived from 1469 to 1538. He is said to have been 27 years of age when he met Kabir, and the year of their meeting has been suggested 1496. Kabir is also believed to have been a contemporary of Sultan Sikandar Lodi who reigned from 1489 to 1517. And according to *The Cambridge History of India*, the Sultan visited Banaras sometime between 1494 to 1495. Since these dates are very close to one another, they seem to enable us to fix Kabir's dates approximately 1440 to 1518, albeit all that can be said with some degree of confidence is that he lived in the fifteenth century.[3]

Notes and References

1. M.A. Macauliff—Kabir pp. 1-8.
2. David C. Scott—Kabir's Mythology. Bharatiya Vidya Prakashan, 1985, pp. 123-124.
3. Muhammad Hedayatullah—Kabir *The Apostle of Hindu Muslim Unity*. Motilal Banarsidas, Delhi, 1977. pp. 165-167.

4

Kabir's Place of Birth

Indu Vashisht in her article 'Kabir" has recorded that there are no accounts or reliable sources giving information about the exact date or year of birth of Kabir. In the 1200-year long history of Hindu literature there has been no other philosopher poet to stand comparison with Kabir except Tulsi, the devotee of Rama. Kabir exerted a lasting influence on Hindu thought and Hindi poetry through his extraordinary intellect, social commitment and magnetic personality. For the Hindus Kabir is a Vaisnavite bhakta, while the Muslims revere him as a peer, the Sikhs call him a bhagat and the Kabir Panthis worship him as an avatar. Modern nationalists respect Kabir as the bridge between Hindus and Muslims; modern philosophers view him as an advocate of the religion of humanity. In the opinion of radicals he was a reformer, an opponent of the caste system, a strong supporter of the downtrodden. He is hailed as a revolutionary who spread the message of universal brotherhood, social justice and equality.

The powerful character of Kabir is greatly appreciated by western scholars. This has been most eloquently summed up by Grierson as follows:

What a wonderful man Kabir must have been! A lovely Muslim weaver who by a strategem gained accession to a Vaishnava community—universally despised and hated by both Mussalman and Hindu, maltreated by the Muslim emperor and persecuted by the Brahminhood of Benaras with unparalleled audacity he dared to set himself face to face against both Islam and Hinduism, the two religions of the 15th century India, and won through. Each he attacked in its tenderest point—its Shibboleths and its rituals—and over both he rode triumphant, teaching and converting thousands who became his devoted followers. Not only did he find an ecletic monotheism that survives in India to this day, but he became the spiritual father of Nanak who founded Sikhism.

Due to this great influence Kabir has been called the "Indian Luther". By the 18th century the voice of Kabir echoed even in Europe. Around the year A.D. 1758 Father Romba, an Italian cleric, translated Kabir's works into Italian. Western Scholars like Macauliff, H.H. Wilson, Garsa-da-Thusy, Smith and others have made deep study of Kabir.

Indian Society at the time of Kabir was full of evils, like blind faith, hypocrisy, caste distinctions and many more. Nineteenth century was the era of Renaissance. It was during this time that institutions like the Brahmo Samaj. Arya Samaj, Ramakrishna Mission and others launched powerful social reforms. Kabir was a great source of inspiration to them. Tagore and Gandhiji too were greatly influenced by Kabir. The latter adopted the doctrines of Truth and Non-violence from Kabir's Philosophy. Kabir considered Kabir's poetical utterances as the highest achievement among all Indian Vernacular literatures. He declared that what Kabir had expressed in Hindi about mysticism has no parallel in Bengali. Gandhiji is said to have claimed that his mother was a Kabirpanthi.

Dr. Peathambardatt Barthwal in his book entitled Gandhi and Kabir has discussed the great influence Kabir had on Gandhiji by saying that "The source of the Ganges of Gandhism is Kabir's teachings, which he inbibed along with his mother's milk".

Comparisons such as these between Kabir and Gandhi abound in the Indian nationalistic literature of the 1930s and 40s. As I Madan writes: :If Gandhi had lived in the times of Kabir, he would have done what Kabir did. And, in turn, Kabir would do in our times exactly what Gandhiji is doing. Like Kabir Gandhiji was also an ardent supporter of Truth.[1]

Vivek Bhattacharya has written that the 15th century was perhaps one of the brightest periods in the cultural history of India. It was a period of emotional integration which was never witnessed before. The great saints of both the South and the North had been preaching the universal brotherhood of man. He did not care for caste or creed, religious rituals or sanctions, and what is more interesting, they had direct communication among themselves in spite of long distances when the only means of transport was on foot. There was a tremendous devotional movement popularly known as the Bhakti movement. In the south it was led by Acharya Ramanuja followed by his equally illustrious disciple Acharya Raghavananda. There was a galaxy of saints Acharya Ramanuja, Ramanand in the South, Guru Nanak in Punjab, Mahaprabhu Sri Chaitanya in Bengal and Kabir Sahib in Uttar Pradesh. Acharya Ramananda brought the message of universal love of Ramanuja to Varanasi and had a galaxy of equally illustrious disciples picked up from all sections irrespective of caste or creed. Among them were, Kabir from weavers family and Ravidas from the family of Cobbler. Both Kabir and Ravidas became great saints. Among the disciples of Ramananda, Kabir became the most outstanding one and his message of love in the form of lucid lyrics reached the hamlets of the Indian villages throughout the country. They are still so popular. Kabir is highly respected even today. His songs are sung with full respect[2].

About the place of Kabir's birth there are three opinions: Magahar, Kashi and Belahara village in Azamgarh. The argument in favour of Magahar is that Kabir refers to this place in his works. He writes that he had seen Magahar first before seeing Kashi and that he had re-visited Magahar before his death. Magahar is near Kashi (modern Banaras or Varanasi) and has the mausoleum of Kabir.

It may be better at this stage to refer to the various sources from which material about Kabir's biography can be sought the first reference to Kabir is in Bhakat Mal by Nabhadas, supposed to have been composed in 1500 and containing accounts of the lives and miracles of several saints. All that can be gathered from the two stanzas devoted to Kabir in this book is that he was a devotee of Ramananda. A commentary on this work by Priyadas reaffirms this fact and maintains that Kabir was born of a Hindu Brahmin widow and was brought up by Niru and Nima, which has already been stated. This work also says that Kabir was a contemporary of Sikandar Lodi. Kabir is also referred to in the writings of Raidas, Garibdas, Dharamdas, Pipa and Tukaram. In the Guru Granth Sahib, the sacred book of the Sikhs, there are several slokas and ragas ascribed to Kabir; and his name occurs in Guru Nanak's verses. Anantda's Parichai written probably in 1600, corroborates that Kabir was a weaver from Kashi and a disciple of Ramanand; a contemporary of the Baghel King, Vir Singh and a victim of Sikandar Lodi's atrocities; and a saint who lived the long life of 120 years.

There are some Persian and Urdu books, too which mention Kabir's name and some legends about his life. Maulvi Ghulam Sarwar's *Khajinat-ul-Asfiya* is referred to earlier. Mohsin Fani's *Dabistan-e-Majahib* and Maulvi Nasiruddin's *Tajkiral Fukra* both note that Kabir was a disciple of Ramanand. *Ain-e-Akbari* refers to the difference of opinion about the tomb of Kabir some placing it in Ratanpur in district Oudh and others in Puri and gives its opinion in favour of the later.

Westcott in his work, *Kabir and the Kabir-Panth* gives eleven references to the name Kabir in several historical works ascribed to different kinds of holy men, and at varying dates;

1. Kabir Chisti of Nagore who died in Gujarat in 1854.
2. Shaik Kabir Julaha who was called Pir Kabir by Muhammadans and Bhagat Kabir by Hindus and who died in 1594.
3. Khwaja Aulia Kabir who visited Bokhara and died in 1229.
4. Syed Kabir-ud-Din Hassan who died in Balakh in 1490.
5. Shaikh Kabir a resident of Bajaora and an opiate.

6. Shaikh Abdul Kabir or Bal-Pir who died in 1539.
7. Shaikh Kabir of Multan who went to Balakh and returned to India and travelled with Akbar, and who died at Fatehpur in 1585.
8. Amir Kabir Mir Syed Ali Hamdani who visited Kashmir in 1379 and died there five years later.
9. Syed Ahmad Kabir, father of Syed Jala-ul-Din.
10. Kabir-ul-Din Ismail, grandson of Syed Jalal-ud-Din who died in 1421.
11. Diwan Shah Kabir in whose memory a mosque was built at Jaunpur during the reign of Humayun.

The first five are mentioned in Khajinat-ul-Asfia, the sixth in Sair-ul-aqitab the seventh in Mankakhal-ul-Tawarikh, the eighth in Akubar-ul-Akhyar and the rest in Ferishta.

It is not only about Kabir's appearance and date that there is such diversity of opinion among historians and literary critics; about his works and his code of beliefs; too, there are many conflicting opinions[3].

According to Scott—Even though Kabir himself tells us nothing concerning whereabouts of his birth, he does refer to himself as a "Julaha from Kasi", and there is a very strong tradition that Kabir was born and spent the major part of his life in Kasi. Further, with very few exceptions[4] modern Indian scholars are prone to accept this tradition. On the surface of it, the strongest evidence to oppose this view would seem to come from an entry in the Benares Gazetteer of 1909 A.D. to the effect that Kabir was born in Belhara, a village in the Azamgarh District of U.P. However, H.R. Nevill the author of the Gazetteer, seems to be the only one who is willing to accept this[5]. It is significant, in this regard, that in this village there is no indication of its being related to Kabir in any special way. There is no monument, nor is there any Kabir math. Based on a verse from the Adi Granth compilation of Kabir bani[6], whose autobiographical pads (couplets) do have a ring of authenticity both in tenor and style, Ram Kumar Verma, G. Trigunayat and P.D. Barthwal think that it probable that Kabir was born in Magahar. Their opinion is based on a translation of the clause 'Pahile darshan Magahara pio (पहले दर्शन मगहर पायओ) as "I first had a sight of Magahar". Chaturvedi has rightly pointed out that the ordinary meaning of the verb darsan pana is not to be born but to have a view or "vision" of some "incarnation" of supreme Reality. P.N. Tiwari suggests that Kabir may have been born at Candavar, a village in the Ballia District of eastern U.P. His opinion is based primarily on several Kabir Panthi documents which Chaturvedi views as highly unreliable[7].

Notes and References

1. Indu Vashisht, An article on 'Kabir' in a book entitled *Poet Saints of India* ed by M.S. Krishna and Sumita Roy, pp. 48-50.
2. Vivek Bhattacharya, Saint Kabir (The Spirit of Indian Culture—Saints of India).
3. M.A. Macauliff, *Kabir.*
4. Among the Indian Scholars consulted only P.D. Barthwal, R.K. Verma, G. Trigunayat and P.N. Tiwari are skeptical about the Kasi tradition.
5. P. Chaturvedi, *Uttari Bharat Ki Sant Parampara,* pp. 140-141.
6. A.G. Ramkali.
7. *Uttari Bharat Ki Sant Parampara and Kabir Vani.*

5

Early Life of Kabir

Muhammad Hedayetullah has mentioned that like his birth and naming concerning Kabir's early life also similar stories are told. In these legends he is said to have performed many miracles even when he was only a baby. According to one tale, Kabir spoke in Hindi in his childhood and told the people that on account of Nima's kindness to him in a previous birth, he had come to their house, and he would deliver them from transmigration. In another story it is said that Kabir grew up without taking any nourishment. When his foster parents saw that he ate nothing they were worried. Yielding to their persuation, Kabir agreed to take milk. This milk was obtained not in the usual manner. An earthen jar was placed under the udder of an uncalved heifer and Kabir looked at the animal thinking of milk. This induced lactation in the heifer and the jar was quickly filled. "Milk obtained thus alone would Kabir drink".

These legends have their basis in faith. The first story appears to have been designed to parallel Kabir with Jesus who is said to have spoken in his childhood. The followers of Kabir who have coined the story must have been familiar with the life history of Jesus. The other story has been made to heighten the spiritual genius of Kabir. It gives the impression that Kabir was a saint by birth. We have no attention of arguing that there has never been any person who showed signs of high spiritual quality and played miracles even as a child. But in the case of Kabir, we have specific evidence in his own sayings that he was not a miracle worker, nor did he like those who lay claim to miracles. However, stories of miracles ascribed to Kabir are but pious fabrications of his faithful disciples, who themselves probably worked miracles.

As regards Kabir's education, the circumstances of his up-bringing in a poor Muslim weavers family make it quite understandable that he did not have any formal education. His speech was a local dialect to which allusion has already been made. Nevertheless, he does not appear to have been apathetic to learning. In place he says: I know that reading is good, but better than reading is meditation <jog> (Granth Sloka, 45) Kabir's aim was not scholarship or philosophy; it was the knowledge of God, and of the things of God, which he sought after with all his heart and mind. He was neither able nor interested in the learning of the schools. A well known proverb says: "What the theologians learn from books, the saints learn it from their hearts".

Now, let us turn to some important events of Kabir's life. Although in Dr. Underhill's sketch of Kabir's life slight reference has been made of most of these events, still they need detailed historical explanations. In passing, it may be mentioned that it is almost impossible to fix any chronological order of events in Kabir's life. In such a situation we will try to describe them in a reasonable chronological order which will be based on our knowledge of a normal life in the society of the Indian sub-continent. Secondly in every event of his life, almost invariably there is an element of his teaching one way or the other[1].

At a very early age Kabir's religious education was far advance. While playing with his companions he used to repeat the name Ram or Hari, Hindu names of God. Musalmans said the child was an infidel. Kabir retorted that an infidel was he—

1. who struck any person without just cause,
2. who wore a religious curb to deceive the world,
3. who drunk wine,
4. who stole,

5. who committed suicide,
6. who smoke tobacco,
7. who committed highway robbery,
8. and who took life.

These became Kabirs commandments. One day he put on the frontal mark and the sacrificial thread of the Hindus. A Brahman called Mukand remonstrated, and said that Kabir having been brought up a Muhammadan, and following moreover, the trade of his foster father, had no concern with Hinduism and was not entitled to wear its distinguishing badge or symbols. Kabir replied with the following hymn:

In my house is thread, I am continually weaving, while only one sacrificial thread is on thy neck.

Thou readest only the Vedas and the Gayatri, while God is in my heart.

On my tongue dwelleth God, in mine eyes dwelleth and in my heart dwelleth God.

When thou art examined, O mad Mukand at Death door, what shall Thou say?

I am the cow, thou the herdsman, lord of the earth, and guardian of man at every birth.

Thou hast not taken me beyond the river to graze; what sort of master have I?

Thou art a Brahman, I am a Banaras weaver, understand my instruction.

Thou biggest from lords and kings, while I meditate on God; which of us is better?

As Kabir grew up, his devotion, spiritual powers and miracles became famous. He deemed everything blasphemy which was opposed to the worship of God. He considered the practice of jog, alms, fasting and the feeding of Brahmans not only useless, but improper, without the repetition of God's name and love for Him. In reality the special tenor of the Shastras is, according to Nabhaji's *Bhagat Mal,* that all the above mentioned religious works are ciphers, and the name of the God is, as it were, a numeral. The practice of jog feeding

Brahmans, are useless without the numeral of God's name. The meaning of the author of the *Bhagat Mal* is, that all religious works should be performed for the acquisition of devotion and love of God, and not for objects of a temporal character.

From Kabir's boyhood his mind was filled with intuitive knowledge and his reasoning faculties were so acute that he vanquished the most learned men of his age, both Hindu and Musalman, in theological and ethical discussions. The Brahmans and the Mullas contrived many expedients to silence him, but all their efforts were baffled. At last they decided that they would call him a nigura, or a person without a spiritual guide and consequently an infidal, with the dubious moral character which that word in the estimation of the vulgar connotes, and that they would thus humble and shame him. Having heard of the Brahman's resolution and of Ramanand's fame Kabir sought him out and became his disciple.

When Kabir's foster-parents found they could not restrain his Hindu proclivities, they determined to circumcise him. Upon this he uttered the following hymn:

Whence have come The Hindus and Musalmans? who hath put them on their different ways?

Having thought and reflected in thy heart, answer this—who shall obtain heaven and who hell?

O Qazi, what expoundest thou?

Such readers and students as thou have failed; none of them hath obtained knowledge.

Thou practisest circumcision for love of woman; I shall never believe in it O brother.

If God had desired to make me a Musalman, I should have been born circumcised.

If a man become a Musalman by circumcision, what is to be done to a woman?

Thou puttest not away thy wife who is half thy body wherefore thou remainest a Hindu.

Give up thy books, O foolish man, and worship God; the practisest grovo oppression.

Kabir hath laid hold of the prop of God; the Musalman have totally failed[2].

Kabir Refused Circumcision

Muhammad Hedayetullah has also described that according to Muslim custom and tradition, a boy is circumcised at the age of 5 or 6. This time limit has not been ordained by the Quran though there are *ahadith* (Muhammad's sayings) which show that that was the practice in early Islam. When Kabir reached that age he was to be circumcised; and a Khalifa[3] was called. But Kabir exhibited such strange potents that the Khalifa was terrified. On this occasion Kabir is said to have uttered the following verses:

Vain-glorious of authority, you make me to
be circumcised; never will I endure it, brother !
If it is God that makes thee to be circumcised,
why came not this cutting of itself ?
If by circumcision one becomes Turk, what
then will be said to you woman ?
Half the body, so the wife is styled;
then you still remain Hindu !
By putting on the sacred thread does one
becomes a Brahman ?
What has thou given to women to wear ?
She from birth is but a Sudra !
Why dost thou eat the food she brings,
O Pandit ? (Bijak Sabad 84)

It is evident in the above poem that in denouncing religious symbols and rites, Kabir showed favour neither to Hindus nor to Muslims. His criticism of each of them is equally severe and categorical. The rites and practices which constitute the two forms of worship—Hinduism and Islam—appeared to him equally useless; it is in the heart that the true faith resides, Kabir instead. One interesting feature of his sayings is that though he starts denouncing any particular rise of one religion, he quickly links it with a similar aspect of the other religion, thus maintaining balance by criticising both the religions simultaneously. His equal denunciation of the Muslim rite of circumcision and Hindu rite of putting on the sacred thread is an example in point.

We are told that as a boy Kabir offended both Hindu and the Muslim playmates by crying "Ram, Ram" and "Hari Hari". Muslims called him a *Kafir* (unbeliever). To this accusation he replied saying that only an evil doer was a Kafir. We are also told that one day he put a tilak on his forehead and put a thread round his neck and cried," Narain, Narain". This action roused the anger of the Brahmans, for it was a sacrilege committed by a low caste "Muslim". To their protest, Kabir retorted: Being a weaver, I wear a thread. You wear the sacred thread, and repeat the Gayatri and Gita daily, but Govind dwells in my heart. You are Brahmans, I am a weaver of Banaras.

It is stated that in his boyhood, one day he found a cow that was slaughtered by a *Mullah.* Kabir objected to it strongly for which the Brahmans felt delighted. On this occasion he uttered the following verses in which, of course, he did not spare either Muslims or Hindus:

O Saints (holy men) ! I have seen the way of both,

Hindus and Turks heed no warning;

to all the taste of their desires is sweet

Hindus keep fast on Ekadasi (the eleventh

day of the half-month, observed as a fast),

they eat only singharas (water chestnuts) and milk

They abstain from grain, but do not check the

mind's desire; next day they eat the flesh of beasts.

Turks keep fast and hour of prayer; they

cry aloud on the name of God. (azhan)

How will they find Paradise ? When evening

comes they slaughter fowls.

Hindus and Turks each has renounced his mercy in his heart.

One kills by halal (the Muslim legal formula of slaughtering an animal), one kills by Jhataka (Hindu method of killing an animal); but fire is kindled in both their houses.

For Hindu and for Turk there is one path; so the sat Guru (True Teacher) has taught;

Says Kabir, Listen, O Sants : cry 'Rama';

cry Khuda (Persian and Urdu name for God)—

it is all one ! (Bijik Sabda 10)[4]

When Kabir's mother found that his attention was directed to the worship of the God of the Hindus in opposition to the God of Islam, she raised lot of complaints. Kabir paid no attention to her, by employed himself as usual in the repetition at remembrance of God's name.[5]

Notes and References

1. Muhammad Hedayetullah—*Kabir : The Apostle of Hindu—Muslim Unity.*, pp. 167-168.
2. Macauliff—*Kabir*, pp. 126-127.
3. Muhammad Hedayetulah—*Kabir : The Apostle of Hindu Muslim Unity*, p. 168.
4. M. Hedayateullah—*Kabir: The Apostle of Hindu —Muslim Unity*, pp. 168-171.
5. Macauliff—*Kabir* (Bhagats of the Granth Sahib), p. 121.

6

Spiritual Guru of Kabir

There is a controversy regarding his spiritual Guru. It is generally agreed that his spiritual Guru was Ramanand though there are some scholars who hold that Kabir was the disciple of Sheikh Taqi, Kabir panthis cite the following Doha (couplet) to show that Kabir was the disciple of Ramanand:

Bhakti Dravid Upaji laya Ramanand

Pragat Kari Kabir the sat deep navkhand

Bhakti originated in the Dravida Desh (the South) and was brought to the North by Ramanand. Kabir diffused it throughout the seven dwipas and nine Khandas).

An interesting story is told as to how he managed to become the disciple of the Great Guru Ramanand, since he was born in a Julaha family Ramanand refused to accept him as his disciple. But as Kabir was greatly devoted to him he remained undaunted even after the rebuffs received at the hands of Ramanand. One day in the Brahma Muhurat (early dawn) he laid himself down on the steps of the Panchaganga Ghat in Kasi. Ramanand, as was his wont went to bathe at the said Ghat at that hour and unknowingly struck Kabir on his head with his foot. Swamiji uttering Ram Ram proceeded towards the river. Kabir declared himself afterwards as the disciple of Ramanand. He related everything truthfully when accosted later on by Ramanand. Ramanand was very much pleased and embraced him[1].

Scott has related the similar story about this incident. Rather early on Kabir seems to have begun the practice of repeating the names of Ram or Gobind or Hari, which distressed his family and Muslim neighbours and friends. Indeed the Muslims accused him of being an infidel. Nor were the Hindus any more pleased when Kabir donned the sacred thread of the "twice born" and applied a tilak to his forehead. For this the Brahmans of Banaras upbraided him maintaining that these were the signs of their religion, not his. They also reproached him for having no guru. To remedy this defect Kabir decided to try and become a disciple of Swami Ramanand, said to be the greatest Vaishnava saint of the time, who was then in Kasi. Fearing that the Swami probably would not accept a Muslim weaver as a disciple, Kabir devised a strategem.

It was the routine of the Swami to bath in the water of the holy Ganga each morning before sunrise. One morning as the saint was on this way down to the river Kabir prostrated himself on the Swamis path. The pre-dawn darkness and the saints meditative mood prevented him from seeing the prostrate figure in his path and one of his wooden sandals accidently struck the would be disciple. When Kabir cried out in pain the compassionate saint stopped and placed his hand on the boy's head admonishing him not to cry but to say "Ram Ram". This Kabir accepted as his Mantra and went home to done the garb of a Vaishnava ascetic, losing no time in informing his critics that he had become a disciple of Swami Ramanand. The Hindus, of course, were incensed that the great Swami had initiated a Muslim weaver into his Vaishnava sect, and went to inquire into the matter. Surprised, Ramanand denied that he had done any such thing and summoned the Julaha lad, to question him. When he arrived at Ramanand's ashram, Kabir related the events which had taken place on the way to the river the previous morning. The Swami maintained that this was not the proper manner for establishing the sacred Guru-shishay relationship. Kabir is supposed to have responded by asking whether there was anything more sacred and more precious than Ramnam. For the worshippers of Ram, of whom Swami Ramanand was the foremost in his time, there is, of course, nothing more sacred and precious than the Name of Ram; and so Kabir pressed his point. What other mystery did the Swami reveal to his disciples at the time of their initiation but Ram-nam? Kabir's point was well taken and Swami Ramanand openly declared Kabir to be his disciple[2].

Thus, succeeded Kabir by attaining the Guruship of Swami Ramanand. But according to the tradition Swami Ramanand never showed his face to Kabir and always had conversation with him behind a curtain. Basically there was a lot of difference between the two saints in their Bhakti Marg. Kabir always gave due regards to his Guru but never followed his way of worship and his traditional rituals. Swami Ramanand used to worship his Lord's statue. One day it had happened while worshipping Swami Ramanand put Mukat on the head of his Lord but forget to put mala around his neck. The garland was not so big that it could be put around the neck of the Lord while bearing a Mukat. Swami Ramanand was in a fix what to do or what not to do. While sitting outside the room's door behind the curtain Kabir was witnessing all this, and requested Swami Ramanand, Gurudev! please loosen the garland's knot and put it around the neck of the Lord. While listening this Swami Ramanand was much surprised and shocked and felt that this poor weaver is not an ordinary man. He shouted at once and said "remove this curtain" just now. There will be no curtain between me and Kabir in future. Seeing this Kabir vowed his head on feet of Swami Ramanand but Swamiji embraced him. This incident has been revealed by Shrimati Shanti Sethi in her book entitled *'Sant Kabir* (a translation of Virendra Sethi's English book Kabir the weaver of God's Name).[3]

Notes and References

1. R.P. Tiwari, *An article on Kabir,* pp. 82-83.

2. David C. Scott, *Kabir Mythology,* pp. 107-108.

3. Shanti Sethi, Sant Kabir (A translation of Virandra Sethi's English book entitled, *'Kabir the Weaver of God's Name,'* Published by Radha Swami Satsang, Vyas, Dera Baba Jaimal Singh, District Amritsar, Punjab, pp. 14.

7

Domestic Life of Kabir

When Kabir grew in age and stature his parents had married him recorded Mahipati in Bhaktavijaya. The mother and father taught him how to carry on his avocation, but he would not take it to heart. He would give no attention to a business life. He could not distinguish what belonged to him and what belonged to others. He did not know what was joy and what was sorrow. He paid the same respect to a Brahman, a prince or a pauper. If he saw a heap of money fall before him, he had no desire to pick it up. If a thief came to rob him of his money, he did nothing to protect himself. Because Kabir worshipped in this way, his business declined. The evil-doers and evil-minded laughed as they saw Kabir's conduct. If a banana tree and a bor tree are planted in the same place it will not be happy for either. How can fire and water dwell together in friendship? How can a prositute and a dutiful wife, a miser and a generous giver, a reviler and a man of intelligence, live together in peace. There will be enmity between the one and the other. How can a fly and dainty food get on well together? A goat herd and a pandit cannot live together in friendship. How can the demon Rahu and the moon, a moth and a flame, the sea and the rishi Agasti, dwell in love.

Kabir continued his worship of God, while his business prosperity grew less. The evil minded laughed at him. You have taken God to your heart, and so has come about this condition of self neglect. It does not appear how you will continue to carry on your domestic affairs. Having that day rubbed paste on the threads, Kabir was made to sit at the loom, but he was not able to think of himself. He was entirely lost in the worship of Ram. Bringing the image of Shri Ram to his imagination, he closed both of his eyes. His full attention was given to the form and name of God. He no longer remembered his own bodily condition. His mother came to him, and tried to awaken him. She said, 'Kabir, I do not know what has happened to you now'. Believing that his mother would beat him, he came to self consciousness and being now awake he wove a hand breadth of cloth. But after a moment he again became unconscious and the image of Shri Rama appeared in his mind. Seeing this to be the case, the Lord of Ayodhya (Shri Ram) himself sat down to weave. Shri Ram said to himself, He has lost himself in contemplating me. His mother will give him beating. So thinking, the Holder of the bow (Shri Ram) sat down to weave the Shela (gold scraf). Now and then awakening, Kabir hastened to begin to weave but soon he lapsed into his usual trauma. Thus, God and his bhakta together wove the garment and folded it and came into the house and gave it to his mother. The mother said 'Go to market and sell it quickly and come back with some money for me. Saying, 'I will do so Kabir started from his home, taking the scraf in his hand, and sat down in the bazar. He closed his eyes and brought to his mind the form of Shri Ram. He lost self consciousness and continued singing the praise of Shri Ram with his lips. He forget completely that he had come to the bazar to sell the scraf. Holding God in his heart, he continued repeating the names of Shri Ram in his love for Him. Merchants came into the bazar and Kabir sat down beside them, but no customers appeared for the purpose of buying the scraf. The customers saw the Shela and left. Kabir was unconcerned but when night fell Kabir awoke from his meditation and realised that the Shela was unsold. He became sad and feared of his mother. He then saw a deserted home and hid himself out of fear of his mother. Just then the pervader of the Universe, seeing his devotion, came to test the truth of it. He took the form of a very aged Brahman, with old and torn clothes. The cold was intense. He entered the house shivering and asked for some clothes from Kabir. Kabir tore the Shela by half and gave it to him. No sooner, this Brahman had left, a Mohammadan Fakir entered carrying in his hands a rosary and opening wide his blood shot eyes. In a violent laughter, he stood at the door and called Kabir and said, "Give me at once a garment". He also said, God is without form and without qualities, both cannot exist with difference. Why do you love him and Shri Ram". Kabir replied coolly. "To be without form and at the same time possess qualities, both can exist without any difference between them. If butter is hardened or melted, it does not thereby lose its character of being butter. So the unmanifested, eternal being had taken form. The pervader of the Universe has assumed visible form for the purpose of His Bhaktas". The Fakir again repeated his request for the garments and Kabir hastened to remove the scarf which remained with him and gave it to the Fakir and himself became unconcerned about the loss of the scarf and again sat worshipping God.

A Brahman informed Kabir's mother all that had happened and told her that I witnessed from a distance, hence have happened to tell you and he consoled her with the words, 'Kabir will not put his mind to worldly affairs. Kabir's mother became very angry and said to herself. "When he comes home, I will give him a sound beating". The Brahman took her to the place where Kabir was engrossed in deep meditation, chanting the name of Shri Ram. The mother said to Kabir, "Bring the scraf and show it to me. If you do not bring it at once, I will punish you". Kabir would, however, give no reply and he was too deeply engrossed in God's concentration. His mother became very angry and said, "In a stupid manner you are sitting here, loving and worshipping Ram". Hearing her say this, the Lord of the Vaikunth said to the old woman, you have used harsh language with your lips but you have love for him at heart. Now take a cane and punish him. The Brahman produced a cane and gave it to Kabir's mother who violently struck Kabir. As she continued to strike Kabir on his back, Shri Hari stood outside trembling with intense pains and explained in the garb of a Brahman. "That is sufficient now, O Mother".

God in the form of a Brahman said unto Himself that, "Kabir is superior to myself and I must show him my visible form, because I have troubled him a lot". The Brahman appeared in a transformed form for Shri Ram and His consort Sita like the thousand dazzling suns. Kabir was thrilled to have darshan of Lord Shri Ram and Sita Mata. His mother was also thrilled to witness such spectacle. Kabir's mother embraced her son and took him home happily.[1]

When Kabir's mother had whipped him it was done in ignorance. After that event she had brought to her the sight of Shri Ram, she became comforted. She was in the habit of persecuting him, but now she said nothing to him. When one has the favour of the pervader of the universe, all troubles pass away. Those who have the king's favour are honoured by the king's ministers. If Ganpati is favourable to anyone, hindrances do not come into his way. So Kabir's mother having received the favour of the Lord of Ayodhya (Shri Ram) no longer persecuted him. And having received divine knowlege, she gave herself to the worship of Hari. Her mind became indifferent to worldly things. In order to conform to public custom she carried on her daily routine in her domestic concerns, but in her heart she was continually repeating the names of God, full of love. Although she had not in her home any food or raiments, her mind felt no anxiety. Kabir's dutiful wife was like the good Ansuya[2].

The question whether Kabir was married or not has been hotly disputed, at first among his Muslim and Hindu disciples, and then among the modern writers. But no doubt he was a married man. While the Muslim traditions regards Loi as his wife, and Kamal as his son and Kamali as daughter. The Hindu traditions considers the latter two as his disciples as well as the first named who, it is argued, was also his disciple having learnt his profession of weaving by frequently visiting his home. However, there are two poems which show clearly that Kabir was married and had children.

In the first of these, Loi being anxious, like Kabir's mother, at the neglect of his weaving and also at his constant entertainment of the saints, addresses him thus:-

Thy threads are broken, thy size is at an end,

Thy needs shine over the door,

Thy poor brush hath gone to pieces,

May death light on this shaven fellows' head !

This shaven fellow hath lost all his property.

I am persecuted by those (Sadhus) coming and going. Kabir now never speaketh of his beam or shuttle; His mind is only concerned with the name of God. His daughter and son have nothing to eat;

Men with shaven heads are crammed in, night and days;

One or two are in the house, and one or two are on the way;

We have only a pallet (on the ground); they get a bed (to sleep on)

We get parched pulse, they have bread (to eat)

These shaven heads and my shaven head (husband) have become all one.

To this complaint Kabir replied thus ;

These shaven heads are the support of the drowning

Hear, O blind misguided Loi !

Kabir hath taken the protection of these shaven heads

(Adi Granth, Gaund 6)

At any rate, the circumstances under which Kabir married Loi are told in great details in Kabir Kasauti. The legend says that at the age of thirty Kabir met Loi, aged about twenty in the cottage of a Bankhandi Bairagi (ascetic who lived in the jungle) on the bank of the Ganges. To her questions as to who he was, what was his caste and sect, Kabir replied: "Kabir". The girl, however, was charmed by Kabir's spiritual quality. Kabir took Loi home, and his mother Nima, thinking that her son brought a wife, accepted her as Kabir's wife.

According to another legend Kabir had two wives, one homely the other pretty. The second wife was called Dhania or Ramjania. As the latter name is also used euphemistically for dancing girls, some scholars suggest that this second consort was probably a courtesan. The Kabirpanthis do not accept the thesis of a second marriage of Kabir.[3]

About the domestic life of Kabir Scott has narrated the under mentioned story in the following words: According to

Muslim tradition, Kabir like other Sufi saints was a married man and had two children. However, some of the Hindu traditions take great pains to explain that the woman named Loi was not his wife, but his disciple. Some accounts omit mention of her altogether. Perhaps the account of Loi recorded in the Kabir Kasauti is as representative and inclusive as any and will thus serve our purpose.

When Kabir was about thirty years old, it is said he was once wandering in the forest along the banks of the river Ganga when he happened to come upon the hut of certain Sadhu, where he sat down to rest a while. After a while a girl of about twenty years of age entered the small enclosure surrounding the hut and inquired about Kabir who he was "Kabir", he replied. In response to questions about his caste and religious order he gave the same answer, "Kabir". Surprised by his strange replies, the girl said she had met many mendicants passing through the woods but never any one who spoke to her in this fashion. Kabir agreed with her and said that all other had a name, a caste and an order but he had none. Meanwhile, a group of six Sadhus had stopped in the enclosure and the girl busied herself preparing seven cups of milk to serve the guests. All drank heartily but Kabir who said he was saving the seventh cup of milk for a Sadhu on the other side of the river, headed towards the hut. The girl assured him that there was sufficient milk but Kabir informed her that he was sustained by the world. Before long, to the astonishment of all, the Sadhu, whose arrival Kabir had predicted, appeared. In further conversation it came out that at one time an elderly sadhu had lived in the hut alone. One day as he was bathing along the edge of the Ganga a bundle wrapped in a woollen cloth bumpered into him. On opening it he found a baby girl, whom he took home and raised on milk, he himself having never touched anything but milk. Because he had found her wrapped in a woollen cloth he named her Loi. Ever since the recent death of her guardian Loi had been living in the forest alone. At the conclusion of the tale the visitors fell silent, but after a few moments Loi, having been deeply impressed by Kabir asked him to teach her something which would give her peace. For his part, Kabir had been impressed by the simple piety of the girl, and in response to her request he urged her to continue her life of humble devotion and service. His kind and straight forward words seem to have had an immediate effect on Loi, for she gave the hut and her few belongings to the visiting Sadhus and vowed she would spend the rest of her days with Kabir. It is said that she learned Kabir's trends and also worked as a weaver. However, there are indications that she, not less than Nama, was alarmed at Kabir's neglect of his weaving and his constant attention to the wandering Sadhus and mendicants. Indeed there are traces of this tradition to be found in the Adi Granth, which as we shall see, indicate that she in her bitterness even confronted Kabir with the circumstances which seemed to partened nothing but hunger and suffering for the family. Afterwards Loi is said to have repented her strong words and begged Kabir's forgiveness.

There are also those who think that Kabir had a second wife or that his wifes name was Dhania or Ramjaniya, not Loi. Support for this is drawn from a tradition preserved in the Adi-Granth as the words of Nima.

> My daughter-in-law was called Dhania
>
> They went and called her Ramjania

Those who maintain that Kabir was celibate mendicant tell a story, whose theme is rather familiar, to support their contention. It seems that Vishnu once called a restless young *apsara* and suggested that she go and try her allurements on Kabir to see if she could distract him from his devotion to God. After a most elaborate preparation, decked in the best finery of the celestial realms, she set out wafting on all sides the most expensive perfume. Indeed she was so charming and alluring that the Lord of Vaikuntha ordered her not to dally lest some pious soul in his realm be tempted. She did not walk but danced and if she even glanced at anyone the victim as paralyzed by the arrow of love.

Approaching Kabir, she bade him took into her eyes as she spoke, "Just think what people do to attain this beauty and love. They make arduous pilgrimages and practice severe austerities. But they do not find me. To you I have come all of my own. Make me yours, just for a moment, and your penances will have come to fruition.

However, Kabir was unmoved. Respected Mother, what made you leave heaven? What hardships do you have to suffer there that you have come to a poor weaver? My calling is extremely humble. You belong with princes, surrounded with the aroma of mask, befitting your great beauty and charm. I am a stone and will not melt. Indeed, sitting with me you will feel ashamed. Further, I see only poison in your eyes, for my soul is united with the divine. There is no place for you in my heart. Please forgive me".

When all her wiles and charm left Kabir utterly unaffected, the frustrated *apsara* returned to Vishnu to report her failure. Vishnu was extremely pleased to hear of the faithfulness of his devoted disciple and appeared to the pious weaver, offering him any boon". A crown can be yours, or all the powers of the occult, or sovereignty over the entire universe. Speak your wish".

But Kabir demurred. "O Tribhuvannathji", I seek nothing at all. How can my finite mind comprehend your infinite will? An ant cannot lift a mountain, nor stars hide the moon. The ocean cannot be cupped in the palm of the hand".

Kabir humility further pleased Vishnu, who placed his hand on Kabir's head in blessing. Vishnu then freed Kabir from age and death before departing for heaven. This is a very common story about Kabir Sahib which needs no comment and explanation[4].

Notes and References

1. Dr. Giri Raj Singh, *Saints, Gurus and Mystics of India*, Vol. I, pp. 304-306.

2. *Kabir's Biography* (Mahipatis Bhakatmal).

3. Muhammad Hedayatullah, *Kabir: The Apostle of Hindu - Muslim Unity*, Delhi, Motilal Banarsidas, 1977.

4. David C. Scott, *Kabirs Mythology*, Delhi, Bharatiya Vidya Prakashan, 1995; pp. 112-115.

8

Birth of Kamal and Kamali

Renowned author Westcott and Keay and Muhammed Hedayatullah and David C Scott have quoted in their books entitled *Kabir; The Apostle of Hindu Muslim Unity and Kabir's Mythology* respectively have narrated the following legends about the birth of the son and daughter of Kabir Sahib:

According to some legends, Kabir's son Kamal and his daughter Kamali were not his actual offspring but children, he found on two different occasions whom he restored to life and adopted as son and daughter. It is also said that both of them used to work with him at the loom.

There are two legends about Kamal's birth: According to one story—one day when Kabir was walking on the banks of the Ganges with Sheikh Taqi the corpse of a child was seen floating by. Sheikh Taqi challenged Kabir to raise it to life. This he did and taking it home he adopted it as his own son. The Sheikh said, "You have indeed shown great perfection (Kamal)". So the boy was named Kamal. According to another story, Kabir caught sight of the child floating down the stream in the Ganges wrapped in a blanket (Kamal or Kammal), and he cried out, "Kammal, Kammal". So he named the child Kamal, which is a corruption of Kammal or Kambal. About the later life Kamal, little is recorded. Like his father, he is said to have been a renowned bhakta and a man of deep spiritual experience, and a poet of high order.

It is also stated that Kamal opposed his father's teaching, and composed verses in refutation of it. One tradition says that Kamal became the guru of Dadu, the founder of the Dalpanthi sect. Another story connects Kamal with Sheikh Taqi, and says that as he differed from his father, Kabir, the Sheikh gave him (Kamal) permission to settle at Jabalpur about ten miles from Jhusi. About 12 miles from Jhusi, the tomb of a certain Sheikh Kamal is shown; but it cannot be certainly identified as being that of Kabir's son. Like Kamal's legend a similar story is told about the coming of Kamali. According to some accounts she was a child who had died in the house of a neighbour and Kabir raised her to life; according to others, the daughter of Sheikh Taqi who had already been eight days in the grave.

According to a tale, when Kamali was twenty years of age, she was one day drawing water from a well. A Brahman, who was thirsty, asked for drink, but was afterwards horrified to find he had taken water from a weaver's daughter. The Brahman rebuked her for breaking his caste. The matter was referred to Kabir Sahib, who replied thus:

O Pandit, think when thou drinkest water,

In the mud-dwelling wherein thou sittest

the universe is contained:

Where fifty six Kotis of Yadavas (one Koti: ten millions. The Yadavas were the tribesmen of Krishna) perished, eighty eight thousand men and munis (sages):

At every step prophets are buried, they decayed to dust therein. Fish, tortoise, and crocodile there gave births,

the water is filled with blood.

Thou, O Pandit, thou didst sit down to drink;

Yet the earthen pot thou accountest defiled;

Renounce the Vedas and the Book, O Pandit;

all these are fictions of the mind.

Kabir says, Hear, O Pandit; these are your pious. The Brahman, named Har Deva, fell at Kabir's feet begged his pardon and became Kabir's disciple. Kabir accepted him, and Kamali was married to him[1].

Notes and References

1. Muhammad Hedayatullah—Kabir—(Footnote at pp. 174-175) and Kabir's Mythology by Scott—pp. 115-117.

9

The Happy Home of Kabir

Kamal from his very childhood was indifferent to worldly things. He was generous, wise, and one of fixed determination. When he heard his father singing the praises of God, so he imitated him in the same worship. When seven years old he said to his father in a humble voice, 'Give me permission to go to Dwarka. Hearing his son's raequest, Kabir said to him, Go and fulfil the desire of your heart and then hasten back. Kamal made an obeisance to his father and mother and then started. As he walked along the easy path, he sang of the names and praiseworthy deeds of God. He had no liking for clothes or ornaments. He had no liking for the best food. All he cared for was the worship of Shri Ram. Every one knew the bhakta Kamal as the son of Kabir. When he entered into the citites, people heard of his coming and went out to meet him. The town people, seeing him, would take him into the town with marks of honour. He would remain their for a night and perform a Hari-Kirtan. In this way, with full experience of knowledge, he hastened to Dwarka[1].

Living in this way, the bhakat Kamal remained for four months at Dwarka and in love composed poetry describing the good deeds of him. With love he prayed, 'O God, give me again the opportunity of coming here to worship and see Thee'. On return, he reached the town of Chitrakut. There he was welcomed by a merchant named Vishnudas who took him home and washed his feet and placed a meal before him. For the night a Hari-Kirtan was arranged and all the people of the town assembled. After the Kirtan, he placed a diamond at the feet of Kamal and said at night time, "If you place it before you, there will be no darkness". Kamal said, 'No' and humbly returned it saying 'My father will be angry. Money should be offered to the Brahmans, Diamonds and other jewels should be offered to Kings and food and gifts should be given to loving beings. One should give to rope dancers, jugglers and players, the old clothes. One should give dry provisions of food to the holy men who are performing austerities. One should give daintily cooked food to Sanyasis. They should be given the yellow robes and loin cloth. The merchant prostrated before Kamal and tied the diamond in Kamal's garment.

Kamal returned home and embraced the feet of his parents and placed the diamond before Kabir after relating everything. Kabir's heart was full of repentence and he fall unconscious. His wife immediately came and grasped her husband and said "Why were you so troubled today"? Turning his back towards his son he said to his wife, "it seems to me that our whole family has shrunk in shame. Our Kamal has sold our good name and brought this diamond. O wife, I think myself that my son, with a sweet desire has brought here this diamond". On hearing this, Kamal returned to Chitrakut and returned the diamond and told his parents about it after his return. Kabir was very happy over this and he embraced his son.[2]

Notes and References

1. Mahipatis, *Bhakta Vijaya*, pp. 94-95.
2. Dr. Giri Raj Singh, *Saints, Gurus and Mystics of India*, pp. 308-309.

10

Kabir and Kamal as Robbers

Once a large number of saints who lived at various sacred places came to Kabir's house. It was at the first half of the night these saints came to Kabir's house. Both father and son came forward and prostrated themselves on the ground. Kamal hastened to bring a woollen blanket for them to sit upon and he said to the saints, 'O Swamis seat yourselves on it. When the saints saw what was being done, the three parties felt joy, just as Indra felt joy when he saw Sanak and the others. Kabir felt great joy as he saw these great saints. Going aside he said to his wife, we must give these saints something to eat. These bhakats of Vishnu who reside at sacred places have come to our home. If we permit them to sleep here empty stomach, our reputation for goodness will be lost. Now there was not the least bit of food in the house, so the distress of the couple was intense, but now listen to what the wife said, when she heard her husband's remark. She said to Kabir, 'O lord of my life, I do not see what is to be done. If we go to our neighbours to borrow, they will give us nothing whatever we could go into the bazar and buy, but we have no money. So take your son with you and go and steal something. Break open the shop of the merchants who seem to have an abundance of materials for food and bring back the food which you steal, and serve a meal to those saints. The bhakta Kabir acceded her proposal. He alongwith his son Kamal went to Bazar and broke open the shop of the merchant. He put his son inside the shop and he himself remained outside. It was now midnight and the merchant was in sound sleep. Kabir called to his son from outside that he should hasten in what he had to do. When Kamal looked into the shop he saw piles of money, garments and ornaments. Seeing them he felt a sense of disgust. The son brought out of the shop, flour, rice, sugar, split peas, melted butter, sugar and gave them to his father Kabir.

As he hastened to come out of the house, a thought came into his mind. The grocer is fast asleep, and one kills him in that state, or if one reviles anyone behind his back, he will fall into the horrors of hell. Being a bhakta of Vishnu and I know what is wrong and what is right. So I will waken the grocer and quickly run away from here. Then taking courage he moved quickly to the side of the grocer and slapped him on his back saying 'You ought to be awake. We are two thieves who have broken open your shop. We are going away with the materials for cooking, I tell you this'.

The grocer got up, but Kamal started to run away. As he was passing through the narrow opening both his feet got caught. When half of his body was outside, the merchant seized him. The child Kamal then called out his father and said to him, Now the grocer will come outside and shout in the bazar. When the people of the town hear him, they will come rushing to see what the matter is. All the men and women will regard us as the thieves of the town, so you cut off my head and hurry back to our home. If you hold in your mind any idea of love (that I am your son), it will be to the loss of your reputation for goodness. If people hear the story of your stealing, saints will not come and sit in your house. So kindly put aside all ideas of love and of my belonging to you, and cut off my head with your own hand. Listening to what his son said, Kabir was pleased in his mind. He took the sword in his hand and cut off his sons head. He then made the bundle of materials for cooking and taking it up, hurried back to his home. There he told his wife what had happened. Kabir put the bundle down on the floor and gave Kamal's head to his wife. He love for him overwhelmed his mother and tears flowed from her eyes. O my child, you are one of the great good fortune. You have sacrified your body for saints. Coming into this worldly existence you have made Shri Ram your own. Thus, you have saved our whole family life.

Saying this, Kabir's wife restrained her feelings by the force of her courage. She took the cooking materials and started to cook. She mixed the nine different kinds of materials into a dainty dish and served the meal to the saints, saying as she served them. This is a blessed day. I have seen the feet of saints. Kabir gave them straw mattresses to sit on, and served these saints. It was now sunrise and these sadhus at once arose.

After their early morning devotions, these Vaishnavas went to their bath. In the meantime the grocer came out of his house and shouted aloud. Hearing the shouting, all the people came there. They came to the place where the thief was, and looked at his condition. They said His head has been cut off and taken away. Who can now recognize him? They remarked to the grocer, your fate works most curiously. One of the thieves has killed this man and taken away his head. The God of all has protected you.

The saints and sadhus had gone to the river side to take bath. They performed their whorship of God and returned to Kabir's hermitages. Finally taking leave of Kabir, these dwellers in sacred places started on their way. Kabir made a *namaskar* to these saints, and accompanied them to see them off. Kabir's wife was bitterly weeping. She prostrated herself on the ground before these saints and said, When shall I see your feet again? Speaking thus humbly to these saints the two accompanied the saints to see them off. As they came out of the city an extraordinary event took place. As the company was hurriedly walking along the path, they suddenly noticed a headless corpse impaled upon a stake. The saints saw it from a distance. As they stood still for a moment to look at the sight, a most extraordinary thing took place. Kamal joined his hands together and made a *namaskar* to the saints and sadhus. The men and women expressed their astonishment as they saw this most unusual act. It seemed to them extraordinary that a headless corpse should make a *namaskar*. The saints and sadhus said to Kabir, 'The corpse is making a *namaskar* to us. How is it that life has been preserved in a body without head? When a tree is cut down what would make its branches suddenly show signs of life? So, seeing a corpse with life in it, seems to our minds a most unusual thing. Kabir joined his hands palm to palm, and said to the saints, when Bhisham Pitamaha fell on the bed of arrows and even then his life was preserved in his body. Similarly Abhimanyu, in order to relate to Arjun his sorrows when he fell on the battlefield, had his life preserved in his body with courage. And in a similar manner when Ravan was making trouble for Jatayu his body was overwhelmed with pain, his desire to see Shri Ram preserved life in his body. So this thief was a Vaishnav. He had a great desire to make a *namaskar* to your feet. Therefore, his life remained in him. The desire of his heart has been fulfilled. Now he will leave his perishable body and live in his everlasting home. Hearing him say this, the saints replied, who indeed was this thief? Then Kabir related to the saints the whole story. The Vaishnavas then said, 'Although we had not asked for food, how is it that Kabir should kill so good a son as Kamal? Hearing them, the noble Vaishnava answered, 'All earthly things are perishable. Whatever is seen to have a form must in the end disappear. Suppose I had not killed Kamal, would he thereby have remained immortal? Listening to this remarks, a sense of compassion arose in the harts of the saints. The saints said to Kabir's wife, 'kindly bring the head and show it to us. Hearing this remark, she hastened back to her home. She took her son's head and brought it back to the saints. When the compassionate saints saw it they were moved with emotion. They took the corpse down from the and placed the head upon it. The people looked on with wonder. As the saints placed their hands upon the head of Kamal, he came to life, arose and made a *namaskar* to the saints. All the inhabitants of Banaras now prostrated themselves on the ground before Kabir. The saints gave him their blessing and started on their way to sacred places[1].

The following most interesting and impressive story have been recorded by Dr. Giri Raj Singh:

> As stated earlier the name of Kabir's wife was Loi. Kamal was his son and Dharam was his disciple. The queen of Chitore, Jhali was also his one of the disciples.

Kabir used to feed the Sadhus and ascetics, who so ever he may be. One day he had nothing in store. Many hungry ascetics came to his hut. Kabir was in an agitated condition. His wife said, "O Lord, if you permit me, I can get some money from a Baniyas". Kabir said, "How can you get the money from him" He is a great miser". His wife said He is very much enamoured of me. He said the other day that he would give me money. Let us take the money and teach him a very good lesson. Kabir replied that it is very good. Go to him immediately and bring some money. The ascetics are very hungry. They have not taken food for the last three days.

Loi went to the house of the moneylender and saw his young son. She promised to meet him at night. He at once gave her the money she needed. Loi came back to her hut and handed over the money to her husband. All the Sadhus were fed sumptuously.

There was a great downpour of rain that night. There was a big storm also. Kabir covered his wife into a blanket and took her on his shoulder, in storm and rain, to the house of the money lender. Loi entered the compartment of the money lender. Kabir waited outside to take her back home. The youngman rejoiced at the sight of Loi. He was quite astonished to see her in his room on such a stormy and raining night. He said to her, "My dear, how have you managed to come to my house? You are not drenched. Your feet are quite clean. There is no mud on your feet. It is great wonder". Loi replied, my husband has carried me here on his shoulder". The youngman was struck with amazement and awe. He became a changed man at once and said, bitterly weeping, "Loi has your husband brought you to me?" He immediately regarded Loi as his mother and at once prostrated at her feet. He said to her, "Thou are my mother. Forgive me for my evil intention". He ran to the place where Kabir was standing. He fell at his feet and cried, "O Venerable Guru ! I am a great sinner. Purify me. Elevate me. Bless me. I take refuge in thy lotus feet. I am a suppliant before thou. I am the humble devotee". From that day the banker's son became one of the faithful followers of Kabir[2].

Notes and References

1. Mahipatis' Bhakatvijaya, pp. 94-95.
2. Dr. Giri Raj Singh, *Saints Gurus and Mystics of India*, pp. 306-307.

11

Banaras Traditions and Kabir

In Banaras, among Hindus, sun dried vessels are replaced daily. It is believed that the night renders them impure. Kabir was anxious to attract holy men, and followed the popular custom of daily renewing his cooking vessels and smearing his cooking places.

One day he was selling a piece of cloth in the market place. He asked five double paise for it, but no one would give him more than three. A broker came up and seeing that Kabir was undervaluing his cloth, began to assist him in its sale. The broker asked intending purchasers twelve double paise. They, forming an idea of the value of the cloth from the price put upon it by the seller, offered seven double paise and at this sum a bargain was struck upon this Kabir uttered the following couplet:-

If I speak the truth,
You beat me down;
the World is pleased
with falsehood.
A sheet worth five double paise is sold for seven.

Kabir, kept his mind continually fixed on God, and worked sufficiently to maintain himself and his family. Another day, as he was standing in the market place selling cloth, a faqir came and begged for wherewithal to cover his nakedness. Kabir offered him half the cloth he had for sale. The faqir replied that that was not enough. Upon this Kabir gave him the whole. Kabir then reflected that his mother and family were waiting for the price of the cloth, and how could he return to them with empty hands? He therefore decided to conceal himself and not return home. His people became very anxious regarding him.

In the meantime God put it into the heart of a corn merchant to take ox-loads of food of every description to Kabir's house, so that his family might not suffer during his absence. Kabir's mother strenuously resented the offering and said My son will not take even a single grain of corn from anyone. Who art thou who throwest such a quantity of provision at my door? The merchant, however, heeded her not but leaving all the provisions took his departure. Two or three men then went in quest of Kabir, and brought him home. When he saw the unexpected supplies and heard the circumstances, he knew it was all due to the kindness of God, and became highly pleased and grateful to the Giver. He then sent for some saints and distributed what he had received among them.

When the Brahmans of Banaras heard that Kabir had given hundreds of mans of corn to holy men, but not even one grain to themselves, they went in a body to his house and thus addressed him:

'Weaver, thou hast become very proud of thy wealth since, without any intimation to us, thou hast distributed provisions among low caste faqirs and sudras. Leave this city at once, and take up thy residence elsewhere Kabir asked why he should leave the city. Had he broken into any one's house or committed highway robbery, that they sought to exile him? The Brahmans replied that, since he had served and done honour to faqirs instead of themselves it was an offence sufficient to merit expulsion from the city. 'Say no more' they continued, it is better for thee either to make us an offering or depart hence'. Kabir replied that his house was all he had and they could take possession of it. Thus saying, he escaped from them, and again concealed himself in a distant forest.

Upon this some admirers of Kabirs sanctity, and sympathizers with his troubles, distributed among the Brahmans such an amount of money and provisions that the name and praises of Kabir resounded throughout the whole city and the Brahmans were highly delighted and gratified on finding their stomachs filled to repletion. After that, a holy man sought out Kabir, and asked him why he spent his days in the forest. Why goest thou not to thine own house? Whoever goeth to thy door obtaineth money and provisions and shall there be nothing for thee? Kabir then went home and finding ample supplies for his family, was grateful for God's mercy and love. When the report of such good fortune and God's bounty was noised abroad, people went in great numbers to the saint. Finding his meditations interrupted by his visitors he resorted to a singular expedient to blacken his own character and keep them at a distance. Pious people were scandalized and said that though Kabir had been a perfect saint, he must now be deemed a wicked man unfit for the association of the virtuous.

While Kabir's desire for seclusion was thus fully attained, and people ceased to throng round him in numbers, ignorant people uttered reproaches and satirized him. Kabir went in strange guise to the king's court and sat down in the midst of the assembly. The king and his courtiers, seeing his strange behaviour, treated him despitefully and ordered him out of their presence. The king, however, on reflection was ashamed of his hasty order and want of consideration for such a saint, not-withstanding the strange guise he had adopted. The king then began to consider how his own sins could be pardoned. He put an axe on his shoulder and a bundle of firewood on his head went bare footed with his queen into Kabir's presence and fell down with great humility and modesty at the saints feet. Kabir pardoned his discourtsy and showed him the way of devotion to God.

12

Atrocities of Sikandar Lodi on Kabir

The bigoted emperor Sikandar Khan Lodi, son of Bahlol Lodi visited Banaras in Samwat 1545, the year he ascended the throne. Owing to the dampness of the locality he contracted a severe fever and ague. Kabir's enemies suggested that he should be called to cure the emperor. Their object was that Kabir should fail in his efforts, and then be punished by the despot. To the dismay of his enemies however, Kabir is said to have cured the monarch by simply presenting himself.

The Musalmans, headed by Shaikh Taqi and the unbelieving Brahmans, subsequently appeared before the emperor to make a complaint against Kabir. They represented that he had so led people astray all over the city, that those who paid heed to what he said, remained neither Hindus nor Musalmans. The emperor summoned Kabir. When he appeared, the courtiers told him to salute and make obeisance to the monarch in the usual manner of subjects. Kabir replied that he was not accustomed to courts and did not know how to make prostrations nor had he any business with the emperor. He but knew the name of the God, who was the support of his soul and only Sovereign of the world. The emperor became enraged on hearing this and forgetting his former obligation to Kabir, loaded him with chains and had him thrown into the river. It is related that, Kabir, who had previously cut off the chains of sin, easily swam to shore leaving his chains behind him. Unbelievers attributed this miracle to magic, so setting some wood on fire they threw the saint into it. By God's grace the fire was completely extinguished and Kabirs' body emerged from it more handsome than before. When these means of destrucion failed, a furious elephant was let loose on him. The elephant, however, not only did not approach Kabir, but fled on seeing him Kabir Sahib compose the following lines on that occasion.

They tied my arms and threw me like a ball;

They beat an infuriated elephant on the head that he might trample on me

But he trumpeted and fled saying

I am a sacrifice to that shape which appeared.

Saith Kabir, 'O my God, Thou at my strength,

The Qazi ordered Drive on the elephant

O driver, or I will make mince-meat of thee;

drive on the elephant, wound him,

The elephant did not move, but kept his attention on God.

And God took possession of his heart.

People asked, 'What crime hath the saint committed,

That you have made a ball of him and thrown him to the elephant?

The elephant lifting up the ball bowed to it;

Even then the infatuated Qazi could not comprehend.

Three times he tried to kill me but failed;

Even then his hard heart would not be satisfied.

Saith Kabir, O God, Thou art my protector;

Thy servant's soul is in the fourth state.

When Kabir had successfully escaped from these ordeals, another charge was invented against him, namely that he had been guilty of the blasphemy of calling himself God. This was deposed by several witnesses, and the emperor was induced to give it credence. He again summoned Kabir. On Kabir's arrival the emperor caused a cow to be slaughtered and ordered Kabir to reanimate her Kabir stroked her with his hand, and then made a noise with his lips as if driving her, upon which, it is related, the cow stood up, and all her wounds and injuries were healed. When the emperor saw the power of Kabir's devotion, it is said he fell at his feet, and thus addressed him : 'I am thy servant and slave. Pardon my offences that I may be saved from God's wrath. Ask what thou desirest money, Lands and other things and I will present them to thee; and do thou in return bestow such kindness on my poor circumstances that I may be happy in this world and the next, Kabir replied that he had no concern with anything but the name of God. Gold and lands were all useless to him. Saying this he went home.

The saints of God were all overjoyed at his safety, but the Brahmans irritated at their failure began to contrive further means of annoyance. They dressed up several persons as holy men, and sent them to various dignitaries to invite them on behalf of Kabir to a banquet on a certain date. Guests came in crowds at the appointed time. Kabir on discovering the trick that had been played, and knowing that on account of his poverty he was unequal to the entertainment of such a multitude, again fled, this time with the approbation of the saint Rav Das, to a neighbouring forest for concealment.

But God did not wish that his saint should be made a laughing-stock. He sent in the guise of Kabir a holy man who performed the duties of host with such grace and dignity as was impossible for any ordinary mortal. As each party of visitors arrived, the holy man met them at the door, and performed for them all the rites of hospitality. He provided them with suitable apartments, washed their feet, and performed all necessary services. When all the guests had fared to their hearts content, and the holy man obtained leisure from attendance on them, he sat down with each group and conversed with its members on sacred subjects. In this way the festival was prolonged for several days. After that he went to Kabir, and gave him a full account of the entertainment. Kabir then went home overjoyed with God's love and kindness to him and composed the following slok:

Kabir, I did not do this, nor will I do it again, nor am I physically able to do it;

How do I know what God may have done? Yet it was all Kabir:

To this Kabir in his thankfulness to God added the following hymn:

Endless salvation awaiteth him

Who hath such a master as God, O brother,

Say, now that my trust is in Thee, O God,

What obligation am I under to any one else?

Why should God who beareth the loud of the three worlds not cherish me?

Saith Kabir, I have obtained one piece of knowledge by reflection-

If a mother will poison her child, who can restrain her?

It is said that the entertainment took place on the spot where since has been built the Chaura Kabir, a temple dedicated to Kabir, in which his writings are said to be preserved.

There was a renowned Brahman disputant, called Pandit Sarva Jit, who at his mother's advice went to Banaras with several ox-loads of books. He had heard of Kabir's fame and proceeded to visit him. On arriving at Lahar Talao, he met Niru's daughter drawing water, and requested her to show him Kabir's place of residence. She said that it was on a lofty place, with a road so narrow that not even an ant could pass, much less the oxen he had brought with him. By her answer he felt sure that she knew where Kabir lived. He took a *lota* of water from her, and requested her to place it in front of Kabir. She did so, upon which Kabir put a needle into it and told her to carry the vessel back to Sarva Jit. There is a proverb that truth is found at the bottom of a well. By the needle Kabir meant that truth was small, exquistely polished, and under-lay much unsubstantial matter.

The Brahmans of Banaras on hearing of Sarva Jit's arrival went to Ramanand and informed him that a Pandit had come with whom nobody could cope. Ramanand was so little impressed with the Pandit's great learning, that he told them to go out into the street and bring in the first person they met; and he undertook that he would vanquish Sarva Jit in argument. The Brahmans went forth into the street. Kabir happened to be the first they met, and they took him to Ramanand. Ramanand declared Kabir invincible and the Brahmans accordingly put him forward as their spiritual champion. Sarva Jit on seeing him inquired his caste, where upon Kabir answered that he was a weaver. The haughty Pandit turned up his nose and asked what a weaver was Kabir replied as follows:

No one knoweth the secret of the weaver;
God hath woven the warp of the whole world.
If thou listen to the Vedas and Purans
Thou shall hear, 'I have stretched the warp so long;
I have made the earth and firmament My workshop;
I have set the moon and sun in alternate motion;
Working My legs I did one work'—with such a weaver my heart is pleased.
The weaver hath looked into his own heart and there recognized God.
Saith Kabir, ' I have broken up my workshop,
And the weaver hath blended his thread with the thread of God.

Sarva Jit admitted himself defeated, and begged Kabir to make him a disciple. Kabir modestly referred him to his guru Ramanand, who gave him the customary initiation.

Tata and Jiwa, two Brahman brothers who lived in retirement on the bank of the river Narbada, doubting the spiritual perfection of their guru, planted a shoot of the Indian fig-tree near their dwelling and vowed that, if it germinated when irrigated with the water in which a holy visitor had washed his feet, they would transfer their spiritual allegiance to such a visitor. Several reputed saints made pilgrimages to the locality, but it was only on Kabir's arrival that the desired result was attained. Upon this Tata and Jiwa had no difficulty in believing in Kabir's super human power.

A young woman of beautiful and bewitching form was sent by Kabir's enemies to test his virtue, but she displayed all her attractions and fascinations in vain. God's image was so firmly seated in Kabir's heart, that the charming damse's wiles produced no effect on him. She therefore departed crestfallen and helpless. God was pleased on beholding the continence and devotion of Kabir, and appeared to him in a vision. He placed His hand on Kabir's head and invited him to go bodily to heaven. Kabir, knowing that he had obtained complete deliverance, prepared himself to accept Gods invitation; but, to show his contempt for Hindu superstitions, and to emphasize the power of devotion to God, he performed a very unusual act before his departure to the celestial realms.

Kabir usually lived, until the last year of his life at Banaras, the sacred city of Shiv, where alone, in the estimation of many Hindus deliverance may be obtained. There is a town called Magahar beyond the Ganges about eighty, five miles to the east of Ajudhia and fifteen miles to the west of Gorakhpur, in which according to Brahmanical belief, those who die have no hope of ultimate beatitude. Kabir's biographer says that they who believe in the religious exercises prescribed in the Shastars, migrate into the bodies of donkeys if they die in Magahar; while for those who are fortunate enough to perform the real worship of God, every country and every place is equal to thousands of cities like the Hindu Banaras. Nay, such is the power of devotion, that God's devotees who die in Magahar go to heaven.

Kabir, on arriving in Magahar, took possession of a saints cell he found on the margin of the river Ami. The river was then dry, but water has flowed in it ever since the day Kabir hallowed it with his presence.

Kabir composed the following hymn at Magahar:

I am as a fish out of water,
Because in a former life I performed no penance.
Now say, O God, what shall be my condition.
People tell me I had little sense to leave Banaras,
That I wasted all my life in that city of Shiv[1];
And now when about to die, I have moved to Magahar.
For many years I did penance to Banaras
But, now that death is at hand, I have come to dwell in Magahar.
I consider Magahar as good as Banaras—
How shell he of scant devotion be saved?

Saith Kabir, my guru Ramanand[2], Ganesh, Shiv[3] and all men know.

That Kabir when dying uttered God's holy name[4]. And also the following :

Thou art my great mountain; O Lord, I have sought Thy shelter.
Thou Shakest not, nor do I fall; Thou hast shelter me, O God;
Now and then and forever more there is but Thou.
By Thy favour I am ever happy.
Relying on Thee I have dwelt in Magahar;
Thou hast quenched the fever of my body
I first obtained a sight of Thee in Banaras, and afterwards I went to live at Magahar.

As Banaras so is Magahar; I deem them both the same. I am a poor man have obtained this wealth on account of which the proud *Pandits* are bursting to death and envy. He who is proud suffereth that torture; there is none to deliver him there form. In this life he crieth bitterly under the torture, and after death he shall be burnt in a frightful hell. What is hell and what heaven, the wretched places? The saints have rejected them both[5]. Through the favour of the guru I pay no regard to any one, I have claimed God's throne and met Him: God and Kabir have become one; no one can distinguish between them.[6]

Notes and References

1. Banaras, where the worship of Shiv specially prevails.
2. Some understand Brihaspati, the teacher of the Gods.
3. Ganesh, it is said, endeavours to bring every one to die in Banaras who has ever visited that place of Hindu pilgrimage. Shiv is said to whisper his *tarak mantar* or farewell spell, 'Ram, Ram' (God God) into the dying man's ear. The idea is that Shiv is also a worshipper of Ram and recommends his friends to that god's protection.
4. Gauri
5. Kabir desired absorption in God, and not heaven where he should be again subject to transmigration.
6. M.A. Macauliff, *History of Sikh—Bhagats of The Granth Sahib*, p. 128.

13

Death of Kabir Sahib

At an advanced old age in 1518 A.D. he passed away at Magahar near Gorakhpur. After Kabir's death a dispute arose between the Hindus and Musalmans for the disposal of his body. Vir Singh Baghela, the king of Banaras, wished to cremate him, while Bijli Khan, the Nawab of Gorakhpur, desired to bury it. They fought over the matter until a voice came from heaven and separated the combatants. When the quarrel was adjusted, it was found that there was no corpse to dispose of. Fragrant flowers were found in its place. The Musalmans, however made a grave, and the Hindus erected a shrine in friendly proximity as if each party were in possession of Kabir's sacred remains.

Kabir lived to such a great age one hundred and nineteen years five months and twenty seven days that there are several fabulous accounts of his duration of life. Indeed some of his followers believe that he is still in existence. The following mnemonic lines, however, which are amply authenticated, show that Kabir went the way of all mortals:

Pandrahi san pachhatar bikhe
Kiya Magahar ko gaun;
Magsar Sudi ekadashi
rali paun mein paun

Kabir went to Magahar in the Samvat year 1575 (A.D. 1518).

On the eleventh day of the bright half of the month of Magahar his spirit blended with the spirit of the world.

Nabhaji wrote on the circumstances:

Trusting to his devotion Kabir relinquished his body in Magahar.

And now rejoiceth in the lap of the Immortal.

The Dadupanthis, or followers of the saint Dadu, also corroborate the fact of Kabir's death at the time above stated and in the town of Magahar.

It is said that Kabir after few days rose from the dead, and appeared to a disciple called Ratan in Mathura, and gave him divine instruction. Kabir then and there met Dharm Das, whom he had previously appointed his successor, and made him more completely acquainted with the principles of his religion. He laid down forty two articles which he called the pillars of faith and having fully explained them to his disciples finally departed to his eternal home.

Besides Kabir's compositions, preserved in the Granth Sahib, there is a long list of works attributed to him, the most famous of which is the Kabir Bijak. Many of his verses are repeated by wandering faqirs.

On the subject of caste Kabir wrote:

The courageous man who effaceth caste and pride shall prove a saint.

On the subject of idolatry he said :

If God be found by worshipping a stone;

I will worship a mountain;

Better than that stone is a hand mill which grindeth corn for the world to eat.

Many similar verses in the mouths of the populace in upper India, and indeed all Kabir's compositions, show him to have been a daring and original thinker. It must be mentioned, however, that his writings are frequently of a mystical character and much concentration of thought and knowledge of the spiritual and social condition of his age are necessary for their elucidation. The author has accepted the interpretation of Kabir's hymns from the gyanis of the Panjab, but possibly the saints followers in other parts of India may differ on some details.

Kabir held the doctrine of ahimsa or the non destruction of life, which extended even to that of flowers. The Sikh Gurus, on the contrary, allowed and even encouraged the use of animal flesh as food (Maculiff).

The visitors to Kabir's temple in Banaras is shown what purports to be his picture. Dharam Das; the man who compiled Kabir's writings, it is said, in Samvat 1521 (A.D. 1464) when Kabir was sixty-six years of age and Surat Gopal, another of his disciples, are represented kneeling at his feet in an attitude of supplication, while his son Kamal, who the Kabirpanthis believe, was a child re-animated by him, is fanning him. The visitor may also see a picture of Kabir and Rav Das, a friend and fellow disciple and townsman. Rav Das is represented as a very attenuated old man, naked except for a red cloth round his middle, wearing a rosary in two folds round his neck, and beads on his wrists and arms. The saintly royal lady Jhali, queen of Chitour, richly dressed, is offering him food on a platter[1].

Notes and References

1. M.A. Macaulif, *History of The Sikhs—Bhagat of the Granth Sahib,* p. 128

14

Kabir Panth

The Kabir Panthis of Northern and Central India recognize two main divisions of the Panth, one with headquarters at the Kabir Choura in Banaras and a branch establishment at Maghar and a second, founded by Dharam Das with headquarters in the Chhattisgarh district, in the Central Provinces. The former is known as baap (father) and the latter as mai (mother). The relations between these two divisions have at times been strained. The Math at Puri, where, in the worship of Jagannath, distinctions of caste are disregarded, is respected by both as a place of pilgrimage.

In the light of the present information to determine the date at which either of these divisions first came into existence, but both were probably established by Hindu followers of Kabir Sahib.

As stated earlier that Kabir died and was buried at Maghar, in the district of Gorakhpur. The shrine at Maghar which has always been in the change of Muhammadans was restored in 1567 by Nawab Fidae Khan, the officer in Command of the imperial army which occupied the city in that year.

There are two memorials (Maths) of Kabir Sahib at Maghar, one for Muhammadans, containing the shrine, and another for Hindus, in the enclosure of which is a hole in which Kabir is said to have sat, awaiting death. Each of these Maths which adjoin one another, has accommodation for 50 Sadhus, though as a rule only one Sadhu lives in each. About 50 Hindu Sadhus live in the neighbouring villages of Balwa and Khurswal where the Panth has landed property.

At Maghar there are more Muhammadan than Hindu Kabir Panthis. The two sections have very little in common, except their devotion to Kabir their Master. Each section receives Prasad in its own Math.

A Mela is arranged by the management of Muhammadan Math which is attended by a large number of people. This Mela is held on the last day of Aghan (November) and a sacred feast is arranged. The Mahant proceeds to the shrine, followed by the Diwan, carrying in both hands a large dish containing Khichri (cooked rice mixed with dal), and by a Bandali carrying an earthenware vessel (Kharwa) containing water and covered over with a white cloth. On reaching the shrine these vessels are placed on the ground and frankincense is burnt upon the tomb, in a fire of cowdung. The Mahant repeals certain prayers in which all present take their part.

On the conclusion of the prayers he takes his seat upon the ground while the Diwan gives to each of the worshippers a small portion of the Khichri and the Bandali pours from the spout of the Karwa a few drops of the water into the palm of their hands. When all have received, the Diwan and Bandali consume what is left. More prayers are held, after which the Mahant departs and the gathering breaks up.

Pilgrims to the shrine are expected to present a rupee to the officer-in-charge and also an offering of rice and dal. They receive in return a small portion of Khichri and a pinch of the ashes that result from the burning of the frankincense and cowdung.

The Kabir Choura Math receives its name from the fact that it occupies the site upon which according to tradition Kabir gave instruction to his disciples. The Math consists of two courtyards, connected by a bridge thrown cross a narrow lane. The main courtyard contains the preaching platform, the Mandar, which is occupied by a pair of wooden sandals (Khadanu) intended to represent the feet of the Guru, the Gaddi, the Samadhis (tombs) of five Mahants and quarters for Sadhus. The courtyard across the lane which occupies the traditional site of Niru's house is made over to the female Bairagis, known as Mai Log. This court contains the Samadhis of three Mahants.

The room in which the Gaddi is placed is immediately opposite the entrance gate. Over the Gaddi hangs the picture of Kabir Sahib. In this picture Surat Gopal and Dharm Dass, the founders of the two main divisions of the Panth, are represented as kneeling before Kabir while Kamal stands behind with a fan in his hand. One side of the picture hangs a portrait of Ramanand and on the other a picture of Rangi Dass, the late Mahant, who died a few years ago.

Above the pictures are hung what appear from the distance to be armorial bearings, but are in reality designs in coloured cloth, intended to symbolise the five elements (earth, air, fire, water and akasa and the nine doors or points of entrance into the human body. In front of the Gaddi are placed two flower - vases and upon the wall at the side hangs a rosary, composed of a thousand beads, which is reserved for the use of Mahant. Morning and evening services are conducted daily in the Math, by the Pujari. Early in the morning, after taking bath the Sadhus assembled in front of the temple. Here takes place the first part of the service which includes the performance of Arti and the washing of the Guru's feet. After this the different Samadhis and the Gaddi are visited and the Sadhus return to the temple for the concluding portion of the service. The morning service is said to occupy thirty minutes and the evening service an hour.

The water in which the wooden sandals have been washed, known as *Charan Amrita,* is poured into a brazen vessel. Three tea spoons full of this water together with three tulsi leaves, are given to all who visit the Math during the day. At 8 P.M. the doors of the Math are closed and any *Charan Amrita* that remains over is offered in the first place to such Sadhus as have not previously received it. The vessel is then presented to the Mahant who after drinking what remains out in the vessel with fresh water and consumes that also.

An annual Mela which lasts over four or five days is held at this Math in the month of January, on this occasion the large courtyard is crowded with devotees. Those who wish to become Bairagis observe a fast for twelve days, eating in the evening a little gur (crude sugar) and rice cooked in milk. These candidates are admitted as Bairagis at the celebration of the *Jot Pershad,* which from a religious point of view, constitute the principal purpose of the Mela. Of the possessions belonging to the Math the Kabir Panthis regard the cap and woollen necklace of Kabir, the picture of Kabir and the Bijak as those of greatest value.

The principal officers of the Math are the Mahant, the Diwan, the Kotwal and the Pujari. The Mahant is responsible for the general arrangements and should be a man of learning, qualified to give religious instruction; the Diwan is the business manager; the Kotwal is responsible for the maintenance of discipline, while the pujari conducts the Puja and keeps clean and in order the Mandar and the Gaddi.

The headquarters of the Dharm Dass section were originally at Bandogarh in the neighbourhood of Jabalpore; from this place they were transferred to Koodarmal and once again in recent years to Dhama Khera.

Dharam Dass, the founder of this section, is said to have first met Kabir Sahib at Banaras and to have been rebuked by him for worshipping idols. He met him subsequently at Brindaban, but failing to recognise him said, "Your words resemble those addressed to me by a Sadhu whom I once met at Banaras". On this occasion Kabir adopted stronger measures and threw into the river the idol which Dharm Dass was worshipping. Once more Kabir appeared to him in his house at Bandogarh.Dharm Dass was a bania by caste and possessed of considerable wealth. Kabir again rebuked him for practising idolatry and asked him how he could worship an idol made out of the same stone as the weights which he made use of in his business. On this occasion Dharam Dass acknowledged the force of his arguments and both he and his wife became his disciples. According to the account given in Sukrit Dhyan,

Dharm Dass was the son of one Mahesh, and was as an infant saved from death by Gyani (i.e. Kabir) who entered into his body. He was originally called Judawan, but objected to this name and received from Kabir permission to change it to Dharam Dass. Narayan Dass, his son, refused to accept Kabir as his Guru, but through the grace of Kabir Sahib a second son was born in 1516 and name Churaman. This son was installed upon the Gaddi by Kabir himself. Upon the occasion of his installation Kabir told in advance that his descendants should sit upon the Gaddi for 42 generations and declared that the right to communicate the Mantra would be confined to his descendants. In accordance with Kabir's instructions the Head Mahant of this section marries and lives with his wife till a son is born. After the birth of the son the wife becomes a Bairagi. The Mahant holds office for a period of 25 years and 20 days and is then succeeded by his son. In one case the son is said to have died and as the mother has become a Bairagi the Mahant lived with another woman by whom he had a son. The father of the present Mahant died after holding office for a period of three years, only and many wished that one of his disciples, Jugla Nand, should officiate as Mahant during the remainder of his term of office. To this proposal the majority of the members strongly objected on the ground that he was not a descendant of Dharm Dass, and Ugranam was duly installed. His grandmother, known as Dadi Sahib, who was responsible for this proposal, still exercises authority at Koodarmal, and Ugranam reigns in the newly established Math at Dhama Khera. Jugla Nand with other discontented sadhus retired to Bombay, where he has published various books bearing upon the Panth. Kabir is said to have given instructions to Dharm Dass regarding the Chauka and the Jot Prasad.

The Kabir Panth exists as a protest against the regions exclusiveness of twice-born castes. As a natural result few but Sudars whose cause it champions have associated themselves with the movement. The Panth contends for a truth which forms part of the Gospel of Creation, viz. that all men have spiritual powers which should find their natural expression in communion with God, now in this life.

The sons of the twice-born as they came to years of discretion are invested with the sacred thread (Janeo) and reminded thereby of their spiritual privileges and responsibilities. The members of this Panth wear round their a *kanthi* (rosary) formed of beads made of Tulsi wood. This *kanthi* is naturally associated with thoughts of prayer and in this way remind those who wear it alike of their relation to God and of the promises which they made at the time of their initiation. Permission to wear a *kanthi* is granted to woman as well as to man, for they too are spiritual beings; but no woman may assume a *kanthi* previous to marriage nor may she become the disciple of her husband's Guru.

Two Brahmins at the time of investiture with the sacred thread is communicated the Brahminical *mantra* which they are not allowed on any account to communicate to those who are not Brahmins. In like manner at the time of initiation a *mantra* is whispered into ear of Kabir Panthis. This mantra serves as a bond of union between members of the Panth and also suggests a position of privilege.

Brahmins wear upon their forehead the sign of the God whom they worship. Kabir Panthis also wear such a mark (tika) as shown in the frontispiece.

In the days of Kabir a knowledge of religious truth was practically confined to those who were acquanted with one or other of the two sacred languages, Arabic and Sanskrit. These two languages were employed both in Public and private worship with the result that the worship of the masses was too often a mere repetition of phrases which were unintelligible to those who used them. Kabir urged that religious books should also be written in the Vernacular that all might obtain that knowledge of God which was essential to spiritual progress.

Again to the illeterate masses teaching contained in books was in accessible and so it is that we find Kabir laying great stress on the importance; of oral teaching. Few men are qualified to become scholars, but all are required to be good; therefore he urged his disciples to associate with good man and through conversation with them to acquire such knowledge as is necessary. The study of books, he thought, was too often productive of pride, to display learning and intelligence scholars were often tempted to enlarge upon topics of little spiritual value, while in private conversation heart speaks heart of its own spiritual needs. Such were the views of Kabir and in consequences the Guru in his Panth occupies a position of extra-ordinary importance.

Kabir was a poet of no mean order and gladly consecrated his literary gifts to the service of God. He knew that religious instruction given in the form of poetry was easily remembered; he knew too that the singing of *bhajans* (hymns) was an occupation in which the people of India took peculiar pleasure. It only remained for him to compose hymns which his followers could sing. This he did, and up to the present day his hymns enjoy great popularity with the people and in the Panth occupy a prominent position in all acts of public worship.

As the Brahmins are required to repeat the Gyatri daily, so as members of this Panth required to use the following hymns, in the morning and evening respectively.

Morning Hymn—Kabir said, spiritual and material blessings attend those who wait upon the Darwesh; their account is sufi. Love you pervades the whole body of your devotees. You are starvation, unmoved by desire, a mendicand. You walk in no one's footsteps, you seek case in no abode. The whole universe is your body. You are boundless (a stream without banks). You pervade the Universe constantly. The love which you cause is profound. The empty universe is in me, says the Guru (Kabir). If we do honour by fire to the true name, the body becomes pure. Dharam Dass taking the Guru's arm walked and found Kabir.

Evening Hymn—Evening having come on, the day having closed, the duck broke into wailing: "O drake let us go to that country where day and night are unknown". If separation takes place at night, the duck is to be met with in the morning, but he who is separated from the name (of God) regains it neither during day nor night. Hear, O Guru, Treasury of kindness, I beseech you with clasped hands. Mercy, humidity, devotion, equality, good nature, constancy, these are the ornaments of a devotee. Devotion to the one without beginning is adornment. The only name, the only Guru is Kabir, the highest Pir.

Anxious as Kabir was to claim for all men spiritual privileges he was no less anxious to impress upon those who desired to become religious that they must live in a way consistent with their profession.

All, therefore, who wish to join the Kabir Panth are required to renounce polytheism and to acknowledge their belief in one only God. They must also promise to eat no meat and drink no wine; to take bath daily and sing hymns to God, both morning and evening to forgive those who trespass against them up to three times; to avoid the company of all woman of bad character and all unseemly jesting in connexion with such subjects; never to turn away from their house, their lawful wife; never to tell lies; never to conceal the property of another man; never to bear false witness against a neighbour or speak evil of another on hearsay evidence.

One prominent trait in Hindu character, viz. personal devotion, finds ample scope for exercise in the devotion to their Guru required of all members of the Panth. All who wish to approach God must, they say, become the disciple must wholly submit himself, mind, soul and body. To Kabir, as the chief Guru, many of the *bhajans* used in Public worship are addressed and marked reverence is also shown to the living Guru as God's representation upon earth.

The above list so far as the name of Mahant, place of Samadhi and tenure of office are concerned was supplied by a Bairagi at Banaras.

The existence of the first three Mahants is highly problematical. Surat Gopal (A.D. 1559) is generally regarded as the founder of the Panth. It is possible that he and the two Mahants who succeeded him did not have their headquarters

List of the Kabir Chaura Mahants

S.No.	*Name of Mahant*	*Samadhi at*	*Year of office*	*Approximate date of installation*
1	2	3	4	5
1.	Shyam Dass	Maghar	28	1491?
2.	Lal Dass	Maghar	22	1519?
3.	Hari Dass	Maghar	18	1541?
4.	Surat Gopal Dass	Jagannath	35	1559
5.	Gyan Dass	Jagannath	25	1594
6.	Sital Dass	Gaya	24	1619
7.	Sukh Dass	Niru Tila	20	1643
8.	Hulas Dass	Niru Tila	26	1663
9.	Madho Dass	Niru Tila	20	1689
10.	Kokil Dass	Niru Tila	21	1709
11.	Ram Dass	Niru Tila	29	1730
12.	Maha Dass	Niru Tila	22	1759
13.	Hari Dass	Niru Tila	20	1781
14.	Sukh Dass	Kabir Chaura	27	1801
15.	Saran Dass	Kabir Chaura	16	1828
16.	Puran Dass	Kabir Chaura	18	1844
17.	Nirmal Dass	Kabir Chaura	22	1862
18.	Ranghir Dass	Kabir Chaura	15	1884
19.	Gur Prasad Dass	-	8	1899

(Courtsey—G.H. Wescott—*Kabir and the Kabir Panth.* Munshi Ram Manohar Lal, New Delhi, pp. 67.)

at Banaras, but that the Niru Tilla compound was acquired during the Mahanti of Sukh Dass. Bulwinder Singh, and his son and successor, Chet Singh, were patrons of the Kabir Panth. The former did in A.D. 1770. The Kabir Chaura compound may have been acquired in their time.

Though seven Mahants are said to, have been buried in the Niru Tila court of the Math at Banaras only three Samadhis are conspicous at the present time.

List of Dharam Dass Mahants

S.No.	*Name*		*Approximate date of installation*
1.	Churamani	Nam	1694
2.	Sudarshan	Nam	1714
3.	Kulpati	Nam	1734
4.	Pramodh	Nam Guru Bala Pir	1754
5.	Kewal	Nam	1774
6.	Amol	Nam	1794
7.	Surat Sanchi	Nam	1814
8.	Haqq	Nam	1834
9.	Pak	Nam	1854
10.	Praghat	Nam	1874
11.	Dhiraj	Nam	1894
12.	Ugra	Nam	1897
13.	Daya	Nam	-

(Courtesy—*Kabir and the Kabir Panth*—G.H. Wescott, Munshi Ram Manohar Lal, New Delhi, pp. 68.

The above have already appeared. Those follow are :-

Girdhmani	Nam
Prakash	Nam
Uditmani	Nam
Mukandmani	Nam
Adh+	Nam
Udai	Nam
Gyan	Nam
Hansmani	Nam
Sukrit	Nam
Agrmahi	Nam
Ras	Nam

Gungmani	Nam
Paras	Nam
Jugrat	Nam
Bhringhmani	Nam
Akah	Nam
Kanthmani	Nam
Santokh	Nam
Chatric	Nam
Dadhi	Nam
Neh	Nam
Adi	Nam
Maha	Nam
Nij	Nam
Sahib Dass	Nam
Udhawa Dass	Nam
Karunra	Nam
Uddhar	Nam
Drigh	Nam
Mahamani	Nam

The dates have been calculated on the assumption that each Mahant held office for 20 years and 25 days except Dhiraj Nam who is known to have died after three years tenure of office. One Mahant stated that the regular tenure of office was for 25 years and 20 days. On such a calculation the date of Churamani would be thrown back to A.D. 1654. In this Kabir Chaura section the average tenure of office has been for 23 years.

The Sudh Nidhan is said to have been written during Pramodh Nams tenure of office (courtsey....)

15

Teaching of Kabir Sahib

In the days of Kabir Sahib the power of the Brahmins was very great. They have the status of a Guru and worshipped every where. Brahmanism have asserted over all authority on the society, until Muslim invaders invaded the country and gradually extended their influence throughout Northern India.

Before considering the character of Kabir's teaching we have first to determine what his teaching was. It is clear that the teaching of Kabir was delivered orally and not reduced to writing till a later age. The earliest writings in which his teaching is recorded are the Bijak and the *Adi Granth*. It is probable that neither of these books was composed till at least fifty years after the death of Kabir, and they can hardly be regarded as retaining in all passages the actual words of the teacher, much less such words without additions Kabir has said:

I neither touched ink nor paper, nor did I take a pen into my hand; to the sages of all four ages Kabir declared his word by mouth.

So far the contents of the *Bijak* have only been made known in part, and all who have studied the book allow that it contains many passages that are practically unintelligible to us of a later age, dark riddles which they are unable to interpret. An exposition of teaching which is based upon a selection from selections, must of necessity be defective; and may possible be misleading, if regarded as an interpretation of the whole.

Illustrations

1. We are idols of clay, to which the name of man is given; we are guests of four days in a very great pit of fuel is our place. (*Adi Granth*).
2. The physician has died, the sickman has died, the whole world has died, One, O Kabir, has not died for whom is no weeper. (*Adi Granth*).
3. O man, thou hast a precious body indeed. The flesh is not used. No ornaments are made of thy bones; no drums are mounted with thy leather. (*Bijak*).
4. Man in this world is wholly sinful from his very birth, and there are many ready to claim his body. The parents say, "He is our child and we have nourished him for our own benefit", the wife says, "He is my husband", and like a tigers wishes to seize him. The children gaze at him, and like the God of death, keep their mouths wide open for support. The vulture and the crow look forward to his death. The pigs and the dogs wait on the road for his bier to pass on its way to the burning ghat. The fire says, "I shall not leave him, until he is utterly consumed". The earth says, 'I shall obtain him". The wind thinks of carryhing him off. O ignorant people, you speak of this body as your house; do you not see that a hundred enemies hang about your throad. Beguiled by the illusion of this world, you regard such a body as your own. So many desire as share in your body that you will live in trouble all your life. O madmen, you do not wake up to a knowledge of this, but repeatedly say, 'It is mine'. It is mine. (*Bijak*)
5. Adding Kauri to Kauri he brings together lakhs and crores. At the time of departure he gets nothing at all, even his *langoti* is plucked away from him. (*Adi Granth*).
6. To the miser wealth is given for the sake of keeping it. The fool says, 'The property is mine'. When the staff of *Yama* strikes his head, the matter is decided in a moment. (*Adi Granth*).

7. Immense riches and a kingdom which extends from the rising of the sun unto the going down thereof could not equal the pleasure arising out of devotion (to God). Of what use than is wealth? (*Bijak*).

8. Fire does not burn it, the wind does not carry it away, no thief come near it; collect the wealth of the name of Ram, that wealth is never lost. (*Adi Granth*)

9. For gold he is not obtained, Ram is obtained for the price of the heart. (*Adi Granth*).

10. Without devotion life is spent to no purpose; without worshipping the Lord in the society of the pious, happiness remains is none. (*Adi Granth*).

11. The poor souls of man is tied to this world with many knots. It cannot unloose itself without the help of God. (*Bijak*).

12. He (God) whom you seek, is near you. He is always near to his devotees and far from those who do not worship him. (*Bijak*).

13. Kabir says, where shall I find a supremely loving saint who will give pleasure, destroy pain and remove all stains of sin. (*Bijak*).

14. Who whilst living, goes on dying, he lives again; in this wise he is absorbed in space; he who remains in the darkness, unaffected by the darkness is no more thrown into the sea of existence. (*Adi Granth*).

15. Now my mind on the contrary has become eternal; then the mind is known, when one dies when living. (*Adi Granth*).

16. At the bank of a river and at a Tirtha there is no reassurance for the mind of him who is clinging to right ways. (*Adi Granth*).

17. What is muttering, what austerity, what vours and

worship to him in whose heart there is another love. (*Adi Granth*).

18. What is muttering, what austerity and control of the passions, what vows and ablutions; so long as the right loving worship of the Lord is not known. (*Adi Granth*).

19. In the heart there is a looking glass, the face is not seen in it; then only you will see the face when the doubleness of the heart is removed. (*Bijak*).

20. The pure diamond is sold for plates of gold. He who knows not its value, what will he do with it? (*Bijak*).

21. The diamond was lying on the road, besmeared with ashes: many in their ignorance passed it by, but the diamond specialist picked it up. (*Bijak*).

22. Pearls are scattered on the road, the blind draw near and depart; without the light of the Lord, the world passes them by. (*Adi Granth*).

23. The black snake is in the heart. It has deposited venom in the souls of all, the new who sincerely worship the true God, will be saved. (*Bijak*).

24. Why should one suffer a dog to listen to the Smritis, why should one sing the praises of Hari in the presence of a *Sakat*? that Ram, Ram is contained in all should on no account be told to a *Sakat*, why should one suffer a crow to feed on camphor? Why should one give a black snake milk to drink? the instruction of the foolish is waste of knowledge; a maund of soap cannot wish charcoal white. (*Adi Granth*).

25. Sandal, restrain thy fragrance, on thy account the wood is cut down, the living slay the living and regard only the dead. (*Bijak*).

26. He is naturally called drunk, who is drinking the juice of Ram and meditating on Divine knowledge. (*Adi Granth*).

27. If one take nectar and be sprinkle a neem tree, its nature does not leave it, says Kabir (*Adi Granth*).

28. Venomous snakes have twined round the sandal tree. What can the sandal do? in every pore Venom has soaked in, where shall nectar enter? (*Bijak*).

29. The snake of separation has attached itself to the body, and darted its fangs into the heart, into the body of the Sadhu it finds no admission: prepare yourself for what may happen. (*Bijak*).

30. In the small pond, O fish, the net is spread by the fisherman; in this small pond thou will not escape, think again of the ocean. (*Adi Granth*).

31. The pride of intellect is manifold, now a swindler, now a thief; now a liar, now a murderer; men, sages and gods have run after it in vain; its mansion has a hundred gates. (*Bijak*).

32. In pride there is adversity, in sin their is sufferings; in kindness there is stability, and in forgiveness there is God. (*Bijak*).

33. Unless you have a forgiving spirit, you will not see God. You may specify as much as you like, but without a forgiving nature you will never reach Him. (*Bijak*).

34. He who enters into intimacy with the highest light, the subdues the fine senses. Religious merit and demerit, both he discards. (*Adi Granth*).

35. What thou art doing tomorrow, do now; what thou art doing now, do at once; afterwards nothing will be done, when death comes on the head. (*Adi Granth*).

36. Now is the time to prepare, henceforth the path is difficult; the travellers all hasten to purchase, where there is neither trade nor market. (*Bijak*).

37. The righteous man does not give up his piety, though he met with crores of wicked persons; even as the sandal

tree is not deprived of its cooling properties though venomous snakes twine round it. (*Bijak*).

38. With the Sakat company should not be kept, one should free far from him; if a black vessel is touched, some stain is received. (*Adi Granth*).

Religion in Life

God is one; how has it come about that there are many religions? All men are of one blood; how comes it about that they are separated by religion and by caste? God is one: the Hindus are therefore at fault in their worship of many Gods. These are in truth the creation of Maya, they have their origin in sin and are themselves the cause of sin in others.

Muhammadans puts their trust in circumcision, Hindus adore the Vedas and the beauties of Nature. The things which are seen are transitory. True worship should have as its object the unseen source of all truth, the unseen creater of the universe.

The Hindus take bath in sacred streams, go on pilgrimage to sacred places, bow down to images of brass and stone, and think that is so doing they are honouring God. In this they are mistaken. What God desires is purity of heart; to rest in symbols that should lead men on to God is to be guilty of idolatry.

Hindus and Muhammadans alike profess to fast, but curb not the desires of the flesh; they praise God with their lips, but their hearts are far from Him. All such religion in vain.

Vain too are the distinctions of caste. All shades of colour are but broken arcs of light, all varieties in human nature are but fragments of true humanity. The right to approach God is not the monopoly of Brahmins but is freely granted to all who are characterised by sincerity of heart. He who reflects on Brahmin is rightly called a Brahmin. The distinctions observed by Hindus are merely productive of that pride which God abhors. The rules regarding impurity deal merely with externals and cleans not the thoughts of the heart.

Hindus believe in transmigration. If they should be free

from the trials of this world, let them meditate on the supreme and attend the courts of His temple.

Above all things let men speak and practise the truth. Suffer all men to worship God according to their convictions. Be not the slaves of tradition and love not controversy for its own sake. Fear not to walk upon unbeaten tracks, if such tracks bring you near to Him who is the truth.

Men are saved by faith and not by works. None can understand the mind of God; put your trust in Him; let him do what seemeth Him good. Spiritual joy is felt, though it cannot be expressed in words, to set forth the glory of God is a task beyond the powers of human language. Those who put their trust in God are no longer subject to fear. Perfect love casteth our fear.

Illustrations

39. God, light, sound and one woman, from these have sprung Hari, Brahma and Tripurari. Innumerable are emblems of Shiva and Bhavani, which they have established, but they know not their own beginning nor end. A dwelling has been prepare for them; Hari, Brahma and Shiva are the three headmen and each has his own village. (*Bijak*).

40. I and you are of only blood, and one life animates as both; from one mother is the world born; what knowledge is this which makes us separate? (*Bijak*).

41. All have come from the same country and have landed at one ghat, but the evil influences of this world have divided us into innumerable sects. (*Bijak*).

42. From whence have Hindus and Turks come? By whom have these ways been started? Having searched and reflected in thy mind tell me. By whom have Paradise and Hell been made? (*Adi Granth*).

43. By force and love circumcision is made: I shall not agree to it, O brother, if God will make me a Turk by him will I be circumcised: If a man becomes a Turk by being

circumcised, what shall be done with a woman? She must remain a Hindu. (*Adi Granth*).

44. If your *khuda* wished circumcision, he would have sent you circumcised into the world, if by circumcision you become a Muhammadan in that case what should you do with your women. A women is said to be the half of man; being so, would she remain a Hindu? If by wearing the sacred thread a man becomes a Brahmin then what do your women wear? They by birth are shudrins, why should you being a pande take the meal placed by them before you? Whence have the Hindus and Muhammadans come? who has started these religious systems. Think well in your hearts who has obtained heaven O mad man, give up the illusion of this world. O brethern, you resist (the warnings of conscience). Kabir is on the road to God and is marching on to his end, forsaking all partial views. (*Bijak*).

45. Is Brahma great, or he by whom he is produced? Is the Veda great or he from whom it has come? (*Adi Granth*).

46. What thou seest, that is passing away: whom thou does not see on him continue to reflect. When in the tenth gate the key is given: then the sight of the merciful one is obtained (*Adi Granth*).

47. A well made picture is of high value: leave the picture and think of the painter. (*Bijak*). Variously coloured in this immense world: leaving the picture, keep the painter in thy thoughts. (*Adi Granth*).

48. O Saints, the world has gone mad; if I tell the truth it comes down upon me to kill me, but believes a lie. I have seen the devout and the pious who regularly bathe in the mornings. They forsake God and worship stones; in them there is no wisdom. They have commenced to worship brass and stones and are proud of their pilgrimages. They wear garlands, caps and frontal marks and chhaps on their arms, and engage in singing the praises of their gods; they have forsaken God. (*Bijak*).

49. The beads are of wood, the gods of stone, the Ganges and the Jumna are water. Rama and Krishna are dead. The four Vedas are fictitious stories. (*Bijak*).

50. If by worshipping stones one can find God, I shall worship a mountain; better than these stones (idols) are the stones of the flour mill with which men grind their corn. (*Bijak*).

51. Although I entreat much even failing at their feet, with tears in my eyes, the Hindus do not forsake idol, worship and the Muhammadans are too stiff-necked to hear anything. (*Bijak*).

52. For the sake of bathing, there are many Tirthas, O foolish mind; for the sake of worshipping there are many idols. Kabir says, No emancipation is thus obtained, emancipation is in the service of Hari. (*Adi Granth*).

53. If by immersion in the water salvation be obtained, the frogs bathe continually. As the frogs, so are these men, again and again they fall into the womb. (*Adi Granth*).

54. A stone is shaped by the hammer and formed into an image, with breasts and feet; If image be true, then it will eat the hammerer. (*Adi Granth*).

55. Kabir says, I am completely at a loss, is the Tirtha great or the servant of Hari. (*Adi Granth*).

56. As long as the sun does not rise the stars sparkle; so as long as perfect knowledge (of God) is not obtained men practice ritualism. (*Bijak*).

57. The water is near but the cattle do not drink in wading through it. By continually remembering Hari water issues. That water is pure, says Kabir. (*Adi Granth*).

58. Within his heart is filthiness though he bathe at a Tirtha, he will not go to Paradise. By the belief of the people nothing is effected, Ram is not ignorant. (*Adi Granth*).

59. The Hindus fast on the 11th of the light half to each month for singhara (as sort of fruit) and milk. They give up food during the day, but do not curb the evil passions of their heart and take meat. The Muhammadan keep fasts, repeat the namaz (early in the morning) cry aloud Bismillah like the crowing of a cock. Kabir says "O saints do not call on Rama or Khuda". (*Bijak*).

60. O Moulvi, what books are you explaining? Although day and night you remain babbling and jabbering you have not found out the one (true) religion (*Bijak*).

61. All have exclaimed, Master, Master, but to me this doubt arises: How can they sit down with the Master, whom they do not know? (*Adi Granth*).

62. The mind knows everything and knowingly commits vices: what is the good of the lamp, if with it in his hand a man falls into the well? (*Adi Granth*).

63. Follow the true Sahib (God) who will uphold you in all your trials. He was not born in Dasraths family and did not oppress the king of Lanka. Yashodha did not fondle him in her lap and he did not enter the womb of Devaki. He did not ravage the world. He did not descend into *Patal* to deceive Bali. He did not fight with king Bali or nor did he kill Hiranyaksh, throwing him down on the ground. He did not assume the form of a boar nor did he destroy the Kshattriyas. He did not hold the Goverdhan on the top of his finger nor did he remain in the jungle with the milkmaids (of Mathura and Brindaban). He is neither *Shalagram*, nor any other stone, he is not fish, nor tortoise, dwellers in the water. He died not at Dwarawali nor was his corpse buried at Jagannath. Kabir proclaims, let non follow such teaching; he whom they believe to be of gross and material elements is of subtle principles. (*Bijak*).

64. Brahma is dead with Shiva who lived in Kashi: the immortals are dead. In Mathura, Krishna, the milkman, died. The ten incarnations are dead. Machhindra Nath

Gorak Nath, Dattatreya and Vyas are no longer living. Kabir says, with a loud voice: "All these persons have fallen into the slip-knot of death". (*Bijak*).

65. Whilst dwelling in the womb, there is no clan nor caste; from the seed of Brahma the whole creation is made.

Say, O Pandit, when were the Brahmins made; by saying, "I am a Brahmin", thy life and religion are lost.

If thou art a Brahmin born of a Brahmin woman; why hast thou not come in another way?

Whose art thou, the Brahmin? whose am I, the Sudra; whose blood am I? whose milk art thou?

Kabir says, who reflects on Brahmin, he by me is called a Brahmin. (*Adi Granth*).

66. Colour proceeds from colour, yet behold all are but one; of what colour then in life? Think well of this. (*Adi Granth*).

67. By the touch of others your Brahmins consider yourselves polluted. Let me ask you, who is lower than you? You are puffed up with pride. Great pride never produces any good. How will he who is called the vanquisher of the proud bear with your pride?

68. There is impurity in water, impurity in earth, there is impurity at the time of birth, there is impurity in the hour of death, there is impurity in destruction (corruption of the body)? In the eyes is impurity, in the speech is impurity and in the ears impurity.

In rising and sitting impurity clings to man, impurity falls into the food. Kabir says, those who reflect in their heart on Ram, in them no impurity is found. (*Adi Granth*).

69. As fixed and movable things, as worms and moths in many and various ways have we been born. Many such houses will be inhabited by us, tell at length we return to the wombs of Ram (*Adi Granth*).

70. Having wondered through the 84 lakhs of wombs he has come into the world; now having gone out of the body he has no spot nor place. (*Adi Granth*).

71. Kabir says, Meditate thou on the Supreme, go to his house, that thou come not again. (*Adi Granth*).

72. Clear away the pain of birth and death, the pleasure of works, that the soul may be liberated from rebirth. (*Adi Granth*).

73. To be truthful is best of all, if the heart be truthful. A man may speak as much as he likes; but there is no pleasure apart from truthfulness. (*Bijak*).

74. He who has no check upon his tounge, no truth in his heart; with such a one keep not company. He will kill you on the highway. (*Bijak*).

75. No act of devotion can equal truth; no crime is so heinous as falsehood; in the heart where truth abides, there is my abode (*Adi Granth*).

76. If you are a true dealer, open the market of veracity; keep clean your inward man, and repeat oppression to a distance. (*Adi Granth*).

77. Put a check upon the tongue, speak not much, associate with the wise; investigate the words of the teacher. (*Adi Granth*).

78. Let truth be your rate of interest, and fix it in your heart; a real diamond should be purchased; the mockgem is waste of capital. (*Adi Granth*).

79. I have examined the religious doctrines of Muhammadans and Hindus. They do not lay aside their bigotry for the sake of relish for their tongues. (*Bijak*).

80. Kabir cries aloud to his fellows. "Ascend the sandal ridge: whether there be a road prepared or not, what matters it to me? (*Adi Granth*).

81. O God, thou knowest thine own movements, I have no power to know them. Kabir says, "In this the world has erred and has been led into doubt". (*Bijak*).

82. Thy name is my support, as the flower will grow out of the lotus stalk. Kabir says, I am the slave of my house, vivify or kill me, as it pleases thee. (*Adi Granth*).

83. As many as are making efforts, they are drowned; the ocean is not crossed by them.

    Though they be performing works, and many abstinences, their mind is burnt by egotism. (*Adi Granth*).

84. Kabir says, I am a sacrifice to my own Guru, by whom I remain in connection with the society of the pious. (*Adi Granth*).

85. O Madhva, my thirst for water does not cease; in drinking the water the fire increases still more.

    Thou art the ocean, I am the fish of the water; I dwell in the water; without the water, I am done for. (*Adi Granth*).

86. In me there is nothing mine; whatever there is, that is thine. In entrusting what is thine to thee, what remains mine. (*Adi Granth*).

87. If a dumb person eats molasses, what can he say about it when questioned. (*Adi Granth*).

88. If I make the seven oceans ink, if I make the trees my pen, if I make the earth the paper, the glory of Hari cannot be written? (*Adi Granth*).

89. If fear of God springs up, fear goes, then fear is absorbed in the fear of God.

    If the fear of God subsides, then fear again cleanes to man; when a man loses the fear of God, fear springs up in his heart; he dies. (*Adi Granth*).

90. Where the fearless one is, there is no fear, where fear is there Hari is not. Kabir says, having reflected in his mind; "Hear this, O saints". (*Adi Granth*).

91. On the day on which I died, on that day joy sprang up. The Lord met with me, Govind honours his own companion. (*Adi Granth*).

92. Death of which the world is afraid, is joy to my mind, by death the full perfect joy is obtained. (*Adi Granth*).

The way to God

Kabir was a great believer in quiet reflection as a means of approach to God. He recognised that the ancient scriptures of both Mohammadans and Hindus were of a certain value, but felt that their value had been greatly over estimated.

Through the understanding of the heart and mind man becomes conscious of God's existence. Thoughts and feelings are expressed in words, words are composed of letters. All that is of use in communicating to man a knowledge of God has a significance that may well be regarded as sacred. What is multiform now will hereafter he seen to be single. The 52 letters will give place to the one letter which denotes man's union with God. The revelation of God, given in Ram, surpasses all other revelations in simplicity and purity, but the unity of Truth has not as yet been fully apprehended.

Through his own powers man cannot attain to a knowledge of God; but God will reveal Himself to those who listen to his voice. He alone overcomes doubts and truly lives who has welcomed this message in his heart.

Strange and sad it seems to those who have experienced a knowledge of the Truth that men should be content to grape on still in darkness.

Men are not equally endowed spiritual insight. The mass of men must seek guidance of those who have, through a knowledge of God, discovered for themselves the way. The Hindus trust in vain to those who wear the symbol of sacrifice while they had lives of pride and self indulgence. Helmsmen of this kind will never bring the boat to the *haven* where it should be. Others there are who practise all kinds of austerities, but mistaking the means for the end find not the true path. Those who escape not themselves from death, are unable to impart to others the gift of life.

The true guide is one whose love is fixed on God; who recognises his own worthlessness apart from God; who lives for others and godlike himself has entered into life. For such a one death has lost its terrors. He is the true ascetic and walks in the path of life.

Illustrations

93. O Qazi, what book is expounded by thee; all such as are pondering on the book are killed; no one has obtained true knowledge; give up the book, adore, Ram, O foolish one; thou are practising heavy oppression. Kabir puts his trust on Ram; the Turks are consumed and defeated.

94. Thou expoundest the book right that Allah is no woman or man; but by reading and perusing nothing is effected; when there is no information in the heart. (*Adi Granth*).

95. By the Turk God is known from worship, by the Hindu from the Veda and Puranas, in order to form the mind divined knowledge should be read to some extent. (*Adi Granth*).

96. Thou shouldst ride on thy own reflection; thou shouldst put thy fool into the steerup of tranquillity of mind. Kabir says, Those are good riders who keep aloof from the Veda and Quran. (*Adi Granth*).

97. I know that reading is good, but better than reading is meditation, the attachment to Ram I do not give up, though people revile me. (*Adi Granth*).

98. The 52 letters are joined together by me, but I am not able to know one letter; Kabir tells the word of the true one! who becomes a Pandit, he remains fearless.

    The profession of the Pandit is for the sake of the people, he who is killed in divine knowledge, he reflects the truth. In whom heart such an understanding is; he will know it, says Kabir. (*Adi Granth*).

99. Remove doubt, put aside the paper; having investigated the 52 letters apply thy mind to the feet of Hari. (*Adi Granth*).

100. As the stars at dawn pass away, so the world passes away; these two letters (Ram) do not pass away them Kabir has seized. (*Adi Granth*).

101. There are many words and there is a great difference between them; accept the true word. Kabir says he who has found the true word, has no pleasure in this life. (*Bijak*).

102. My word is of the word; hear it, go not astray; if man wishes to know the truth, let him investigate the word. (*Adi Granth*).

103. By the power of the word the sin of this world is destroyed. The word makes kings forsake their kingdoms. He who has investigated the word has done his work well. (*Bijak*).

104. Without hearing the word it is utter darkness; say, whether shall anyone go; without finding the gateway of the word, man will ever be astray. (*Adi Granth*).

105. Without the word the Shastras are blind. Say whether shall one go? They do not find the gateway of the word but grope on still in darkness. (*Bijak*).

106. There are many words, but take the pith of them; he who takes not the essence, says Kabir, will live a profitless life. (*Adi Granth*).

107. Doubt has triumphed over the whole world. No one has overcome it. He who finds out the word will overcome it. (*Bijak*).

108. Think whence the world has come and where has it established itself. Kabir says, I am a lover of the word which has shown me the unseen (God). (*Bijak*).

109. I have wept for this world but no one has wept with me;

he alone will weep with me who understood the word. (*Bijak*).

110. All speak of God, but to me this doubt arises, how can they sit down with God whom they do not know? (*Bijak*).

111. Thou pasturest us, never bringing us, to the other side; Thou are a Brahmin, I am a weaver of Kashi, understand my divine knowledge. Thou petitionest Kings and Rajas, my meditation is with Hari. (*Adi Granth*).

112. The jogis ascetics, austeres devotees and Sanyasis wander about at many tirthas, those with plucked out hair, those with munj cord, the silent ones, those who are wearing piated hair, all are dying at the end; the Tantras are attended to by them, but not Ram; on whose tongue is put the name of Ram. What can Yama do to him? The Shastras, Vedas, astrology and many, many grammar they know; they know the Tantras, Mantras and all medicines, yet at the end they must die; they enjoy dominion, an umbrella and many beautiful women; betel camphor, perfume and sandal. yet at the end they must die; all the Vedas, Puranas and Smritis are searched by them but in no wise at they spared; Kabir says, Utter Ram, he extinguishes birth and death. (*Adi Granth*).

113. The Pandits are in error by reading the Vedas. They have no common sense. They daily go through their morning and evening rites and other ceremonies with great punctuality and regularity. They have caused the Gayatri to be read and repeated in the four yugas; as them who has obtained freedom from sin by doing so?

They consider themselves polluted by the touch or others; ask them who is lower then they are? (*Bijak*).

114. Who wear dhotis of three yards and a half and three fold cords; on whose necks are rosaries, and whose hands are white lotus; these cheats of Banaras are not called the saints of Hari. Having scoured the vessels they put them

on, having washed the wood they light it; digging out the earth they make two fire places, but eat whole men. (Adi Granth).

115. If by wandering about naked union with Hari be obtained; then every deer of the forest will become emanicipated.

What are the naked? What are those with skins? When they do not know the Supreme?

If by shaving the head, perfection is obtained; the sheep is emancipated no one is lost.

Kabir says, Hear, O man and brother; without the name of Ram no one has obtained salvation. (Adi Granth).

116. In our house the string of the body is continually stretched out; on the breast is a sacrificial thread; Thou readest the Veda and Gyatri; in our heart dwells Govind.

On my tongue is Visnu, in my eyes Narayan, in my heart dwells Govind; when at the gate of Yama he will ask thee, O fool, what will thou say to Mukand?

We are the cattle, thou art the cowherd, O Lord, who are our keeper through the several births.

117. What can he do whose teacher is blind? The blind pushes the blind and both fall into a well. (*Bijak*).

118. How is it possible to reach the city when the guide cannot point out the road; when the boat is crazy, how shall the passengers get clear of the ghat? (*Adi Granth*).

119. The man who fixes his love on the true teacher is contained in him. They could not be separated they have two bodies but one spirit. (*Bijak*).

120. I am the worst of all, every one is good except me; who considers himself in this light, he is my friend. (*Adi Granth*).

121. The tree bears not fruit for itself, nor for itself does the

stream collect its waters; for the benefit of others alone does the sadhu assume a bodily shape. (*Adi Granth*).

122. The body is wounded by a spear; the head is broken off and left in the flesh; it cannot be extracted without the loadstone; a thousand other stones are of no avail. (*Adi Granth*).

123. From heaven and hell I am fried by the favour of the true Guru I remain in the wave of the lotus foot at the end and the beginning. (*Adi Granth*).

124. In this society thou will not die; if thou knowest his order, thou will be united with the Lord. (*Adi Granth*).

125. Death, by which the whole world is frightened; that death is lighted up by the word of the Guru. (*Adi Granth*).

16

Kabir and Guru Nanak

Sant Tradition and Guru Nanak

It is said that Kabir had profound influence on Guru Nanak's thought and as a corollary to it many a strand of Nanakism can be discerned as borrowings from the thought pattern of Kabir, the greatest exponent of Sant tradition in India. The protagonists of this view reinforce their point of view by stating that the Guru had a meeting with Kabir.

On analysis and scrutiny, the above view does not sound correct, even if the two *saints* had a meeting and a discussion, it does not follow that one must have borrowed from the other. In certain matters such as caste, idolatry, formalism, faith in monotheistic God both the teachers resemble in their approach, so are they in agreement regarding the final objective i.e. say Sahay. Both emphasise the need of a Guru but not as human link. Both understand by Shabad, the same meaning, although Guru Nanak is clearer in his expression. But similarities do not go far.

On issues like rejection of the authority of the Vedas and disapproval of ascertism. Kabir was inclined towards compromise while the Guru did not mince words while rejecting them. Both looked at life from fundamentally different points of view. Guru Nanak was not a visionary like Kabir, he was far too deeply interested in the fate of his fellow beings upon earth than to linger upon in the rare mystic regions. Furthermore, Kabir was deeply impressed by the futility and misery of life and sought as much isolation from life as possible instead of framing a constructive programme of reconciliation of man's spiritual and material needs. Guru Nanak regards life a beautiful thing to be enjoyed in fulness. Kabir does not distinguish between the psychological notion of mind and metaphysical idea of soul because for him mind undergoes the process of transmigration of souls, but for the Guru mind is gross in the sense that it is attached with the body and is the outcome or five element (In man panch tat te janma).

Kabir's teachings bear an imprint of Tarik beliefs and faiths, handed over to him probably through Nath tradition. He uses the imagery of Ganga and Yamuna to mean the right and left nerve channels, the Triveni to mean the middle channel and the hundred-petal lotus the sun and the moon etc. and expresses his intense dislike of women, Guru Nanak does not make use of such words, phrases and images nor does he harbour hatred for woman. Nanak, in fact, considers woman as man's equal.

Guru Nanak's Guru?

Who was Guru Nanak's Guru there is a difference of opinion on this subject among the scholars of Sikh history. Generally the Sikhs are of the opinion that there was no person who has been named as Guru of Guru Nanak Dev? They are of the firm opinion in a jungle near black Beain Guru Nanak was blessed with a spiritual power and was assigned the job of propagating the real spiritual knowledge among the people. On the contrary certain scholars stressed that there was a person must had been Guru of Guru Nanak. The author of the book entitled, Siyaraul - Mutakhrin, Ghulam Husain is of the opinion that Syyed Hasan was the Guru of Guru Nanak. A recently published books author have confirmed this view point. He said that Ghulam Husain has disclosed a new story about Guru Nanak that during his childhood in Talwandi there was his teacher named Syyed Husain who was a Muslim intellectual and a saint.

The followers of Kabir Sahib—Kabirpanthis are of the firm opinion that Guru Nanak had achieved much knowledge from Kabir. Westcott said, that those who followed Kabir Sahib as their spiritual Guru, Guru Nanak; the founder of Sikhism was one of them. Another scholar had written that there is no doubt that near about all the writers have attached Kabir's name with Guru Nanak. While describing this that author had mentioned the name of A.S. Garden and J.N.Farquhar who confirmed the idea that Guru Nanak was the disciple of Kabir Sahib. The author named wheel while accepting this theory that there must have been one person as Guru of Guru Nanak had strengthened this idea that Syyed Hasan was Nanak's Guru. He has also mentioned that according to certain researchers that Kabir was the Guru of Guru Nanak. An another scholar while mentioning Guru Nanak's Bagdad visit has said that there was an inscription on a stone slab (शिललिख) on it—it had written that "Guru Murad had expired". Guru Nanak had helped in the construction of this building; which shows the dedication and love of a disciple towards his Guru. The period mentioned on it is Hijari 127. According to this Shilalikh (शिललिख) Murad was the spiritual Guru of Guru Nanak on the contrary majority of the scholars condemn this theory that ever Guru Nanak had attained any spiritual power from the above quoted peoples. Principal Jodh Singh and Doctor Ganda Singh and so many other scholars also did not agree to this theory that there was any body who was a Guru of Guru Nanak Dev[1].

Regarding meeting of Guru Nanak with Kabir Sahib Doctor P.N. Tiwari in his book entitled 'Kabir' has mentioned that if the dates of Kabir's birth (1399 A.D.) and death (1518 A.D.) are as accepted by most of his followers there is a possibility of their having met at Banaras, but no historical record suggest this thesis, nor any other Janam Sakhi or chronicle dealing with the life of Kabir. Recent researchers, however, reveal that Kabir lived only 50 years and died in 1450 A.D. i.e. 19 years before Nanak's birth[2].

From Gorakhmata; now called Nanakmata and has a Gurdwara commemorating the memory of Guru Nanak's visit. This place is about twenty miles away from Pilibhit (Uttar Pradesh), which was a great centre of Nath Yogis, he proceeded towards Banaras, alongwith his bard, Mardana, the holiest of Hindu centres of pilgrimage. The birth place of Kabir and Ravidas, two renowned devotees of God, and a great centre of Sanskrit learning, housed a learned Pandit, Chatar Das by name. While going towards the Ganga for a holy dip, he saw the Guru in his unusual dress and said with a snear; "What kind of a holy man are you? You neither wear the necklace of Tulsi, nor have a rosary in your hand, nor possess a saligram (the sacred quartz stone representing the God Vishnu). How will you be emancipated? During Guru Nanak's visit to Banaras there is no mention of Kabir Sahib. This shows that Guru Nanak had never met Kabir, as is alleged by several European historians, nor accepted his influence upon him, otherwise even if dead, the places or people connected with him must have been visited by Guru Nanak. Doctor P.N. Tiwari, quoting a report in the Archacological Survey of India says that Bijli Khan got a tomb of Kabir erected on the right bank of the river Ami (in the Basti District of Uttar Pradesh) in 1450 A.D. i.e. 19 years before Guru Nanak was born[3].

From the historical point of view the most significant contribution of the Bhakti Movement during this period came from Kabir and Nanak, who expressed the sentiments of the urban class in towns and of the artisans in the villages who were in contact with the towns.[4]

It is said that Vaishnav reformer of Bhakti movement like Ramanand, Chaitanya Mahaprabhu, Goswami Tulsidasa, Vallabhacharya, Guru Nanak Dev had also visited Banaras and met Kabir Sahib. Related to this are the questions of whether Guru Nanak was acquainted with the works of Kabir with regard to the first, MacLeod says "Neither the works of Guru Nanak nor those of Kabir offer the remotest hint of a meeting between the two, and such evidence as the Janam Sakhis offer is entirely inadequate to establish on". As far as the second is concerned McLeod concludes, "The examples of verbal correspondence are sufficient to suggest that Guru Nanak may have known some of the compositions of Kabir, but they do not more than established it as a remote possibility[5].

Muhammad Hedayatullah have described relations between Kabir and Nanak like this :- When one passes from Kabir to Nanak one is not conscious of any changes of atmosphere. The main ideas of the two teachers are the same, and both teach principles of inwardness and devotion, and commend the way of quietism and of meditation. They are alike in betraying evident traces of both Hindu and Muslim influence, and at the same time they agree in standing apart from these two faiths, criticising them in the forms in which they see them, and seeking to reconcile them.

Thus, like Kabir, Nanak says: "I am neither Hindu nor Muhammadan, but a worshipper of the Nirakar or the Formless. Adi Granth or Granth Sahib is taken as an evidence of the former's influence on the latter. Nanak is said to have been 27 years of age when he met Kabir. As Nanak was born in 1469 A.D. the year of their meeting would have been 1496, the very year in which Sikandar Lodhi, the Sultan of Delhi, visited Jaunpur and other cities in that neighbourhood. But Farquhar finds no evidence of their meeting[6].

Notes and References

1. Professor J.R. Puri—Guru Nanak Ka Ruhani Updesh. Radha Swami Satsang Vyas—1983 pp. 12-13.
2. Kabir by Doctor P.N. Tiwari, Published by N.B.T. pp. 47 and quoted by Dr. Gopal Singh in his book entitled History of the Sikh People (1469-1978), p. 65.
3. Ibid. pp. 82.
4. Romila Thapar—A History of India, 1966 p. 308 also quoted by David c. Scott—Kabir's Mythology - Bhartiya Vidya Prakashan, Delhi, 1985, pp. 3 and 41.
5. Guru Nanak and Sikh Religion—W.H. MacLeod, Oxford University Press, 1966 pp. 39, 56, 64, 66 and Proceedings of the Punjab History Conference—First Session, Patiala, 1966 for 1965 and also quoted by David C. Scott—Kabir's Mythology, Bhartiya Vidya Prakashan, Delhi, 1985 pp. 13 and 45-46. (Fn.) 58.
6. Kabir: The Apostle of Hindu—Muslim Unity—Muhammad Hedayetullah, pp. 122-123.

17

Works of Kabir Sahib

Near about all sources fully agree that Kabir was an illiterate person and his teaching was mainly oral. In this regard, Kabir himself is reported to have said:

I am not skilled in book knowledge,

nor do I understand controversy[1]

He says further:

I touch not ink nor paper,

nor take pen in my hand;

of the greatness of the four ages

Kabir has given instructions

with his lips[2]

The circumstances in which Kabir was born and brought up make it quite probable that he was unable to read and write. However his saying has been called in a book entitled 'Bijik"; which means (1) essence or seed, (2) an invoice, and (3) a key to a hidden treasure or a document by which a hidden treasure can be located. It is the third meaning which is probable here. It is said that in the neighbourhood of Banaras, there is a group of people who are in the habit of burying treasure for safety and the place of concealment is remembered by the secret sign of a chart which is called bijack. This custom may have been in vague elsewhere. For sure, it is still (prevalent among) the fishermen of Bangladesh. It was evident in the film called 'Jago Hua Savera' an academic award winner film, depicting the life of fishermen of the then East Pakistan (now Bangla Desh). Kabir seems to have been familiar with the name Bijak, and the compiler of his sayings probably found this name as a suitable title for his (Kabir's) verses which were considered to reveal the hidden treasures of religious knowledge. There is a verse which says :-

The Bijak tells the secret of that treasure which is hidden; the word tells of jiva (soul or life); few are they who understand[3].

These sayings of Kabir was compiles after 50 years of his death. One Bhagwan Das is supposed to be the compiles of this book. Some scholars are of the opinion that perhaps Kabir himself dictated his sayings to his disciple, Bhagwan Das. This book has been acknowledged most authenticated record of Kabir's teaching.

The Bijak consists of the following divisions:

1. The Adi Mangal (a short introductory poem)
2. Ramainis (Short doctrinal poems consisting of an indefinite number of Chaupais)
3. Sakhis (evidence or rhyming couplets bearing witness to the truth)
4. Sabads (words of the same character)
5. The chauntisi (or the 34 consonants of the Nagari alphabet, with their religious significations);
6. The Vipramatisi (an attack, in thirty short verses on the orthodox religious system of the Brahmans);
7. Kaharas, Basantas, Chaucharis, Belis, Birhulis and Hindolas (all religious songs in various meters);
8. The Sayar Bijak Ko Pad (Summing up of the whole Bijak).

The Bijak ends with the following verse:

Kabir said, within the creater is all,

and the Creater permeates all;

without the secret all are sunk in error;

only the holy man, the wise can comprehend[4].

Though there are several printed editions of the Bijak are available, but the two best known editions are--one by Raja of Rewa; Maharajah Biswanath and the second by Baba Puran Das of Burhanpur. These editions were printed at Banaras in the year 1868 and at Lucknow and Allahabad in 1905.

Adi Granth

The second most important source of information is the Sikh scripture, namely the Adi Granth, "Adi" means "The First" and "Granth" means "Book". It is called Adi-Granth (First Book) to distinguish it from the Granth of the tenth Guru, Govind Singh, which was compiled at a later date). Compiled in 1604 by the orders of Guru Arjun Dev, the fifth Guru of the Sikhs. The Granth contains, in addition to the compositions of the Sikh Gurus from Nanak to Tegh Bahadur.

Only the works of the first five Gurus are significantly represented in the Adi Granth. It seems that the sixth, seventh and eighth guru were not poets, while the ninth and tenth gurus have been given a rather minor representation in the Granth Sahib.

Fifteen Bhakatas are represented by compositions in the sacred volume:

Beni, Bhikan, Dhanna, Farid, Jay Dev, Kabir, Namdev, Pipa, Premanand, Ramanand, Ravidas, Sadna, Sain, Surdas, and Trilochan.

Of these the largest collection is more extensive than those of a couple of the Sikh gurus are those of Namdev—Sixty Pads, Sheikh Farid—four Pads, and one hundred thirty shlokas. (The shloka is a couplet, also known as doha or Sakhi).

The wide difference of opinion as to the number of Kabir's works included in the Adi Granth is amazing e.g.

S.S. Kohli—292 pads and 249 Shlokas

R.K. Verma—228 pads and 243 Shlokas

P.D. Barthwal—227 pads and 240 Shlokas

W.H. MacLeod—226 pads and 237 or 239 Shlokas

Kabir Granthavali

Kabir Granthavali edited by Babu Shyam Sundar Das, is based on two manuscripts in the possession of Kashi Nagri Pracharni Sabha, one of them supposedly compiled and written in 1504 A.D. and the other in 1824 A.D.

According to Babu Shyam Sundar Das Granthvali contains 812 Sakhis and 403 pads and according to Dr. P.N. Tiwari it contains 744 Sakhis, 200 pads.

In addition to these works attributed to Kabir, there is a book by Rabindranath Tagore, entitled one Hundred Poems of Kabir. This translation is supposed to be based upon the Hindi text with a Bengali translation by Kashiti Mohan Sen, who has gathered from many sources a large collection of poems and hymns to which the name of Kabir is attached. (Kashiti Mohan Sen's translation is in four volumes and contains 341 poems. The hundred poems translated by Tagore are taken from the first three volumes, which contain 264 poems.[6]

Dr. Giri Raj Singh has said about the works of Kabir that, Kabir's works are mostly collection of songs compared in the various meters of old Kurdi. There are in all seventy two works, the most famous being Kabir Bijato, Sukhnidhan, Shabads, Sakhis, Rekhitees, Mangal, Vasantald Holi Agams. Kabir's language is very simple and he expressed his thoughts in a lucid style. His couplets are pregnant with deep significance and the use of similes and metaphors is appropriate. The expressions have emanated straight from Kabir's heart.

He mostly wrote in two-line couplets, known as dohas expressing his intimate love for the Almighty.

Kabir was essentially a mystic, he had no teacher. His spiritual insights and philosophical thoughts were intutive.

Kabir's poems are contained in Adi Granth, the holy scripture of the Sikhs.

The mystic songs of Kabir, preaching the omnipresence of God, and expressing a heartfelt desire for Union with Him are a precious legacy of not only India, but all the world.

O! Mind! worship Rama, Govind Hari!

Japa (repeated recital of God's name) and penance (prolonged meditation)

do not cost anything;

There is no spending out of your Pocket.

To think children and wealth are the means to happiness is the mistake you make.

Remember the name of Rama

Death is waiting on the wings.

Says Kabir: Listen O! Friends O! Good men !

That face which is not turned towards Rama is worth nothing[7].

According to Bhattacharya—The most outstanding contribution of Saint Kabir was that he brought the highest thoughts of the land to the masses through his simple and lucid expositions in their own language. So long these thoughts were restricted only to the Sanskrit knowing scholars most of whom were Brahmins. His presentation in a popular form and in a sincere and simple style and in a common language opened a new window to the masses. They were so long denied. Kabir did it perhaps consciously. The saint says, "O Kabir, Sanskrit is the water in a well, the language of the people is the flowing stream". The simple presentation of the poet had tremendous force and could travel long distances just over the people's lips.

One of the stalwarts of the Bhakti Movement, Kabir was very much against caste system and deciared caste distinctions of the Hindus to be vain and productive of that pride which God abhor's.

Like Guru Nanak, Kabir deprecated the practice of Sàti concernation of widows on the pyres of the dead husbands. Kabir discouraged the practice by pointing out the futility of the universal belief that the woman who immolated herself on her husband's pyre would obtain salvation. Kabir was deadly opposed to use of intoxication like wine.

Truth like a flower is to be enjoyed with inner glow of spiritual light. It can never be the monopoly of any section of society. The Brahmins unfortunately were claiming supermacy. Caste system took a virulent turn. The saint opposed it. In the following song Kabir lodges his protest against this ill practice. He denounces the 'touch me not' attitudes of the Brahmins; He says:

Oh Pande : why are you so sensitive to touch?

of touch the whole world is born.

Is there blood in me and milk in you?

How are you a Brahmin and I a Sudra?

So scrupulous about touch from birth.

Why came you through the unclean womb?

Is there impurity at birth and impurity at death?

Says Kabir, only God's glory shines pure.

Kabir's claim to a pride of place in Indian history is assured as a great saint with a message of universal brotherhood of Man. He made the most earnest efforts to foster a spirit of harmony between the two premier communities of this sub-continent. He endeavoured to combine the strict monotheism of Islam with its abhorence of idolatry with whatever was best and most deeply rooted in the creed of Hinduism. Basing his teachings on the monotheism of the Upanishads, he attempted to form a composite creed out of the best elements of the two great religions. He was a great singer, and avadhuta, an advocate of Advaitavada who "places the Law of the universe in the heart of man as his higher self where alone the soul can discover Him".

In the religious history of India Kabir occupies a place of great importance. He was the founder of the deistic movement; and while he used the name 'Ram' (as well as other names such as Hari, Govinda, Allah etc.) for God and propagated Vedantic ideas he rejected entirely the doctrine of incarnation. He condemned idolatry and most of the Hindu ceremonies and rites with no unsparing voice. He took the Muslims also to task for their intolerance of other faiths. One of his typical songs in this strain reads as follows:

O servant where don't thou seek Me?

Lo! I am beside Thee,

I am neither in temple nor in mosque;

I am neither in Kaaba nor in Kailash;

Neither am I in rites and ceremonies,

Nor in Yoga and renunciation

In the same piece the saint repeats,

If thou art a true seeker, thou shalt at once see Me;

thou shalt meet me in a moment of time.

Kabir says : O Sadhu ! God is the breath of all breath. There is nothing but water at the holy bathing places; and I know that they are useless, for I have bathed in them. The images are all lifeless, they cannot speak; I know, for I have cried aloud to them.

The Purana and Koran are mere words; lifting up the curtain. I have seen.

Kabir gives utterances to the words of experience; and he knows very well that all other things are untrue.

(From Rabindranath Tagore's One hundred poems of Kabir)

The most significant point noticed in the Saints singings is that in their essence Kabir's teachings are another instance of the revolt of simple minds against the deadening weight of ritual, mystery and confusing complications of thought with which Brahmanism and Islam of those days were overlaid.

In his famous Hibbert lectures for 1930 delivered at Oxford entitled Religion of Man Tagore made special mention of this great saint and quoted Kabir's message on Spiritual Freedom where he (Kabir) sings:

By saying that Supreme Realaity only dwells in the inner realm of spirit we shame the outer world of matter and also when we say that he is only in the outside, we do not speak the truth.

Truth lies in unity and freedom flows from this like all great sages of India Kabir says that the human heart is the paradise. It is the dwelling place of God. Says Kabir:

In this body is the garden of Paradise; herein are comprised the seven seas and the myriad stars; Here is the creator manifest".

There are numerous poems composed byKabir. It is probable that he himself did not commit them to writing but that they were remembered and treasured up by his disciples. Among various collections of Kabir, one is to be found in the Adi Granth of the Sikhs, compiled in 1604 A.D. Another collection is contained in the Bijak, a work produced in connection with the Kabir Panth after its founder's death, probably as a book of instruction. Among other collections, mention may be made of the Ramainis (short doctrinal poems) the Shabads (similar poems in a different metre) and the *Chaunties* (an exposition on the religious significance of the consonants of the Nagari alphabet). Besides these there are a large number of Sakhis or rhyming couplets, bearing witness to the truth.

Although the poetry of Kabir is rough and unpolished and his language not always easy to understand, he must be given a very high place in the Hindi literature. To quote F.E. Keay the author of Hindi literature in the *Heritage* of Indian Series:

"The amazing boldness with which he attacked the religious practices of his day, tolerating no shame and demanding reality in all those who were seeking after God, and the moral earnestness of his appeal to men to put the things of God first, would in itself give his work an outstanding importance. But besides this, stringing satire which he has epigrams and the fascinating rhythm of his verse all combine to give a wonderful power to his poetry. He has been called the pioneer of Hindi literature and the father of all Hindi hymns; but though, in view of the predecessors we have already mentioned such a claim can hardly be allowed, it is certainly true to say that it was he, more than any others before him, who popularized Hindi religious literature and vastly extended its influence and Hindi literature of the same type subsequent to Kabir owes to him a great debt".

When Sikandar Lodhi spared his life, in the interest of peace, he was banished from the city of Varanasi. Thereafter he appears to have moved about amongst the various cities of North India and ultimately settled at Maghar near Gorakhpur. He was approached by a large number of his followers to return to Varanasi. Kabir told them, "why do you unnecessarily get disturbed"?

Jas Kashi tosh Maghar usar
Hiradoi Ram Soti hoira

Whether it is Varanasi or Maghar both are meaningless. The real truth is the presence of Shri Ramchandra, who is dwelling in my heart. So it does not matter whether I stay at Maghar or Varanasi. In Maghar he breathed his last in 1518.

He was convinced that Truth was universal. Truth was light. Truth was love and Truth was God.

He had practised it himself. He did not like any external rituals to discover or search his Truth. To him it was not necessary. It was not necessary because when Truth reveals itself it will manifest itself as a flood of light washing away all ignorance and would not wait for any outer traditional ortho dox rituals. This deep denial of traditional approach was perhaps more of an indifference than hatred. To him the greatest instrument, rather the easiest vehicle was deep devotion, devotion with utmost yearning for the light. He did not preach although he himself became one of the outstanding preaches of the country. He only practised and that too in silence. But when he was enlightened his ecstacy knew no bounds. He was overwhelmed with inner emotion, inner light. He proclaimed like the great saints of ancient times *Shrinyantu Vishy amritasya putrah.* Oh listen ! My dear sons of the immortal, here is the heavenly nectar. Here it is in the very soil of your holy land. That is dwelling in your very heart that great flood of light. You have only to enkindle it with your pure mind, clean heart and above all deep yearning blended with unstinted devotion. Saith Kabir is immortal.[8]

According to Indu Vashishat—Kabir belonged to the community of weavers which was considered as a low caste. There are not many authentic sources narrating Kabir's life. The writing of this contemporary and successive generations of bhakti poets speak of Kabir more with reverence and devotion than with historic authenticity. There are a few references by Kabir himself, that he was born in Maghar and then came to Banaras. After extensive research it was widely accepted now that the birth place of Kabir is a place called Lahartara in Banaras. Kabir called himself neither a Hindu nor a Muslim. He preferred to be called a weaver. He may look a Muslim by appearance but he was a Hindu by Sanskara. He has constantly used the names of Hindu gods and goddesses, sages and other references from Hindu mythology in his writings.

Inducted into the sant dharma Kabir spent most of his time in sadhana and satsang. Even his married life was more oriented towards spirituality than worldly preoccupations. Inspite of his being a *grihasth* he spent long hours in activities of inner transformation.

Kabir was greatly influenced by Hindu traditions. He was a strong supporter of satya (truth) and ahinsa (non-violence). He gave the utmost importance to the guru (teacher). He said that the path of sadhna cannot be pursued without the teacher. Teachers, according to him, are of three kinds:

manav guru
Siddha guru and
divya guru

The manav guru of Kabir was Ramanand from whom he received the initiation of Ramanama. His divya guru was none other than God himself. It is possible that he was blessed with his darshan, the vision of the Divine.

The works of Kabir can be classified into three categories: Ramaini, Sakshi or Sakhi and Shabad.The Ramaini describes the wanderings of the soul (jeeva) in this world; the Sakshi or the observer is a doha or couplet; and the Shabad is the word of the Master.

In Ramaini Kabir has mainly dealt with the creation, the soul and the world or jagat. Doha and Pada forms of verse are used to express these. There is much space devoted in these verses to Kabir's ideas about maya.

The word Sakhi originates from the Sanskrit form sakshi meaning the witness of truth. Kabir has chosen this name because in these verses he has mentioned only those incidents which he witnessed through his senses and grasped / analysed through his intellect. There is no reference here to knowledge acquired through books.

Shabad can be used in two different senses: It can refer to the word of the Master or to a form of Pada.

Kabir's sadhana was of the Advaita variety; he elaborated this in the Ramaini, Sakhi and Shabad . In Advaita the dominent feeling is that of the union of the atman with the paramatman. Kabir described the soul as a part of the paramatman. The atman is created by and finally unites with the supreme paramatman at the time of the body's destruction. To explain this idea Kabir has used a beautiful simile; a pot filled with water is floating in a river; once the pot is broken the water inside and the water outside mingle to become an inseparable whole.

Kabir acquired all this knowledge through "love" and not through books. He was illiterate. He believed that yoga was one of the means of attaining to the Supreme. Of course, he was not in favour of the difficult or tortuous ways of yoga sadhana practised by cults such as the Nathas and Siddhas. He vehemently condemned all hypocrisy[9].

According to R.P. Tiwari—The lists of Kabir's works given in different sketches of Kabir's life are numerous. H.H. Wilson (1846) mentions eight works while Westcott (1906) forty two and Dr. Ram Kumar Verma (1957) fifty six. In these works are collected the Sakhis, the Padas and the Ramainis. It is said that Kabir was unlettered and that his utterances were written down by his disciples. Naturally there is scope for his utterances getting mixed up with those of other saints. Even the devoted followers of the saints have contributed much to this confusion. They considered it a privilege to be able to compose verses by way of elucidating the words of their Gurus and their compositions also passed under the names of the saints. There have been interpolations too. Sacts and sub sacts grew and developed in course of time found it easy to resort to these means in order to gain their own ends. It is therefore very difficult to distinguish the authentic form the spurious. A modern researcher Dr. Parasnath Tiwari, has taken great pains and devoted several years to study this complex problem. In his book Kabir Granthavali (1961) he accepts only two hundred padas, twenty Ramainis, one chauntisi Ramaini and seven hundred and forty Sakhis to be genuine. There are three works of Kabir which occupy a place of honour in the numerous writings attributed to the saint. They are Bijak, writings of Kabir which found place in the Adi Granth of the Sikhs and Kabir Granthavali. The Bijak of Kabir is considered to be genuine by his followers. These works provide material for understanding the personality, philosophy and the importance of Kabir. For centuries Kabir has been an inspiration to a huge mass of people in India and is still living in the faith of a large number of his followers[10].

Literature on the Life and Teaching of Kabir

1. Achhar Bhed Ki Ramaini
2. Achhar Khand Ki Ramaini
3. Agadh Mangal
4. Agam Ujiyar
5. Alif Nama (1)

6. Alif Nama (2)
7. Alif Nama (3)
8. Allab Tok
9. Amar Mul
10. Ambu Sagar (Bombay)
11. Anu Rag Sagar (Bombay)
12. Asar Grabi Ko ang
13. Atam Anubhav
14. Balakh Paij
15. Bhakti Ko ang
16. Bhau Taran
17. Bhopal Bodh
18. Barah Masa
19. Basant
20. Bijak with commentary by Raja of Rewah (Lucknow, Benares and Bombay).
21. Bijak with commentary by Puran Dass (Lucknow and Allahabad).
22. Bijak with notes by Prem Chand (Calcutta).
23. Chauka Ki Ramaini
24. Chauntisi
25. Garur Bodh
26. Gauri
27. Gorakh Gusht
28. Gur Updesh (Bombay)
29. Gyan Dipak

30. Gyan Godri
31. Gyan Sagar (Bombay)
32. Hansawali
33. Hanuman Bodh
34. Hori
35. Hari Ram Lila
36. Kabir Charitra Bodh (Bombay)
37. Kabir Kasauti (Bombay)
38. Kabir Manshur (Bombay)
39. Kabir Upasna (Bombay)
40. Kabir Sahib Ki Sakhi (Lucknow)
41. Kamal Gusht
42. Karni Bina Kathni Ko ang
43. Karni Sahit Kathni Ko ang
44. Kusangit Ko ang
45. Kurmauli
46. Madad Bodh
47. Mangal
48. Mukti Mal
49. Muhammad Bodh
50. Mul Ramaini (Lucknow)
51. Musa Bodh
52. Nam Mahatam
53. Nanak Gusht
54. Niranjan Gusht

55. Nirbhai Gyan
56. Piya Pahchan Ko ang
57. Puno Mahatam
58. Ramanand Gusht
59. Rekhta
60. Sadhu Ko ang
61. Sam Darsi Ko ang
62. Samjhe Ghat Ko ang
63. Santokh Bodh (27 writings, Bombay)
64. Sarab Gyata Ko ang
65. Sar Grabi Ko ang
66. Sar Sangarh Prishotar (Lucknow)
67. Sarwag Sangar Sanyukat
68. Sat Kabir Ki Sakhi
69. Sat Kabir Ki Shatak Satik (Benares)
70. Sat Sang Ko ang
71. Sat Sang Mahima Ko ang
72. Shabad Bhawani
73. Shabad Chaunitisi
74. Shabad Pukar
75. Sikandar Bodh
76. Sowansa Gunjar
77. Sukh Nidhan
78. Sukrit Dhyan
79. Ugr Gita (Lucknow)

80. Vasist Muni Gusht
81. Vivek Sagar (Bombay)
82. Vivek Sangram

In addition to the above H.H. Wilson in Essays on the Religion of the Hindus—Vol. I pp. 76-77 mentions:

Anand Ram Sagar

Balakh Ki Ramaini

Chancharas

Hindolas

Jhulanas

Kabir Panji

Kaharas

Shabdawali

Every poet chooses his own idiom, and addresses his own imaginary audience. The greatness of Kabir lies in the fact that he did not care for the language of the sophisticated in these days, namely sanskrit or the court language Persian, but composed his verses and songs in a mixed language of his own which is now called by Hindi scholars Sadhukari (language of the Sadhus). As Dr. Govind Trigunayat says in his Kabir Ki Vichardhara, 'Kabir did not use one language. In his bani, one comes across a mixture of Hindi, Urdu, Persian and many dialects like Bhojpuri, Punjabi, Marwari and so on. The first authentic collection of Kabir's works in Kabir Granthavali, edited by Dr. Shyam Sundar Das on the basis of two manuscripts dated Samwat 1561 and 1881 (A.D. 1508 and A.D. 1828); the other in Sant Kabir by Dr. Ram Kumar Verma which contains Kabir's writings in the Granth Sahib too. In both these works we find: (1) Punjabiness, (2) noun and very forms of Bhojpuri, (3) some Khari Boli forms, (4) language according to subject matter (5) many words from regional languages, (6) simple and direct expression, (7) symbolism and technical allusiveness, (8) no adherence to any one standardised form.

Acharya Ramchandra Shukla writes in his Hindi Sahitya Ka Itihas that the saint poets of Hindi used Khari Boli which they received as a legacy from the Siddhas. But Dr. Trigunayat differs from this opinion and maintains that Kabir did not confine himself to Purbi (eastern U.P. dialect of Banaras) only but made use of many other dialects so as to make himself more communicable to saints coming from other regions. Kabir uses Persianized Hindi when he talks of Hindu Pandits. In his language one comes across Bengali verb forms like 'achhilo'. There are also words from Rajasthani and Lahanda. His language has a peculiarity that it is at once simple and yet difficult to interpret; Added to it is the great difficulty which scholars have to contend with, namely, the different forms of the same text due, may be to oral transmission. Many words have undergone such transformation and even corruption that it is difficult to decipher and excavate the correct original form. Kabir's language in ult-bansiyan is also called, on account of its obscurity and vagueness of meaning. Sandhabhasha (according to Vidhusekhra Bhattacharya) or Sandhya Bhasha, the language of the meeting point or the language of the evening. Dr. Das Gupta has discussed it in his obscure Religious cults, and given different reasons for such riddle like usages. Either they were deliberately done to confound the opponent, or because of the mixture of Apabhramsha and Hindi, or such was the language on the borders of Bengal and Bihar. In Sanskrit `Sandhi' is used even for an allegorical language and, may be, poets like Kabir used it consciously, as the Tantriks did, to hide some secret notions or esoteric practices not considered proper in ordinary society. Whatever the reasons, in Kabir one comes across many such poems which apparently seem to be contrary to all rational meaning. May be, Kabir did it is fun to confound the Pandit who took recourse to very intricate Sanskrit. Some examples of this kind of Sandhabhasha are given below under paradoxes.

These couplets (Padas) of Kabir are also called ult-bansiya or ult-batiya (inverted bamboos or inverted talks). One example is in Kabir Granthavali:

Such wonderment did the guru tell

I remained stunned
The mouse fought the elephant
one rarely sees
The mouse entered into a hole
serpent afraid ran
Contrarily, mouse devoured the serpent
It was a great wonder
The ants uprooted the mountain
and brought it open
The cock fought the human
the fish ran after water
The cow was milking the calf
the Calf was giving milk
Such wonderment happened
the deer killed the tiger
The hunter hid himself in the thicket
the rabbit shot arrow
Kabir says make him a guru
who tells you the meaning of this Poem.

Dr. Hazari Prasad Dwivedi discusses these poems in a chapter entitled 'Yogic Allegories and Ult-bansiya; and quotes from Kabir Granthavali another passage, given below, and gives a chart of three different interpretations by Vishwanath, Vichardas and the traditionalists of 23 such symbolic terms in this pad:

(Santan jugat neend na Kyai...)
Saint don't sleep while awake
Death does not eat, epochs don't cover
the body is not eroded by old age

Contrary wise the Ganges absorbs the ocean
and darkness eclipses the sun
The sick man kills nine constellations
the reflection in water gives light
without feet one runs in tens directions
without eyes sees the world
The rabbit devours the lion, such wonder who can solved?
The inverted pitcher does not sink in water
the straight one is filled with it
The reason why men are different
with guru's grace they get through
Inside the cave one sees the whole world
outside nothing is seen
The arrow argument and client the
only the brave can follow
The singer when requested cannot sing
the dumb sings always
The jugglers game is seeing the on lookers
Anhad cause is increased
The statement inspects itself
all this is an inexpressible tala
The earth enters into the sky
this is the word of a man
Without glasses nectar oozes
the river keeps away the water stored
Kabir says he alone is immoral
Who drinks Ram rasa

Obviously in their first reading such compositions sound very much lime irrational mutterings. But all these words have some symbolic meanings: the mind is generally compared with fish, weaver, hunter, elephant, niranjan; the soul is referred to as son, calf, hunt, lion, mouse, bee, yogi; the maya is harlot, woman, she-goat, cow and cat; the world is like a forest or an ocean; the senses are the five maidens and friends and so on. Such songs also refer to certain numbers; five stands for elements or senses; three for qualities or three tenses or worlds; eight for the Hathyogis eight centres in the body, more or less like the glandular endocrinic seats secretring harmones. In a doha like -

Sixty-four lamps lighted in fourteen moons

What moon is there in the house when Govind is not

Sixty-four stands for arts and fourteen for Vidyas or achievements.

Such paradoxes have a long tradition dating from the Upanishads. The inverted tree and the two birds are well known. In Taittiriyopanishad there is a passage which says, the sky rests in the earth and the earth rests in the sky. It was carried further by Vajrana Buddhists. Perhaps Kabir got it through them[11].

Mahatma Gandhi and Kabir

Gandhiji included the following song of Kabir in his daily prayer book:

Jhine Jhine bini chadriya !

Kah-e Ke tana Kah-e- Ke Bharni,

Kaun Chadar Se bini Chadriya,

Ingla Pingla tana bharni

Sukhman tar se bini Chadriya,

Aath Kanwal dal charkha dolein,

Pauch tat gun बीनी Chadriya

Sai ko siyat mas dus lage

Thok thok ke bini Chadriya

So chadar sur nar muni oodhe

Oodh-e-ke maile kinhe Chadriya

Das Kabir Jattan se Oodhe

Jiyon ki Tiyon dhar dini Chadriya

(What is the wrap and what is the woof

what are the threads from which the Chadar is woven?

Ingla and Pingla are the wrap and woof

Sushaman are the threads from which the Chadar is woven

Eight are the lotuses and ten are the spinning wheels

five are the elements and three the qualities of the Chadar

The Master required ten months to weave it

and made it well woven by hitting it and beating it.

This Chadar the gods, men and sages used

and used and soiled the chadar

Kabir Das has used it very carefully

and kept the chadar back as it is

Weaving was the profession of Kabir. Gandhiji also gave much weight to spinning and weaving. In several matters there is great similarity in these two great men of India, though functioning in different periods of history and in different circumstances.

Notes and References

1. *Adi-Granth,* Bilavaluz.
2. *Bijak,* Sakhi 188.
3. *Bijak,* Ramaini 37 quoted by M. Hedayetullah, pp. 132-133.
4. Quoted by Keay, p. 53.
5. *Scott Mythology of Kabir,* B.V. Prakashan, Delhi, 1985.

6. M. Hedyatullaha—Kabir, p. 142.
7. Dr. Giri Raj Singh, *Saints, Gurus and Mystics of India*, p. 317-318.
8. Vivek Bhattacharya, *The Spirit of Indian Culture—Saints of India*, pp. 182-186 and 194.
9. Indu Vashishat, *Kabir (Poet - Saints of India)*. Ed. by M. Sivarama Krishna and Sumit Roy 1996. pp. 50-52.
10. *Kabir,* R.P. Tiwari (Devotional Poets and Mystics, General Editor, V. Raghavan, Publication Division, New Delhi, 1978).
11. Prabhakar Machwe

18

Kabir Hymns

SRI RA

Without God's assistance men are lost in worldly love.

1

The mother thinketh that her son is growing big,

But this she thinketh not, that day by day his life is decreasing.

She called him her own and fondleth him excessively, while the god of death looketh on and laugheth.

So much hast Thou, *O God,* illuded the world;

How can it ever know Thee since mammon hath bewitched it[1]?

Saith Kabir, abandon the pleasure of sin, *for* in such companionship thou must assuredly die.

O mortal, repeat the name of the Lord, put aside mention of others, so shalt thou pass over the terrible ocean of *this world.*

If it please God, man feeleth divine love,

The error of supersition departeth from within him,

Divine knowledge is spontaneously produced, intelligence awakened,

And by the favour of the guru the heart is touched by God's love.

In such companionship there is no death;

Obey the Master's order and thou shalt meet Him.

The following was addressed to a Jogi who offered wine to Kabir.

2

Hear a wonderful thing, O Pandit, I cannot now describe *Maya.*

Who hath bewitched demigods, men, celestial heralds, and musicians, and girdled the three worlds.

The sovereign God's lyre playeth without being struck;[2] And he on whom He looketh *with favour* loveth its sound.I have made my brain a furnace, the breath of my left and right nostrills *two stills*, and *my heart* the golden vat, Into which a very pure stream hath trickled; I have distilled the sweetest essence;[3]

And--what is without parallel--I have made *suspension* of my breath my wine-cup.

Say is there any Jogi in the three worlds who would be satisfied *and not long for more.*[4]

Suck Knowledge of the Supreme Being hath manifested itself; Saith Kabir, I am imbued with it.

All the rest of the world is led astray in error, but my mind is intoxicated with God's elixir.

Notes and References

1.It is explained that this passage does not cast blame on God, because it is men's acts which really lead them astray.

2.God gladdens man's heart by divine knowledge without any perceptible interference with him.

3.God's name.

4.The line is also translated--He is a unique Jogi in the three words who hath tasted such essence. Is there any king *equal to him*?

GAURI

Devotion is the water which has quenched Kabir's burning thirst for God.

1

I have been on fire, and have now found the *name* of God as water to *extinguish it*:

The *name* of God is the water which hath cooled my burning body.
Men go to the forest to chasten their hearts,
But without God they cannot find such water *as will do so.*
The water of God's *name* hath saved His burning slave.
From the fire which hath consumed demigods and men.
In the terrible ocean there is an ocean of happiness;[1]
I continue to drink, but the water is not exhausted.

Saith Kabir, worship God.
God's *name* is the water which hath extinguished my thirst.
Yet Kabir's thirst for God increases.

O God, thirst for the water of *Thy name* departeth not from me;

2

Nay for that water my ardour rageth the more.
Thou art the ocean, I am a fish therein ;
I dwell in the water, I perish without it.
Thou art the cage, I am Thy parrot;
What can the cat Death do to me ?
Thou art a tree, I am the bird thereon ;
Unfortunate is he who seeth Thee not.
Thou art the True Guru, I am Thy novice.
Saith Kabir, meet me, O God, at the last moment.

A thief when hotly pressed sought refuge in Kabir's house. It would have been foreign to Kabir's character to refuse shelter to any one who sought it. Moreover he did not know the character of his guest, and accordingly have him the usual permission to remain in his house. It happened that Kabir's daughter was then on a visit to him, and when he entertained the thief at the same time, the circumstance led to much unfavourable comment. Kabir addressed the following hymn to his detractors :--

3

Since I recognized *both the thief and my son-in-law* as one,
Why are people distressed at it ?
If I am dishonoured and have lost my honour, Let no one follow in my footsteps.
If I am bad the badness is confined to myself;
I have no partnership or connexion with any of you.
You know nothing about honour or dishonour;
But you shall know when your gilding is laid bare.[2]
Saith Kabir, that is honour which is acceptable to God;
Forsaking all else worship only Him.

A satire on the ritualistic practices of the Hindus.

4

If union with God be obtained by going about naked,
All the deer[3] of the forest shall be saved.
What mattereth it whether man goeth naked or wearoeth a deerskin,
If he recognize not God in his heart?
If perfection be obtained by shaving the head,
Why should not sheep obtain salvation ?
If, O brethren, the continent man is saved,
Why should not a eunuch obtain the supreme reward ?
Saith Kabir, hear, O my brethren,
Who hath obtained salvation without God's name ?

5

They who bathe in the evening and the morning,
Are like frogs in the water.
When men have no love for God's name,
They shall all go to the god of death.
They who love their persons and deck themselves out in various guises,
Feel not mercy even in their dreams.
Many leading *religious* men call them quadrupeds,
And say that only holy men shall obtain happiness in this ocean of trouble.
Saith Kabir, why perform so many ceremonies ?
Forsaking all other essences quaff the great essence *of God's name.*

God 'prefers before all temples the upright heart and pure'.

6

What availeth devotion, what penance, what fasting and worship.
To him in whose heart there is worldly love?
O man, apply thy heart to God;
Thou shalt not obtain Him by artifice.
Put away covetousness and the example of others;
Lay aside lust, wrath, and pride.
By the religious practices of *the superstitious* boasting is increased;
They join together and worship a stone.
Saith Kabir, by devotion I have obtained *the Lord;*
By becoming simple *in heart* I have met God.

The name Brahman should only be applied to a holy man.

7

While dwelling in the womb man hath not family or caste;
All men have sprung from the seed of Brahm.
Say, O Pandit, since when hast thou been a Brahman;
Waste not thy life in calling thyself a Brahman.
If thou art a Brahman born of a Brahmani mother,
Why hast thou not come by some other way?[4]
How art thou a Brahman? How am I Sudar?
How am I of blood and you of milk?[5]
Saith Kabir, only he who meditateth on God
Is a Brahman in my estimation.

'All are men condemned alike to groan'.

8

Man can never sleep comfortably in *spiritual* ignorance;
The rich and the poor both weep alike.
When *man's* tongue no *longer* uttereth God's name,
He shall continue to bewail birth and death.
When life departeth, say whose shall be man's wealth
Which appeareth like the shadow of a tree? [6]
As the life of a musical instrument is contained in itself,
How can any one know the secrets of the dead?[7]
As the swan *presideth over* the lake, so doth Death over the body.
Drink God's elixir, O Kabir.

Without purification of the heart pilgrimages are of no avail.

9

The Lord of light having created the races *of men* infused light into them,

Which sometimes produceth glass ornaments, and some-times pearls.[8]

What abode is that which is called secure,

Where fear is dispelled, and one abideth without fear?

The heart is not satisfied with pilgrimages to the banks of *sacred streams;*

Man remaineth entangled with good and bad acts.
Demerits and merits are both the same;[9]
In thine own heart is God, the philosopher's stone; abandon *the hope of obtaining* merits from any one else.
O Kabir, chide not the name of Him who is without qualities;
Enjoy thyself in intercourse with that Lord.

Kabir desires not heaven but absorption in God.

10

The men who have no *correct notion* of the Supreme Being,
Think of entering heaven by mere words.
whither it has gone. When human life fails, the soul departs, and no mortal knows its destination.
I know not where heaven is;
Everybody saith he longeth to go there,
But there is no satisfaction in *such* conversation--
The heart is *only* satisfied when pride departeth.
As long as man desireth to go to heaven,
So long *shall he find* no dwelling at *God's* feet.
Saith Kabir, to whom shall I tell this,
That heaven is in the company of the saints?

The body is perishable.

11

Man is born and groweth up, and when he hath grown up he dieth;;
We see that the world passeth away *in this wise.*
Diest thou not of shame talking of thy house?
At the last moment nothing is thine.
With great efforts the body is cherished,
But after death it is burned in the fire.
The limbs to which thou appliest ground aloe-wood, sandal, and fragrant soap,
Shall all be burned with wood.
Saith Kabir, hear me, O virtuous man[10],
While the whole world looketh on thy body shall be consumed.

Since all must die, why mourn ? There is no death for the holy.

12

When another dieth why mournest thou?
Do so, if thou art to live thyself.
I shall not die like the rest of the world;
I have now met Him who reanimateth.
The body is perfumed with sandal ;
In such pleasures the Primal Joy is forgotten.
There is one well and five water-carriers;
Even when the well rope[11] is broken, the silly beings still draw water.[12]
Saith Kabir, *I have gained one piece of* wisdom by reflection--
There is no more a well or water-carriers for me.[13]

Kabir's transmigration.

13

I was in immobile and mobile creatures, in worms and in moths;
I passed through many births of various kinds.
In this way I occupied many bodies,
But when, O God, I assumed *human* birth,
I was a Jogi, a Jati, a penitent, a Brahmachari,
Sometimes a king, an emperor, and sometimes a beggar.
The apostates shall die, but the saints shall all live,
And drink the elixir of God with their tongues.
Saith Kabir, O God, have mercy on us;
We have grown weary ; make us now whole !

Deadly sins veiled under allegories.

14

Kabir hath beheld such wonderful things--
Water churned by mistake for cream;[14]
A donkey grazing on a green crop,[15]
Which on rising every morning killeth itself laughing and braying;
A mad buffalo which could not be guided,[16]
Gambolling as it grazed and falling into hell;
A sheep ever sucking its lamb's milk.[17]
Saith Kabir, *such* sport hath been shown.
By repeating God's *name* my understanding hath become enlightened:

Saith Kabir, I have obtained understanding from the guru.[18]

(Hymn No. 15 is in Kabir's Life).[19]

The body is false, God alone is true.

16

The limbs *anointed with* ground aloe-wood, sandal, and fragrant soap,

Shall be burnt with wood.

What is there to be proud of in this body and in wealth?

Both shall remain on earth and not go *with the soul* to the other world.

They who sleep at night and work by day,

Who utter not God's name for a moment,

Who eat betel, and stretch out their hands *for more,*

Shall at the hour of death be firmly bound as thieves.

If under the guru's instruction thou joyfully sing the praises of God,

And utter the name of Him who filleth all creation, thou shalt be happy.

He in whose heart God mercifully establisheth His name,

Giveth the odour and perfume of God a place in *his heart.*

Saith Kabir, think, O blind man,

God is true, all worldly occupations are false.

The blissful peace of the holy.

17

Instead of death it is God who hath come for me;

Sorrow hath been removed and I have found a refuge in happiness.

Mine enemies have turned into friends;

The minds of the infidels have altered and become well disposed towards me.

I have now obtained all comfort,

And peace hath come over me since I have known God.

My body suffered millions of ills;

They have now been converted into permanent happiness and composure.

When man knoweth himself,

He shall not suffer from illness or the three fevers.

My mind hath now returned to the Eternal;

When in life I was dead,[20] it was then I knew God.

Saith Kabir, I have now entered happiness and rest;
I have no fear myself, and I inspire no fear in others.[21]

It is said that Krishan Das Bairagi asked Kabir:--

18

When the body dieth, to what abode shall the *pious man's* soul go?

Kabir--It shall unite with Him who is beyond expression and indestructible :

He who knoweth God understandeth this,

As the dumb man when pleased with sugar *must keep his pleasure to himself.*

Such divine knowledge *only* God Himself expoundeth.
O man, arrest thy breath at the junction of the nostrils ;
Appoint such a guru as shall render another unnecessary ;
Utter such a word as shall render another unnecessary ;
Embrace such divine knowledge as shall render any more unnecessary ;
So die that thou shalt not have to die again ;
Turn back the Ganges and unite it with the Jamna[22];
And think that thou art bathing without water at their confluence.[23]
Be it thy duty to look on all men as equal ;
Reflect upon the Real Thing ; what *else is there* to reflect on ?
Water, fire, wind, earth, and the firmament--
If thou abide like these[24], thou shalt be near God.
Saith Kabir, meditate on the Stainless One,
And go to that place whence there shall be no returning.

How Kabir found God.

19

God cannot be obtained *even by offering* one's weight in gold ;
But I have purchased Him with my soul ;
And now that I recognize Him as mine own,
My mind is naturally at ease.
Brahma, however much he talketh, hath not found God's limit;
But by my devotion God came to me as I sat at home.
Saith Kabir, I have cast off my wavering disposition ;
It is only in God's service I am now a sleeping partner.

The holy cannot die for they are saved by divine knowledge.

20

That death which terrifieth the whole world,
The guru's instruction hath set before me in a clear light.
Now how shall I die although my mind accepteth death ?
It is they who know not God who are always dying.
Everybody talketh of dying,
It is they who die in divine knowledge who are immortal.
Saith Kabir, my mind is happy ;
Doubt is dispelled, and supreme happiness abideth.

Kabir's body is burning all over to meet God; it is useless to try to heal any particular part of it.

21

There is no *special* part of *my body* to which I may apply *healing* ointment ;
I have examined my body but found no *such* place.
He who feeleth pain knoweth it ;
The service of God is a barbed arrow ;
I consider all women[25] to be alike ;
Who knoweth which shall be dear to the Bridegroom ?
Saith Kabir, the Husband, forsaking all other *women,*
Shall meet her on whose forehead *such* lot *hath been written.*

It was believed that widows who immolated themselves on their husbands' pyres obtained salvation. Kabir traverses this belief.

23

How can a woman without chastity be a sati ?
O Pandit, see and consider this in thy heart.
If a woman have no love *for her husband,* how can *her husband's* love for her increase ?
As long as there is *worldly* love, there can be no *divine* love.
He who in his heart believeth mammon to be real,
Shall not even in his dreams meet God.
Kabir calleth her a happy wife,
Who giveth up to God her body, soul, wealth, and household.

Devotion to God is the only dispeller of the deadly sins.

24

The whole world is subject to the deadly sins ;
The deadly sins have ruined *whole* families.
O man, where hast thou wrecked and sunk thy boat ?
Having broken with God thou hast joined the deadly sins,
In whose fire demigods and men burn.
Water[26] is near, but, O beasts, why not drink it, *removing* its scum[27]?
By contemplation water fit *for drinking* issueth forth ;
That water alone is pure, saith Kabir.

Only the holy who meditate on God are useful in the world.

25

Why was not the mother of the family barren[28],
Whose sons meditate not on divine knowledge ?
Why did not the wicked man who hath performed no service for God,
Die at his birth ?
Many[29] miscarriages have occurred--how is it he escaped?
He liveth, *it is true*, but like a raven in the world.
Saith Kabir, they who are beautiful and shapely,
Shall become hunchbacked and deformed without God's name.

Kabir's devotion to the saints.

26

I am ever a sacrifice.
To those who repeat the Master's name.
He is pure who singeth the praises of the pure God;
He is my brother and dear to my heart.
I am the dust of the lotus feet.
Of those whose hearts are filled with God.
My caste, *it is true, is that* of weaver, but my heart is resigned ;
Kabir very tranquilly repeateth God's praises.

Kabir, thus, addressed a Jogi who advised him to drink wine to concentrate his thoughts.

27

I collected much molasses[30], and turned my body into firewood ;

Then wine trickled from the roof of the house of pleasure[31] *by means of the* furnace *of my heart.*

Describe him as intoxicated *with the wine* of divine love
Who drinketh the sweetness of God's *name and* meditateth on divine knowledge.

Since the server[32] *of the wine* of divine love met me and *gave it to me,*
My days and nights are passing away intoxicated with pleasure.
I carefully applied my thoughts to the Pure One,
And then, saith Kabir, I obtained Him the Fearless.

A Jogi maintained that deliverance could not be obtained without chastening the heart, and that the heart could not be chastened without the practice of Jog. Kabir criticizes the statement.

28

Without devotion the qualities of the heart cling to the heart.
Who secureth perfection by *merely* chastening his heart[33] ?
What holy man *hath succeeded* in chastening his heart ?
Say who hath saved any one by *merely* chastening his heart.
Every one thinketh in his heart that he is *going to chasten it,*
But the heart is not chastened without devotion.
Saith Kabir, let him who knoweth this secret,
Worship in his heart God, the Lord of the three worlds.

The following was addressed to an atheist who maintained the theory of spontaneous creation.

29

Who was the painter who painted
The stars which appear in the sky[34] ?
Say, O Pandit, to what is the sky attached[35] ?
Fortunate is the wise man who knoweth this.
The sun and moon diffuse light ;
God hadth extended Himself in everything.
Saith Kabir, he shall know this.
In whose heart is God, and in whose mouth is God.

The evil wrought by the Simritis.

30

O my brethren, the Simriti is the daughter of the Veds ;
She hath brought a chain and a rope *for men,*
And hath of herself imprisoned them in her capital[36];
She hath flung the noose of worldly love, and discharged the arrow of death ;
The former cannot be cut, and the latter cannot be broken.
The *Simriti* hath become a serpent, eaten the world,
And plundered the whole universe before my very eyes ;
But, saith Kabir, I have escaped *from her* by uttering God's *name.*

The following was addressed to an admirer who had offered Kabir a horse.

31

Let me put a bit and bride *on my steed,*[37]
And abandoning all else course him in heaven[38].
Let me make self-reflection my saddle,
And put my foot in the stirrup of divine love.
Come, *my steel,* let me drive thee to heaven ;
If thou jib, I will strike thee with the whip of love.
Saith Kabir, they are good riders.
Who keep themselves aloof from the Veds and the books *of the Musalmans.*

The following was written after witnessing a cremation:--

32

I have seen fire applied to the mouth
Which used to eat the five nectars[39].
Remove, O God, my one misery
Of abiding in the womb and being burned in its fire.
The body is destroyed in various ways and manners--
Some burn it, and some bury it in the earth.
Saith Kabir, O God, show me Thy feet ;
Afterwards why not send death[40] ?

Kabir was engaged in his devotions when a hostile neighbour took the opportunity to set his house on fire. Kabir heard of it and returning home succeeded in extinguishing the flames. It is said that the hostile neighbour's house took fire from Kabir and was totally consumed. The following hymn was composed on the occasion :-

33

God Himself is the fire, Himself the wind ;
When the Master setteth fire *to the house,* who can save it.
What if even my body burn when I am repeating God name ?
My mind was absorbed in God's name ;
Whose house burneth, and who suffereth loss[41] ?
God playeth like an acrobat.
Saith Kabir, utter two letters[42] ;
As sure as I have a Master, He will save me.

Kabir thinks he has not performed sufficient worship.

34

I have not applied my mind to the science of union was God or contemplation of Him ;
Without hate of the world I shall not escape from mamm
How shall I live.
If I have not God's name as my support ?
Saith Kabir, I have searched in heaven,
And have seen none equal to God.

The following was written on seeing ravens sitting on a skull and feeding on its contents:--

35

Ravens were cleaning their beaks on the skull.
On which a turban had been *once* very daintily bound.
Why be proud of this body and of wealth?
Why dost thou not hold fast God's name?
Saith Kabir, hear, O my man,
This shall be thy condition at last.

Kabir discourses on the soul.

Gauri Ashtapadi

36

Man prayeth for temporal happiness, but sorrow cometh to meet him.

It pleaseth me not to pray for such happiness *as shall bring sorrow.*

Man still intent on sin hopeth for happiness;

How shall he find his dwelling in the Supreme God ?

The happiness which even Shiv and Brahma would dread, I supposed to be real.

Even the four sons of Brahma, the muni Narad, and Sheshnag.

Never found their minds *stable* in their bodies *until they had given up hopes of such happiness.*

O my brethren, let any one inquire into *the condition of the soul.*

When it escapeth from the body, where shall it be ?

By the favour of the guru, Jaidev and Namdev

Discovered that, by love and devotion to God,

The soul shall not suffer transmigration.

He whose doubts are dispelled knoweth the truth--

This soul hath no shape or outline ;

By God's order it was created, and by understanding God's order it shall be absorbed in Him.

If any one understand the secret of the soul,

It shall *only* obtain divine happiness when absorbed in God.

There is but one Soul[43] which occupieth all bodies.

Kabir worshippeth that Soul.

God's name is the tree of life.

37

Of those who watch day and night *to utter* the one Name.

How many have become perfect by the love they bore to God !

Sidhs and their disciples and all the munis have grown weary *in their efforts without God's name :*

The one Name like the tree of life saveth *mankind.*

They who are regenerated by God shall never alter.

Saith Kabir, I have recognized God's name.

The worship of the one God inculcated.

Gauri And Sorath

38

O shameless man, art thou not ashamed ?

Why dost thou forsake God, and go to some one else[44]?

It becometh not him whose God is the Most High

To go to a strange temple.
That Lord pervadeth *all space,*
Is ever present, and never distant.
Say, O man, what is there not in His palace
At whose feet Lakshmi taketh refuge ?
Every one speaketh of Him :
He is ommipotent, our own Lord, and our Benefactor.
Saith Kabir, that man is perfect in the world,
In whose heart no other than God abideth.

They who are absorbed in God feel not joy or sorrow for relations.

39

Who hath a son? Who hath a father?
Who dieth? who inflicteth pain ?
God is the Illusionist who hath illuded the world[45].
If separated from God how shall I survive, my mother?
Who hath a husband? who hath a wife ? reflect on this truth in thy heart.
Saith Kabir, I have become reconciled with the Illusionist;
The illusion vanished when I recognized Him.

Kabir's satisfaction on feeling that he had obtained salvation.

40

The sovereign God hath now become my helper;
Having cut away birth and death I have obtained the supreme state.
God hath united me with the guild of the saints,
And freed me from the five deadly sins.
The ambrosial name I repeat with my tongue;
God hath made me His unbought[46] slave.
The True Guru did me a favour
By rescuing me from the ocean of the world.
I have begun to love God's lotus feet,
And God ever and ever dwelleth in my heart.
The sparks of the fire of worldly love have become extinguished,
And my mind hath obtained resignation by the support of the Name.

In sea and land the Lord God is fully contained;
Wherever I look, there is the Searcher of hearts.
It is He Himself who implanteth His service *in my heart*;
God is obtained, my brethren, according to primal destiny.
The man to whom He showeth favour succeedeth in his affairs.
Kabir's Lord is the Chreisher of the poor.

The following was a remonstrance to a Brahman who had found impurity and caste defilement in almost everything.

41

There is impurity in water, there is impurity in land, there is impurity in whatever is born.

There is impurity in birth, and again in death ;

God's subjects are ruined by this impurity[47].

O Pandit, tell me who is pure ;

Explain to me such knowledge *as thou hast on the subject,* my friend.

There is impurity in the eyes, there is impurity in the tongue, there is impurity in the ears ;

Standing or sitting there is impurity, impurity entereth the kitchen.

Every one knoweth how to be caught *in impurity,* but few how to escape from it.

Saith Kabir, no impurity attacheth to those who meditate on God in their hearts.

God is greater than any creature, and His saint than any place of pilgrimage.

42

Decide one controversy, O Ramanand,
If thou *desire* any service from thy slave.
Is this soul or He to whom it is attached the greater?
Is God or he who knoweth God the greater?
Is Brahma or He who created him the greater?
Are the Veds or the source whence they came the greater?
Is the pilgrimage or God's saint the greater?
Saith Kabir, I have been unhappy *on this subject.*

The effects of the influx of divine, knowledge. Kabir likens his mind to a hut.

43

Lo ! my brethren, a storm of divine knowledge hath come ;

The screens of doubt have all been blown away, and even the ropes of mammon have not been left ;

The two props of indecision[48] have been thrown down, and the beam[49] of worldly love hath been broken ;

The thatched roof of avarice hath fallen to the ground ; and the vessel of evil inclinations hath burst.

Saith Kabir, thy slave, O Lord, hath become saturated by the rain[50] which fell after the storm.

And when *next* he saw the sun appear[51], his mind was illumined.

The following was addressed to a Brahman. Kabir did not desire his followers to associate with infidels.

44

What shall one say to such people.

As neither hear God's praises nor sing His attributes,

But who knock down the heavens by their hoasting ?

They whom God hath excluded from His service should always be feared.

They who give not a handful of water *to the thirsty*

Slander him[52] who brought down the Ganges.

Sitting or standing crooked are their ways ;

They have ruined themselves and ruined others ;

They know nothing save evil converse ;

They obey not even Brahma's bidding ;

They have gone astray themselves and are leading others astray.

They set fire to their houses and sleep in them[53];

They laugh at others, though they have only one eye themselves ;

Kabir is ashamed on beholding them.

A lecture against the shradhs and idolatry of the Hindus.

45

Nobody obeyeth his parents when alive, yet he giveth them feasts when dead ;

Say how shall the poor parents obtain what the ravens and the dogs have eaten.

Let some one explain to me what kushal[54] means ;

The world dieth talking of kushal ; however shall kushal be obtained ?

Men make goddesses and gods of clay, and offer them living sacrifices--

As your lifeless gods, so your deceased, who ask not for what they want themselves.

You kill living things, and you worship lifeless things ; at the last moment great *shall be your suffering.*

You know not the worth of God's name, and you shall be drowned *in the sea* of terror.

You waver and know not the supreme God, *wherefore* you worship gods and goddesses.

Saith Kabir, you have not thought of the Unknowable, and have become entangled in the deadly sins.

The holy obtain their great reward.

46

If while living thou be dead, while dead return to life by *means of divine knowledge,* and thus become absorbed in God ;

If thou abide pure amid impurity, thou shalt not again fall into the terrible ocean *of the world.*

My God, such milk should be churned--[55]

Keep thy mind steadfast under the guru's instruction; in this way shalt thou quaff nectar[56].

The guru's arrow hath pierced this adamantine age, and let in the light of God's word.

The doubt *which I felt, through* the power of ignorance *whether this world was a snake or a rope,* is at an end ; I have a permanent abode in God's house.

The guru without putting an arrow on his bow hath pierced this world, my brethren.

In all directions the kite[57] fluttereth in the wind, but its string is fixed in the love of God.

My perturbed mind is absorbed in God ; duality and evil inclinations depart.

Saith Kabir, I have seen the Fearless One by fixing my attention on His name.

Rather than practise Jog search for God through the guru.

47

When I turned my thoughts towards God, I restrained my mind and my senses[58], and my attention became lovingly fixed on Him.

O Bairagi, search for Him who neither cometh nor goeth, who neither dieth nor is born.

My soul turning away from sin is absorbed in the *universal Soul* ;

By the favour of the guru I have *now* obtained a different understanding ; otherwise I should become estranged from God.

What was near[59] hath become distant, what was distant[60] hath become near for him who accepteth God as He is.

As sharbat made from sugar--only he who drinketh it knoweth *its flavour.*

O Thou devoid of qualities, is there any discriminating person to whom I may speak of Thee ?

Saith Kabir, only he who applieth the spiritual fuse seeth the blast.

Heaven described by negatives.

48

There (*with God*) is no rainy season, no ocean, no sun shine, noshade; there is no creation and no destruction ;

No life, no death ; nor are sorrow and joy felt ; nor is there either retirement or contemplation--

A description of celestial rest would be impossible and peculiar to itself--

There nothing is weighed in the balance, and nothing is exhausted; there is nothing light, nothing heavy.

There are no nether or upper regions, neither night no day ;

There is no water, wind, or fire ; the True Guru is there contained.

Inaccessible and inapprehensible, He dwelleth uninter ruptedly in everything ;

He is found by the favour of the guru.

Saith Kabir, I am a sacrifice to my guru ; may I remain attached to his society !

Human life under the allegory of an ox and his burden.

49

With merits and demerits an ox is purchased[61] ; life appeareth as the capital[62] ;

In this way a herd is purchased[63]; covetousness which filleth man's heart is as a sack *on the ox's back.*

So *potent* a master is my God.

Who made the whole world dealers[64].

Lust and wrath are both tax-gatherers[65] ; the whims of the mind are highway robbers.

The herd, which spring from the five elements, pay the tax[66], and are saved.

Saith Kabir, hear, O saints, this is now the state of things--

One ox[67] hath grown weary of travelling the steep road, and dropping his sack, proceedeth on his journey[68].

The world under the allegory of a well, human life under that of a well-rope.

50

A woman hath four days in her father's house ; she must *then* go to her father-in-law's--

The blind, the stupid, and the silly know not this--

The bride with her *sarhi* round her is ready to go ;

The guests arrive ; her husband hath come to take her home[69].

Who is that we see letting down the rope into the well.

When the rope breaketh by the weight of the water, the water-drawer departeth.

If the Lord be compassionate and show mercy, *won* shall settle her affairs;

She is known as a happy wife who pondereth on guru's instructions.

All men bound by their acts transmigrate ; attentive consider this.

Why blame woman ? what can the poor creature do.

Without hope she departeth ; she hath not the firm of *faith* in her heart.

Cling to the feet of God, and flee to His asylum, O Kabir.

It is the truly pious and not the Jogis or His Sectaries who shall be saved.

51

The Jogi says that jog and nothing else is good sweet;

They who shave their bodies, and the Ekshabdis, that they *alone* have obtained perfection.

Without God thou art lost in error, O blind one ;

They to whom I go to release myself, are themself bound by many toils.

You call yourselves pandits, virtuous, brave, general and assert that you alone are great ;

It is only when *this pride of yours* is forgotten that shall be absorbed in Him from whom you sprang.

Only he understandeth whom Thou, O God, causes understand ; how can man obtain permanence with understanding ?

When the true guru is found, darkness is dispelled this way the gem[70] is obtained.

Lay aside the sins of thy left hand and thy right[71]; firm hold of God's feet.

Saith Kabir, if a dumb man eat molasses, what can he say if questioned[72] ?

The following was composed by Kabir on the death of a Jogi :--

52

Where there was something there is nothing ; *the body of* five elements is no more.

What availeth thee now the suspension of thy breath in the left and right nostrils and their junction ?

The string[73] is broken, thy brain destroyed ; whether hath thy speech gone ?

I feel this anxiety night and day; who will explain and ease my mind?

The body is no longer in the world ; thy creative *mind* is no more.

The Joiner dwelleth ever separate *from the world*; say who else hath this *power* ?

If *I try* to join the *elements of the body* ; I cannot join them ;

if *I try* to separate them, they will not be separated until they perish.

Who hath a master ? who hath a servant ? who waiteth on any one else[74] ?

Saith Kabir, my attention is directed to that place where *God* dwelleth night and day;

His secret He Himself fully knoweth ; He is ever imperishable.

Kabir was advised to become a Jogi ; the following was his reply:--

53

Meditation and remembrance of *God* are my two ear-rings, independence of the world my patched coat ;

Dwelling in a silent cave my devotional posture, the abandonment of worldly desires my sect.

My king[75], I am a Jogi without temporal love ; I repine not at death and separation.

In the regions of the universe *I find* my horn ; the whole world, which I hold as ashes, is my wallet ;

Riddance of the three qualities and release from the world are my contemplative attitude.

I have made by heart and breath the two gourds of impyre, and unbroken atatention on God its frame.

The strings are strong and break not ; the lyre playet spontaneously

On hearing it the perfect are enraptured, and I no longer feel the swaying of worldly love.

Saith Kabir, the soul which hath played in this way shall not be born again.

The body under the allegory of a full piece of cloth.

54

Reason went to the soul to order *a body* to be woven--

Let a full piece of nine yards, ten yards, and twenty-one yards be woven[76].

Let there be sixty threads, nine joinings, and seventy two cross threads[77] added ;

The weaver[78] then cometh, leaving his last abode.

Is not *the body* measured by yards, weighed by weigh and starched by two and a half sers of flour[79] ?

If the body obtain not starch quickly, it will quarrel and destroy its abode[80] ?

O man, how many days are there for thee to sit *idly* ?

When shalt thou, who art adverse to the Lord, again have the present opportunity ?

The vessels[81] and the wetted bobbins shall fall to pieces, and the weaver depart in anger ;

Thread cometh not out of an empty bobbin[82], and *the cloth* will not remain wound around the beam.

O wretched man, abide in the world, but renounce display--Kabir *giveth thee this* advice[83].

The light of God has an affinity for the light of man.

55

Can one light which is absorbed in another be separated from it ?

May that man burst and die in whose heart the name of God springeth not up !

Dark and beautiful God, my soul is attached to Thee.

When a holy man is found, supernatural perfection obtained ; this is both union with God and worldy enjoyment.

When two, *the guru and the disciple*, meet by means of God's name, the *disciple's* business is accomplished[84].

People think this is a song ; it is a meditation on God,

Like the instruction given to men at Banaras when they are on the point of death.

He who attentively heareth or singeth God's name.

Saith Kabir, shall certainly obtain the supreme state last.

Salvation can only be obtained by true devotion.

56

However great man's exertions *without God's name*, shall be drowned in the terrible ocean and not cross over.

Thou hast practised thy religious duties and great austerties, yet pride consumeth thy soul.

Why hast thou forgotten the Lord who is the Giver life and food ?

Human birth is a priceless diamond or ruby ; thouth lost it for a kauri.

Not having thought of God in thy heart, thou suffer from the thirst of covetousness and the hunger of error.

The intoxication of pride deceiveth those who keep the word of the guru in their hearts.

Sinful are they who are led away by pleasure, who tempted by sensual delights, and who enjoy the savour of wine.

They who by destiny keep the company of the saints, float over like iron attached to timber.

Through error I have wandered among human and lower births ; I am now weary and overspent with travail.

Saith Kabir, on meeting the guru *I have felt* great joy, and my love and devotion have saved me.

The deceits of the world.

57

Like the semblance of a female elephant, O foolish man, the Lord of the world made this play[85].

The elephant *impelled by* the sweets of love is captured, O foolish man, and his head hath to endure the goad.

Flee from evil passions, attach thyself to God ; heed this *advice*, O foolish man.

Why dost thou not, O foolish man, fearlessly worship God, and take possession of His ship[86] ?

The monkey stretcheth out his hand, O foolish man, and taketh a handful of corn[87] ;

He is anxious to escape, O foolish man, but he shall be made to dance at the door of every house.

As the parrot is caught by a trap[88], O foolish man, so is man by worldly occupations[89].

As the *fleeting* dye of the safflower, O foolish man, so hath this world been shown.

There are many places for ablutions, O foolish man, and many gods to worship.

Saith Kabir, thou shalt not be saved by *means of these* O foolish man; thou shalt be saved by the worship of God.

A raja offered temporal wealth to Kabir. The following was his reply--

58

Lay up for yourselves the wealth of God's name, which fire will not burn, which hot winds will not dry up,

And which thieves will not approach ; that wealth shall never depart.

My wealth is God, the Supporter of the earth ; He is the real wealth.

The pleasure obtained from the service of God is not to be found in regal state ;

Shiv and the four sons of Brahma in their search for this wealth abandoned the world.He in whose heart is God and on whose tongue is God falleth not into Death's noose.

The guru's private wealth of divine knowledge and devotion is like water to the thirsty, like a prop to the fickle mind ;

The minds of those on whom He bestoweth it, conceived good resolutions, and their doubts, entanglements, and fear depart.

Saith Kabir, O you who are intoxicated with wealth reflect in your hearts and understand this.

In your mansions are hundreds of thousands and millions of horses and elephants ; in mine is the one God.

The love of worldly things leads men to damnation.

59

A monkey through greed will not let go the pulse in his hand.

Man is responsible for acts done through greed.

Without devotion to God human life passeth in vain.

Without association with the saints and worship of God, truth nowhere abideth.

As the flowers of the desert bloom, and no one enjoyeth their odour.

So men wander *idly* in many births, and Death destroyeth them again and again.

God hath given wealth, youth, sons, and women *fair* to view ;

By these man, prompted by the senses, becometh arrested and entangled.

The body is a house of grass, life's end the fire which assaileth it on every side.

Saith Kabir to cross over the terrible ocean I have taken the shelter of the true guru.

A brief account of the process of procreation.

60

There is a dirty water and white earth ;

From this earth a puppet is made.

I am nothing and I have nothing ;

My body, my wealth, all that is dear *to me* is Thine, O God--

Into this earth breath is infused,

And forcibly setteth the false contrivance in motion.

Such and such a person may have accumulated five lakhs, *of treasure,*

But at last his pitcher bursteth[90].

Saith Kabir, the sole foundation thou hast laid.

Shall be destroyed in a moment, O thou proud one.

By devotion to God through the guru Kabir has obtained salvation.

61

O my soul, repeat God's name

As did Dhru and Prahlad *of old.*

O Thou compassionate to the poor, my reliance is on Thee.

I have *therefore* embarked all my family on the guru's raft.

If it please God He will have His order obeyed,

And cause this raft to float over.
By the favour of the guru such knowledge hath filled me.
That all my transmigration is at an end.
Saith Kabir, worship God ;
In this world and the next, everywhere, it is He alone who knoweth[91].

The soul having obtained a human body has obtained its last chance of salvation.

62

When *man* leaveth the womb and cometh into the world,
As soon as the air toucheth him, he forgetteth his Master--
O my soul, sing God's praises !
When thou didst penance reversed in the womb.
Thou didst escape its fire.
Having wandered through the eighty-four lakhs of existences,
If thou stumble now, thou shalt find nor house nor home.
Saith Kabir, worship God.
Who is not seen coming or going, and who knoweth all things.

Think not of heaven or hell, of prosperity or adversity ; leave everything to God.

63

Long not for a dwelling in heaven, and fear not to dwell in hell ;
What will be, will be; O my soul, hope not at all.
Sing the praises of God from whom the supreme reward is obtained.
What is devotion, what penance and austerities, what fasting and ablutions,
Unless thou know the way to love and serve God ?
Be not glad at the sight of prosperity and grieve not at the sight of adversity ;
As is prosperity so is adversity ; what God proposeth shall be accomplished.
Saith Kabir, through the saints I now know in my heart.
That the worshipper in whose heart God dwelleth, *performeth* the best worship.

Commit not sin for the sake of thy relations or others and mourn not for them.

64

O my soul, thou hast no *helper* ; drag not the weight of *others' sins* behind thee.

As a bird percheth on a tree, such is the world[92].

I have drunk the elixir of God.

By which other elixirs are forgotten.

Since we are not permanent ourselves, why should we mourn the death of others ?

Whatever is born perisheth ; why should we be sorry and weep for that ?

When man becometh attached to holy men, he drinketh *God's elixir,* and is devoted to Him from whom he hath sprung.

Saith Kabir, I have thought of God in my heart ; resigning the world remember Him.

Kabir longs for God as a loving wife for her absent spouse.

65

Woman with her eyes filled *with tears* and heaving sighs awaiteth *her lord* ;

Her heart is not happy ; she retraceth not her steps in the hope of seeing him.

Why fliest thou not away, O black raven[93], so that I may quickly meet my beloved ?

Saith Kabir, perform God's service to obtain the dignity of eternal life ;

The name of God is the one support ; repeat it with thy tongue.

There are many excellences in the body ; God resides within it and Kabir is delighted to behold Him.

66

There are many shrubs of sweet basil ; near and within them is the village of Barsana[94].

The milkmaid *Radha* on seeing *Krishan's* beauty became enamoured ; Leave me not; go not hither and thither.

My heart is attached to thy feet ; O holder of the bow, very fortunate is she who meeteth thee'.

Enchanting in Bindraban where the fascinating Krishan grazed his kine.

Since thou art my Lord, O holder of the bow, Kabir (great) is my name.

Vain is the devotion of anchorets and idolaters.

67

How many wear the bark of trees as clothes, but what availeth it to dwell in the forest ?

What availeth it to man to offer incense *to idols* ? What to drench his body with ablutions ?

O my soul, I know that thou shalt depart ;

O silly one, think of thy fall[95].

Wheresoever I look, I see none but those who are entangled in worldly love ;

Men of divine knowledge and meditation, great preachers are all *engrossed* in this world's affairs.

Saith Kabir, without the name of the one God this world is blinded by mammon.

Fearlessly worship God.

68

O man victim of mammon, abandon doubt, come forth and dance[96].

Doth a hero dread the conflict of the battle-field, doth a sati collect utensils *when she is about to die* ?

Cease to waver, O foolish man ;

Now that thou hast taken the red lead[97] in thy hand, burn and die, and obtain perfection.

The world is ruined by being absorbed in lust, wrath, and mammon.

Saith Kabir, forsake not the sovereign God who is the highest of all the high.

Kabir places himself altogether in God's power.

69

Thy commands are acceptable to men ; I consider not their propriety.

Thou art the river, Thou art the pilot, from Thee is salvation.

O man, embrace the service *of God.*

Whether He be angry with thee or love thee.

Thy name, O God, is my support, as a woman rejoiceth on *beholding* her son[98].

Saith Kabir, I am the slave of Thy house, preserve me or destroy me.

A homily against the worship of Krishan.

70

Nand[99] became very weary wandering through the wombs of the eighty-four lakhs of existences ;

Through his devotion *Krishan* became incarnate ; great was the poor man's good fortune.

You who say that *God* was the son of Nand, whose son was Nand?

When the earth and the firmament and the ten quarters of the world were not, then where was this Nand ?

He whose name is the Bright One falleth not into trouble, and undergoeth not birth.

Kabir's Master is such a Lord as hath neither father nor mother.

Kabir hails slander to preserve his humility and lead him to God.

71

Slander, slander me, ye people, slander !
Slander is right pleasing to God's servant.
Slander is my father, slander my mother[100] ;
If I am slandered and store in my heart.
The wealth of God's name, I shall go to heaven.
If I am slandered my heart becometh pure,
The slander washeth my clothes for me[101].
He who slandereth me is my friend ;
My heart goeth out to the slanderer ;
He is the slanderer who preventeth my being slandered.
The slanderer desireth *long* life *for me* ;
I bear love and affection to *him who* slandereth me ;
Slander effecteth my salvation.
To God's servant, Kabir, slander is the best thing ;
The slanderer is lost, I am saved.

Kabir feels that he has parted with egoism and become absorbed in God.

72

O sovereign God, Thou art very fearless ; Thou art a raft to save the world, O God.

When I was proud, Thou *wert* not *in me* ; now that Thou art *in me* I am not proud.

Now Thou and I have become one ; seeing that we are both one, my mind is satisfied.

When there is *worldly* wisdom, how can there be *spiritual* strength.

Now I have *spiritual* wisdom, but no bodily strength.

Saith Kabir, God hath taken away my *worldly* wisdom, and instead of it I have obtained perfection.

The human body under the allegory of a house.

73

The Creator made the six mystical chambers[102] into a house, and in it He put a peerless thing[103] ;

Without delay He made *divine knowledge* its key, *spiritual ignorance* its lock, and life its watchman.

Now my brother, let thy mind remain awake ;

Through carelessness thou hast lost thy *human* life ; thy house is being robbed by thieves[104].

Thy five *senses* stand as sentinels at the gate, but they cannot be trusted.

Carefully think of God, and thou shalt obtain the light of divine knowledge.

If woman go astray through only heeding the body of nine apertures, she shall not obtain the peerless thing-- God's name.

Saith Kabir, thieves may plunder the body of nine apertures ; *God's* spirit dwelleth in the tenth.

Kabir obtained perfection and complete faith on meeting the guru.

74

O mother, I know none beside *God* ;

My soul dwelleth in that *God* whose praises Shiv and the sons of Brahma sing.

On meeting the guru enlightenment and divine knowledge entered my heart, and I meditated on God in my brain ;

The disease of the deadly sins, fear, and worldly entanglements fled away, and my soul knew happiness in itself.

Imbued with devotion I know and obey the one *God*, and think of none beside.

Having abandoned the pride of my heart, my soul is perfumed with the perfume of sandal.

God dwelleth in him who hath sung and meditated on His praises.

Very fortunate are they in whose heart *He* dwelleth, and distinguished is the destiny recorded on their foreheads.

I have destroyed Maya, divine knowledge is kindled in my heart, and I have become absorbed in the one God.

Saith Kabir, on meeting the guru I have felt great comfort ; my mind hath ceased to wander and is happy.

Notes and References

1. The terrible ocean is very bitter--within it is found the sweet water of God's name.

2. Also translated--

   My honour or dishonour bringeth no shame on you. You shall know who is in the right when all gilding is cast off.

3. *Mirg* also means beasts generally.

4. That is, why wert thou born of woman ? The Brahmans are supposed to have issued from Brahma's mouth.

5. Among the Hindus blood is considered impure, and milk pure.

6. Man's wealth shall pass away with his life like the shadow of a tree.

7. The life or sound of a musical instrument is contained within it. If the string breaks, no life or sound remains, and no one can tell whether it has gone. When human life fails, the soul departs, and no mortal knows its destination.

8. Good and bad fruit spring from human acts, which again proceed from the light or understanding that God has given. The first verse of this hymn is also translated :--

   There is a species of animal for every spark of light, and a spark of light for every species of animal.

9. Good acts are compared to gold, bad acts to iron fetters ; but both good and bad acts retard man's progress towards absorption in God. These two lines are also translated :--

   They are entangled in *religious* ceremonies good and bad,

   And their acts whether bad or good have the same result.

   That is, they commit sins of various descriptions at places of pilgrimage, and their pilgrimages are therefore of no avail.

10. Spoken ironically.

11. Here the well is the body; the well-rope, life; the five water-carriers the five evil passions. Others understand the well to mean the world, and translate this line as follows :--

    When the well-rope (sensual desire) is broken, the water-carriers (the five organs of perception) grow weary of doing evil.

12. Even when life is drawing to a close the evil passions are still active.

13. Since Kabir has obtained salvation during life.

14. Stones are worshipped instead of God.

15. Men in power extorting money from the poor.

16. The perverse who listen not to the advice of their spiritual guides.

17. Women who sell their daughters and live on the proceeds.

18. The fifth Guru is said to have composed a portion of this hymn.

19. Hymns missing from this collection will be found either in the Life of Kabir or that of Guru Nanak.

20. When I abandoned pride.

21. I do not threaten men with spiritual tortures for themselves or their deceased relatives if I do not receive money for my ministrations.

22. Unite the breath of the left and right nostrils, as the Jogis do.

23. Make the breath of both nostrils meet in the brain, and thus obtain exaltation of spirit without bathing at the confluence of the Ganges and Jamna, as so many pilgrims do.

24. if thou adopt their properties, and remain sinless like them.

25. That is, all human beings.

26. Divine knowledge.

27. Man's evil passions which conceal the water of divine knowledge.

28. *Vidhwa.* Literally--a widow not allowed to marry.

29. In the original *much much,* as in Spanish.

30. From which spirits are made.

31. The Brain.

32. *Kalalin,* corresponding to the European barmaid. Even in India in

former times the distiller or publican used to employ a woman to serve wine to his customers. She probably here means Ramanand, Kabir's guru.

33. Man must also repeat God's name.

34. According to the Muhammadan conception of the heavens, the sky is a fixed vault on which the stars are painted.

35. What supports the sky ?

36. Probably Banaras is meant.

37. The mind.

38. The brain.

39. These are *bhakshya,* what is masticated by the front teeth, the back teeth, and the tongue ; *bhojya,* what is masticated by the back teeth and the tongue ; *lehiya,* what is licked or sipped by the tongue alone; *peya,* what is drunk ; and *choshya,* what is sucked.

    Another list of the five nectars is--milk, cream, clarified by honey, and sugar.

40. Kabir does not fear death provided he has first seen God's.

41. All property belongs to God.

42. *R* and *m* which with a long vowel make Ram, God.

43. The Soul of the world.

44. To worship idols.

45. Kabir believed with the Vedantists that everything was illusion. As all things emanated from God, it is He who continues the illusion, hence Kabir familiarly compares Him to an illusionist or actor.

46. As such I shall serve Him all the better.

47. When there is impurity in everything according to the Brahmans, they must be very well remunerated to purify men.

48. Whether man inclines to God or the world.

49. On which the rafters rested.

50. Internal peace or happiness.

51. When he saw God after the attainment of divine knowledge.

52. Bhagirath.

53. They commit sin, and feel no compunction or repentance.

54. A feeling of satisfaction after repletion.

55. Such good actions should be performed as shall ensure man against being born again.

56. That is, obtain the great boon of unswerving faith.

57. The mind.

58. *Chakr khat* is here understood to be the mind and the five senses, not the six mystical divisions of the body.

59. The deadily sins are meant.

60. God.

61. The soul enters a human body.

62. To earn further merits or demerits.

63. The mass of mankind are born.

64. Who gave every one life as his capital.

65. They subject the soul to punishment.

66. Are punished by the god of death.

67. Kabir himself, who obtained salvation while alive.

68. The following is an alternative translation of this very difficult hymn. A friend of Kabir suggested to him to speculate in bullocks. They could at the time be purchased cheap, and Kabir could afterwards sell them at a profit, and thus provide himself with funds for the entertainment of holy men. Kabir replied :--

    Men have purchased the bullocks of *their bodies* with bad and good acts, the breath *of life* is their capital.

    Desires and packed in the sack of the heart, and thus are the *good and evil produced by which oxen* are purchased.

    Our God is such a head of the firm that He hath made the whole world His traders.

    Both lust and wrath become tax-gatherers, and mental vagaries high-way robbers.

The man who associateth with the elect who know God, payeth the tax and his ox crosseth over.

Saith Kabir, hear O ye saints, it hath now come to this with me.

That is scaling the pass *of divine knowledge one ox at least* hath cast away his sack *of desires* and proceeded on *his journey*.

69. In the East, as still among the peasant classes in Ireland, women are allowed to remain sometime after marriage with their parents.

70. God's name.

71. Thy besetting sins.

72. He cannot describe his sensations. In the same way a man who has obtained God will be silent with pleasure.

73. Thy life has departed.

74. The meaning apparently is, that there are no earthly masters or servants, and that man should only acknowledge God as his Master.

75. Applied respectfully to the Jogi.

76. A full piece of cloth generally measures forty yards. The yards mean the nine apertures of the body; the ten yards, the organs of action and perception ; and the twenty-one yards, the subtle elements, the five gross elements, the ten breaths of the body and the mind. The twenty-one yards may also be the twenty- vertebrae of some Indian anatomists. The whole forty make up body which, in weaver's parlance, is compared to a full piece of cloth.

77. The sixty threads are supposed to be sixty blood-vessels, though Indian anatomists count one hundred and seventy five blood vessel altogether. The nine sections are the four pieces of the legs, the of the arms, and the head; and the seventy-two cross threads seventy-two chambers of the body according to the Jogis.

78. The soul leaves its last abode, and takes possession of a new

79. One *ser* of the present standard ; as much as a man can eat is said to be applied as starch to the tissues of his body.

80. And then the soul and body shall separate.

81. *Kunda* is an earthen pan which holds water to wet the thread.

The thread, when wetted, is put into the bobbins. Here, *Kunda* is understood to mean worldly possessions.

82. No breath issueth from the throat after death.

83. The following is an alternative translation of this most difficult hymn. Some pandits spoke contemptuously of Kabir's social position and said it was gross impudence on the part of a weaver to dare mention God's name. Kabir replied, that every one must be a weaver in a mystical sense in order to gain salvation. The pandits inquired how all men could become weavers. Kabir explained :--

The weaver's wife (reason) went to her spouse (the mind) to have a piece woven.

But the weaver was always leaving his home.

Kabir was then asked how he could compare the body to a piece of cloth. He replied :--

It is consisteth of nine yards, ten yards, and twenty-one yards.

Sixty threads of the warp, nine joinings, sixty-two cross threads.

Is not the body measured by yards, weighed by weight, and starched by two and a half sers of flour ?

If the body obtain not starch quickly, its spouse (the mind) will quarrel.

When shall such an opportunity come again? The days of life soon end and the soul departeth.

Thou must leave thy pans and thy wet bobbins, and the soul will depart in anger.

Thread issueth not from the empty bobbin, and the cloth will not remain wound round the beam.

Saith the mind to reason, O wretched one, leave off this wrangling, abide with me here; Kabir hath given this explanation.

84. Also translated--(a) When both meet, this work is accomplish namely, an alliance with Him whose name is God. (b) Blessings result from meeting God or obtaining His name.

85. The play of the world. A likeness of a female elephant is made out of cardboard to catch wild elephants. They are allured by the likeness to the verge of a pit into which they fall and are secured.

86. To float thee over the terrible ocean of the world.

87. Monkeys are caught by putting dry grain into a vessel and partially

burying it in the earth. The monkey puts in his hand, and fills it with grain. He is then caught, not having with enough to open his fingers and let go his grasp. So, too if man would abandon his vices, he would be saved.

88. The *nalni* is a contrivance made of bamboo put over water. When the parrot perches on it, it revolves, and the bird's body is below it and immediately over the water. The parrot clings to the nalni so as to avoid falling into the water, and is thus caught.

89. Literally--this is Maya's doing.

90. The body dies.

91. The verses is a so translated--I deem this world and the next all the same.

92. Temporary or transitory.

93. If a raven come to a woman's casement when her husband is absent, she says 'Fly away, O raven'. If it fly away in obedience to her order, it is an women that her husband will soon return. Here the word raven is understood to mean man's evil passions.

94. In the neighbourhood of Mathura and Bindraban. The original has Banaras, but the word does not suit the context. *Bana ras gaon* is also read--In the midst of them is made an excellent village.

95. *Abigat* means descent, but the word may also here mean God, from the Sanskrit *avyakl,* imperceptible, transcendental.

96. Scorn the opinion of the world.

97. It was the custom for a sati on the pyre to take some vermillion paint (*sindur*) in her hand, make a tilak on her forehead with it, then apply it to the foreheads of the bystanders and sprinkle it on them. After this ceremony she might not change her mind and must die. The sindur is generally carried in the rind of a coco-nut and is employed at marriages. Its use at the concremation of widows was emblematic of a second marriage to which death is likened.

98. Also translated--As a flower bloometh in the water.

99. The adoptive father of Krishan.

100. Is dear to me as my father and mother.

101. That is, he takes my impurity on himself.

102. The six mystical chambers of the body are--*Muladhara,* the parts about the pubis ; *Swadhshthanam,* or umbilical region ; *Manipuram,* or pit of the stomach or epigastrium ; *Anahalam,* the root of the nose ; *Visuddham,* the hollow between the frontal sinuses ; and *Ajnyakhyam,* the fontenelle or union of the coronal and sagittal sutures.

103. The Soul.

104. Thy evil passions.

KABIR'S ACROSTIC

1

Everything connected with the three worlds is contained in the fifty-two letters ;

These letters shall perish, but He who is beyond letters is not in them.

2

Where there is speech, there letters are used ;

Where there is no speech there no mind abideth.

God is contained both where there is speech and where there is not;

Nobody appeareth like unto Him[2].

3

If I obtain God, what shall I say ? and if I say anything what kindness *do I show God,*

Who is diffused through the three worlds *as well as* in the *tiny* seed of the banyan-tree[3] ?

4

For him who hath obtained God, any knoweth to some extent God's secret, the difference *between God and himself* hath disappeared.

God's secret penetrated my heart when it turned away *from the world* ; and I have obtained Him who is Indestructible and Impenetrable.

5

The Musalmans accept the Tariqat ; the Hindus the Veds and Purans; *but for me the books of both religions are useless.*

A man ought to study divine knowledge to some extent to instruct this heart.

6

I know the one God who was in the beginning ;

I do not believe in what can be written and erased.

Whoever beholdeth the one God,
Becometh as God, and shall not pass away.

7

K. When the rays of *divine knowledge* fall on the lotus of *the heart,*
It closeth not even at the rising of the moon[4] ;
And if *man* obtain the sweetness of that flower,
He would grow mute in describing it, *yea,* to whom could he explain it ?

8

KH. My mind hath entered God's cave[5] ;
It leaveth it not to wander in every direction.
He who, knowing the Master, practiseth resignation,
Shall become imperishable, and obtain the imperishable dignity.

9

G. They who understand the guru's instruction,
Lend their ears to nothing else.
He who graspeth the Ungraspable[6], and having grasped
Him keepeth Him in his brain,
Shall abide *wealthless* as a bird, and wander nowhere.

10

G.H. God's dwelling is in every heart ;
Even though the heart break, *God* is never *thereby* diminished.
When man findeth a way *to God* in his heart,
Why should he leave that way and follow a difficult one ?

11

NG. Grasp the love of *God,* dismiss doubts.
Even though thou *see no way to God,* flee not away ;
this is the highest cleverness.

12

C.H. *God* painted the great picture of the world ;
Dismiss the picture, and think of the Painter.
This painted picture is an *abode* of strife ;
Dismiss the picture, and keep thy mind on the Painter

13

CHH. God the Lord of the umbrella is near ;
Why dost thou not abandon desires and be happy ?

O man, I admonish thee every moment ;
Why dost thou leave God and entangle thyself *with the world* ?

14

J. If a man burn his body alive,
And efface his youth, he shall find the *right* way
When man burneth the wealth of this and the next world[7],
He shall then proceed and obtain *God's* bright light.

15

JH. Thou art entangled *with the world,* and knowest not how to disentangle thyself ;

Thou shrinkest back, and art not accepted of *God.*

Why talk nonsense trying to convince others ?

Since thou stirrest up controversy, controversy thou shalt have.

16

NY. Since *God* dwelleth near thee in thy heart, why leave Him and go far *to find Him*[8] ?

Him for whom thou searchest the world, thou shalt find near thee.

17

T. The difficult way *to God* is in man's heart.

Why open not the doors of thine *understanding,* and repair to His court ?

There shalt thou behold the Immovable One, and thou shalt not move elsewhere.

Thou shalt remain attached *to God,* and thy heart shall be glad.

18

TH. Keep the world, which is a deceitful mirage, at a distance--
I have with difficulty rendered my mind patient--
The cheat which cheated and devoured the whole world
I have myself cheated, and my mind is now at ease.

19

D. When the fear of *God* is produced, *all other* fears depart ;
All other fears are absorbed in that fear.
If man reject the fear of *God,* then he hath fear of *man* ;
When he no longer feareth man, the fears of his heart flee away.

20

D.H. Search for God near thee ; why *search* elsewhere ?

While searching for Him elsewhere life departeth.

When I ascended the mountain to search for Him, and returned *home disappointed.*

I found Him in the fortress[9] which He Himself had made.

21

N. The life of him is accounted happy

Who, though surrounded in the battle-field, standeth fast like a man[10],

Who doth not quail or retreat[11],

But killeth the opposing chief, upon which has army fleeth away[12].

22

T. The world is unfordable ; it cannot be forded.

My soul is absorbed in the Lord of the three worlds.

If *the Lord of* the three worlds enter into my heart,

My soul shall blend with Him, and I shall find the True One.

23

TH. The Unfathomable cannot be fathomed.

God is unfathomable ; this *body* shall not abide for ever.

Though man's span of life be brief, he beginneth *to build* many a mansion[13]--

But can mansions be supported without pillars ?

24

D. Evertything we see is perishable;

Meditate on Him who is Unseen.

When thou appliest the key of *divine knowledge* to the tenth gate,

Thou shalt then behold the merciful One.

25

DH. Everything is settled when the soul *blendeth* with God

Who dwelleth in earth and heaven.

When the soul leaving earth goeth to heaven.

The soul and God shall meet and happiness be obtained.

26

N. Man's nights and days pass away waiting for *God* ;

His eyes grow blood-shot by such waiting.
When man findeth God after long waiting,
He who waiteth is blended with Him who is waited for.

27

P. The Boundless One hath no bounds ;
I am gladdened with the Supreme Light ;
I have controlled the five senses,
And relinquished *all idea of* demerits and merits.

28

PH. Fruit is produced without the blossom[14] ;
If any one looked at a section of that fruit[15],
And reflected on it, he would not contract duality.
That section of fruit shall destroy all bodies[16].

29

B. Blend drop with drop[17],
When drop is *blended with* drop, both cannot be separated.
Let man, becoming *God's* servant, embrace His service,
And He becoming a friend will take care of His servant.

30

BH. Remove the difference between thyself and God, and
thou shalt be united *with Him ;*
Then shall thy fear be shattered, and thou shalt gain confidence.
Him whom I thought without me I *now* find within me ;
When I found this secret, I recognized the Lord of the world.

31

M. He who graspeth the First Principle[18] shall be happy at heart ;
He who is in this secret knoweth his own mind.
Let no one delay to attach his heart *to God* ;
He who obtaineth the True One shall be immersed *in delight.*

32

M. Man's business is with his heart ; he who chastenth is obtaineth perfection.

Kabir communeth with his heart, 'I have found nothing like thee, O my heart !'

33

This heart is power ; this mind is God[19] ;

This heart is the life of the five elements *of the body.*
If man restrain his heart and remain in a state of exaltation[20],
He can tell the secrets of the three worlds.

34

Y. If thou know anything, destroy thine evil propensities and conquer the citadel of the body ;

Thou who art surrounded *by foes* in battle and fleest no away, shalt be called a hero.

35

R. He knoweth the real pleasure, who spurneth the pleasure *of this world* ;

Having spurned the pleasures of the world he recognizeth the Real Pleasure ;

When he abandoneth the former, he obtaineth the latter
And when he quaffeth the latter, the former please him not.

36

L. O man, so apply thy heart to God,
That thou mayest not go elsewhere, but obtain the primal True One.
If thou heartily love Him,
Thou shalt obtain Him, and, obtaining Him, become absorbed in His feet.

37

W. Every moment remember God ;
Remember God and defeat shall not come to thee,
I am a sacrifice to those who sing the praises of the sons of God[21] ;
He who meeteth God shall obtain all truth.

38

W. Know God ; by knowing him thou shalt become *as* He. When the soul and God are blended, no one can distinguish them.

39

S. Carefully strive to know Him ;
Restrain every thought which allureth the heart.
When love for God springeth up, there is mental happiness,
And the Lord of the three worlds will fill thy heart.

40

KH. He who searcheth,

He who searcheth for God shall not return.
He who searcheth and knoweth God by meditation,
Shall cross over the terrible ocean without delay.

41

SH. She who dispelleth *all* doubts *of her spouse's affection for her.*
Shall adorn his bed.
She resigneth a little comfort and obtaineth the highest gratification.
Then is she *justly* styled a wife and he a husband.

42

H. *God* existeth, *but the spiritually ignorant* know not of His existence.

From the moment man *knoweth that God* existeth his heart is satisfied.

God certainly doth exist, if any one could see Him ;
But in that case God alone would exist, and man exist not at all.

43

Everybody goeth about saying, 'I will take this, and I will take that'.
They therefore feel great sorrow *when they are disappointed.*
He who fixeth his attention on God,
Shall obtain all happiness and his sorrows shall depart.

44

KSH. How many have pined away and perished !
But, despite such destruction, man will not even now think of *God.*

If any one *even* now know that the world is *fleeting* and restrain his heart,

He shall obtain an abiding place with Him from whom he is separated.

45

The *Pandits* have in another way joined the fifty-two letters,
But they cannot recognize one letter[22].
Kabir uttereth the word of the True One--
He is a pandit who abideth without fear--
To join letters[23] is the business of the Pandits ;
To meditate on God *is the business* of the holy man.
Saith Kabir, man will understand *which to do*
According to his intelligence.

Notes and References

1. *Shakti Shiv.* Literally--the energy of Shiv; but Shiv may also be a separate world, meaning bliss or happiness, and the next clause of the verse would then be translated--happiness was being kindled in my heart, and God naturally appeared to me.

2. Also translated--No one knows Him as He is.

3. Also translated--He whose expansion the three worlds are, is contained in the tiny seed of the banyan-tree.

4. Once a man has obtained divine knowledge he is not again subject to spiritual ignorance.

5. Has become attached to God.

6. God.

7. When man only thinks of God, and not of rewards in this or the next world.

8. Why lead the life of an anchoret in the forest.

9. My body.

10. Happy are they who are victorious over their evil passions.

11. The gyanis generally translate capitulate.

12. When the heart is subdued, the evil passions flee away.

13. Man's ambition is too great for the brief span of his life.

14. If God pleases, divine knowledge may be obtained without effort.

15. *Phank*, a natural division of fruit as seen, for instance, in the orange.

16. Shall remove all transmigration. It is believed that bodies are made for the soul, but, when the soul is absorbed in God, bodies will of course not be necessary for it.

17. Blend thy soul with God.

18. God.

19. Even Shiv and his consort are not superior to the human intellectual which decides on the worship of one God.

20. *Unman.* The gyanis generally translate this word--to turn away from the world and direct one's thoughts to God.

21. *Bishantana,* an equivalent of the Persian *ahl-i-khuda*--sons of God, saints.

22. They cannot recognize the Imperishable One (*Akshar*), a play on the Sanskrit word.

23. To write essays and theological disquisitions.

Kabir's calendar is arranged according to lunar days. The lunar month has thirty days. Fifteen of them are called *shudi,* the light half, and the other fifteen *wadi,* the dark half of the month. In this composition, however, sixteen days are counted.

KABIR'S LUNAR DAYS

1

There are fifteen lunar days and seven week days.
Saith Kabir, they have no limits[1].
The Strivers and Sidhs who know their secrets,
Are creators and gods themselves.

2

On the day when there is no moon remove worldly desires;
Remember God the Searcher of hearts,
So shalt thou *even* in life obtain the gate of salvation,
And the real word of the Fearless. One which is the essence of everything.
He who loveth God's lotus feet,
And is night and day watchful in His praises, becometh pure in heart by the favour of the saints.

1

On the first day of *the moon* meditate on the Beloved ;
He who cannot be lessened, and who hath no equal, sporteth in the heart.
He who is absorbed in the primal God,
Shall never suffer the pain of death.

2

On the second day know that there are two parts of the body,
Maya and God[2], who are contained in everything.
God doth not increase or diminish;
He is unknowable, spotless, and changeless.

3

On the third day let man apply his mind to God *in the three states of waking, dreaming, and sleeping*[3].
Thus shall he obtain the Root of Joy and the Supreme Delight.
In the company of the saints ariseth the faith in man
That *God's* light is ever within and without him.

4

On the fourth day restrain thy fickle mind;
Never associate with lust and anger.
God is all in all in sea and land;
He repeateth His own praises[4].

5

On the fifth day *know that* the world was extended from the five elements,
And that the pursuit of gold and women form its occupation.
Whoever quaffeth the nectar of *God's* love,
Shall not again feel the pains of old age and death.

6

On the sixth day the mind and the senses run in six directions;
The *mind* will not be restrained without the love *of God.*
Efface duality and hold fast endurance;
Endure not the torture of *absurd* religious ceremonies.

7

On the seventh day know that the Word is true,
And the Supreme Spirit will hold thee accepted;
So shall thy doubts and troubles be effaced,
And thou shalt obtain happiness in the celestial sea.

8

On the eighth day know that the body is made of eight ingredients.
In it is the Unknowable, the King of great treasures.
The guru who is versed in divine knowledge discloseth the secret.
How man may turn away *from the world,* and remain *absorbed in* the Infrangible and the Indivisible.[5]

9

On the ninth day keep watch over the nine gates,

And restrain thy flowing desires ;
Forget all covetousness and worldly love,
And thou shalt eat the immortal fruit and live through all ages.

10

On the tenth day joy prevaileth in the ten directions;[6]
Doubts are dispelled and God is found.
God is light, the essence *of all things,* incomparable,
Pure without a stain; *where He dwelleth* is neither shade nor sunshine.

11

On the eleventh day, if man run in one direction[7],
He shall not again suffer the pain of birth;
His heart shall become cool and pure,
And God, *whom men* say is distant, he shall find near.

12

On the twelfth day let twelve suns[8] arise for thee,
And day and night trumpets shall play spontaneous music.
Thou shalt behold the Father of the three worlds;
A miracle shall be wrought *for thee,* and from man this shalt become God.

13

On the thirteenth day they who repeat *the name of this* Inaccessible escape *transmigration;*
Know that God is equally diffused below and above.
God is neither low nor high, in Him is neither honour dishonour;
He is equally contained in all things.

14

On the fourteenth day *remember that God* filleth fourteen worlds,
And that He dwelleth in every hair of man's body.
Meditate on truth and patience,
And recite the legend of divine knowledge.

15

On the day of the full moon the moon is full in the heaven
And there is gentle light *diffused* from its beams[9].
God is firmly fixed in the beginning, the middle, and end *of all things.*
Kabir is absorbed in the ocean of happiness.

Notes and References

1. Literally--they have no hither and thither sides; a metaphor from the banks of a river. The meaning is that time has no limits.

2. Matter and spirit.

3. Also translated--Let man bring together the ira, pingla, and sukhmana.

4. Contained as He is in man.

5. Also translated--

   When a man meeteth a guru the latter discloseth to him the secret of divine knowledge,

   And man turneth away from the world and remaineth absorbed in the Infrangible and Indivisible.

6. A Hindi idiom for everywhere.

7. Towards God.

8. The Hindus believe that every month has a sun of its own. On the last day the twelve suns shall shine together and burn the world. The twelve suns of the text mean the bright lights of divine knowledge.

9. Also translated--divisions. The Hindus divide the moon sixteen sections. During the full moon the whole sixteen section seen. *Solah kala sampuran*--It is complete in its sixteen division. The same expression is applied to men of eminent virtue goodness.

KABIR'S WEEK DAYS

Sing God's praises all the days *of the week;*
On meeting the guru thou shalt obtain God's secret.

1

On Sunday begin *God's* service,
Restrain the desires in the temple of thy body.
Let man day and night keep *his attention* on the Infrange One,
And the lute shall tranquilly play spontaneous music.

2

On Monday nectar trickleth from the moon;[1]
When tasted, it is a speedy antidote to all poison;

He who drinketh it shall become intoxicated.
Let thy mouth remain closed *to idle converse*[2].

3

On Tuesday learn what thou really art;
Know how to guard against thine evil passions[3].
Leave not the God who is in thine own home[4] to wander *abroad;*
If thou do, He will be exceeding wroth.

4

So Wednesday let man enlighten his understanding,
So that God's dwelling may be in the lotus of his heart.
Let him, on meeting his guru, consider both his soul and God as the same,
And set erect the inverted lotus of his heart[5].

5

On Thursday let him throw his evil passions into the river,
And consider the three gods *of the Hindus* the same[6].
Why doth he not day and night wash away his sins
At the junction where the three rivers[7] meet?

6

On Friday by the practice of endurance man shall attain his object.
By struggling with himself daily,
And carefully restraining all his five senses,
He shall never fall into duality.

7

On Saturday if man keep strong within him
The wick of God's light which shineth in his heart,
He shall be illumined without and within,
And all his sins shall be erased.

8

Know that as long as man hath duality in his heart,
He shall not attain God's court.
Let him love the omnipresent God,
And then, saith Kabir, his heart shall be pure.

Notes and Reference

1. That is, from the guru.
2. Literally--let the door of thy speech be locked up.
3. Literally--know the way of the five thieves, that is, the way by which they approach.
4. Heart.
5. Inverted owing to its devotion to the world.
6. Being, as the great God's creatures, equally impotent for good or evil.
7. The ira, pingla, and sukhmana, i.e. by the practice of Jog.

ASA

The first three lines of the following were addressed by Kabir to his Guru Ramanand. The remain of the hymn contains Ramanand's replies as instruction.

1

Touching my guru's feet I bow and ask him why soul was made,

Why man was born and why he shall perish--tell explain to me.

O divine one, show mercy to me and put me in them of escaping from worldly entanglements and the fear *transmigration*.

The pain of transmigration resulteth from deeds do and happiness cometh when the soul is released from it.

Man bursteth not the entanglements of worldly love, *therefore* is not absorbed in God.

He knoweth nothing of the rank of nirvan, and so fears are not dispelled[1].

The soul is not born, though men think it is; it is free from birth and death[2].

When the idea of birth and death[3] departeth from man's mind, he shall for ever be absorbed in God.

As the reflection *of an object* in a vessel of water blendeth with the object when the vessel is broken;

So, saith Kabir, through virtue doubts flee away, and the soul is absorbed in God[4].

The following is a satire on the Brahmans of Banaras:--

2

They wear loin-cloths three and a half yards long and sacrificial threads of three strands;

They carry rosaries on their necks and glittering *brass* utensils in their hands;

They should not be called saints of God, *but* cheats of Banaras--

Such saints are not pleasing to me--

They gulp down trees with their branches;

They scrub their vessels, and put them on fires whose wood hath been washed[5];

They dig up the earth, make two fire-places,[6] and eat up men whole!

Those sinners ever wander in evil deeds, yet they call themselves Aparas.

Ever and ever they wander about in their pride and ruin all their families.

Man is attached to what *God* hath attached him, and his acts correspond.

Saith Kabir, he who meeteth the true guru shall not be born again.

Thanks giving to God the father.

3

The Father gave me *this* consolation--
He *made* me a comfortable bed and put ambrosia into my mouth.
Why should I forget that Father?
When I go to the next world I shall not lose my game.
My mother[7] is dead, and I am quite happy.
I do not put on a beggar's coat; I feel not the frost.
I am a sacrifice to that Father who begot me,
Who put an end to my companionship with the five *deadly sins*,
Who enabled me to subdue, and trample on them.
When I remember God, my soul and body are happy.
My Father is the great Lord of the earth.
To that Father how shall I go?
When I met the true guru, he showed me the way--
The Father of the world then became dear to my mind
I am Thy son, Thou art my Father;
We both live in the same place.
Saith Kabir, *God's* slave knoweth the one *God*;
By the guru's favour I know everything.

The central idea of the following is the worship of Maya. She is represented in a hideous and repulsive guise, her nose having been cut off for her infidelity. The first two lines of the hymn describe Tantric ceremonies.

4

Into one vessel they put a slaughtered cock, and another they fill with liquor.

Five Jogis sit round, and the noseless queen in the mids.

The bell of the noseless one resoundeth in both worlds.

But some discriminating person cut off thy *nose, O Maya*

The noseless one hath her dwelling everywhere; she killeth every one and looketh out for more.

'I am,' *saith she,* 'the sister and niece of all[8]; I am the handmaiden of him who weddeth me[9].

My husband is very wise and calleth himself a saint[10].

He standeth continually over me; no one else cometh near me'.

It was I, saith Kabir, who cut off her nose and her ears, and assaulted and expelled her,

Because, though dear to the three worlds, she was an enemy of the saints.

All must die at last; God's name is their only salvation.

5

Jogis, celibates, penitents, anchorets, they who wander on many pilgrimages,

They who pluck out and shave their hair, they who practise silence, and they who wear matted locks, must all die at last;

Wherefore worship God.

What can the Jamna do for those whose tongues love God's name[11]?

They who know the Shastars, the Veds, astrology, and various languages,

Who know written and spoken incantations, and all medical science, must die at last.

They who enjoy empires, umbrellas, thrones, many beautiful women,

Betel, camphor, and highly fragrant sandal, must die at last.

The Veds,Purans, and Simritis I have all searched, but there is no salvation anywhere *in them.*

Saith Kabir, so repeat God's name that transmigration may be at an end.

Kabir was asked whether the world was real unreal. The following hymn was his reply. Meaning is that the world is unreal like the possibilities mentioned.

6

Can an elephant be a rebeck-player, or an ox a drumn can a raven play the cymbals?

Can an ass put on a dancer's skirt and dance? a buffalo perform worship?

Can Raja Ram[12] cook cakes of ice?

Can any man in his sense seat them?

Can a lion seated in his denprepare betel? Can a moth rat serve it when made up?

Can a mouse sing a song of rejoicing from house to house. Can a tortoise blow a shell?

Can a barren woman's son go to wed, and build a man in the sky?

Can he marry a fair and beautiful virgin? Can they and the lion sing their eulogies?

Saith Kabir, hear, O saints, hath an ant eaten a retain?

Can the tortoise say, 'I want fire'? Can the gnaclaim God's word[13]?

The following was addressed to a Jogi who maintained the superiority of his sect and the advantage of its external accessories.

7

I have one wallet which containeth seventy-two chamber and one door[14].

In the whole world he *alone* is a Jogi.

Who craveth *for God* in the earth containing nine

That Jogi shall obtain the nine treasures

Who lifteth his soul from below to heaven,

Who maketh divine knowledge his patched coat, meditation his needle,

Who twisteth the thread of the Word and putteth it therein,

Who maketh the five elements his deer-skin *jacket,* and walketh in the way of his guru.

Who maketh mercy his fire-shovel, his body his fire-wood, and applieth to it the light of knowledge.

Who loveth God within his heart, and ever sitteth in the attitude of contemplation.

All the Jogi's craft consisteth in the name of God, to whom belong the body and soul.

Saith Kabir, if *God* be merciful, He will give man a true mark.

Trust to God alone and not to thy relations.

8

As long as the oil and the wick[15] are in the lamp, everything is visible;

When the oil is spent, and the wick goeth out, the chamber is dark.

O madman, *when thy lamp is out,* no one will keep thee even for a ghari.

Therefore repeat the name of God.

Who hath a mother? who hath a father? what man hath a wife?

When the vessel bursteth[16] no one asketh about thee;

it is all 'Take him out ! Take him out !'

Thy mother sitteth and weepeth on the threshold, thy brother taketh away thy bier.

Thy wife openeth the plaits of her hair and weepeth; the soul departeth alone.

Saith Kabir, hear, ye saints, regarding this terrible ocean.

The slave man suffereth torture, and the lord of death retireth not from him, O God.

The body under the allegory of a churn from which salvation is obtained through the Word.

9

Sanak and Sanand, *sons of Brahma,* never found *God's* limits.

Nor did Brahma himself *though* he spent his life reading the Veds.

Churn God's churn[17], my brethren.

Gently churn it that the butter may not be lost[18].

Make thy body the churn, thy heart the churning-staff;

Into the churn *put* the Word *instead of milk;*

Make hearty meditation on God thy churning.

Pour the guru's favour into it as thy cold water.

Saith Kabir, he on whom the King looketh with favour,

And who clingeth to His name, shall gain the shore.

When the deadly sins are subdued man arrives at a knowledge of the one God and obtains salvation.

10

When the wick *of pride* is dry and the oil *of worldly love* is spent;

When the drum *of boasting* is not heard, and the mind[19] is fast asleep,

When the fire *of avarice* is out, and the smoke of *desires* no longer issueth,

Then shall man know that one God is everywhere contained, and that there is no second.

When the strings are broken, the rebeck no longer playeth[20].
Man hath ruined his affairs by error--
When man obtaineth understanding he shall forget
Preaching, ranting, arguing, and intoning.
Saith Kabir, the highest dignity shall not be far from those
Who crush their deadly sins.

If Kabir commits sin the hopes that God will pardon him as a mother pardons her child, when he prays for forgiveness.

11

A mother beareth not in mind
All the faults her son committeth.
O God, I am Thy child;
Why destroyest Thou not my demerits[21]?
If a son in great anger rush at *his mother,*
Even then she breath it not in mind.
Since I have fallen into the prison of anxiety,
How shall I be saved without *God's* name?
O God, ever cleanse my mind and body,
And Kabir will tranquilly sing Thy praises.

12

My pilgrimage is to the bank of the Gomti,
Where dwelleth the yellow-robed priest[22].
Bravo ! bravo ! how sweetly he singeth
God's name delighteth my soul ;
Narad and Saraswati wait on him,
And near him sits lady Lakshmi as his handmaiden.
With my rosary on my neck and God on my tongue
I repeat His thousand names and salute Him.
Saith Kabir, I sing God's praises,

And instruct both Hindus and Musalmans.

Kabir deprecated the destruction of life in any form for idol worship.

13

Thou cuttest leaves, O flower-girl; in every leaf there is life.

The stone for which thou gatherest the leaves is lifeless.

Thou art in error, O flower-girl, in this;

The true Guru is a living God.

Brahma is in the leaves, Vishnu in the branches, and Shiv in the flowers.

Thou destroyest three gods in our presence; whom dost thou worship?

The *sculptor* carving the stone turned it into an idol; and, *in doing so,* put his foot upon its breast.

If it were a real God, it would have destroyed him.

Men cook rice, dal, lapasi, pancakes, kasar[23];

The Brahman feasters feast on these things, and put ashes into the idol's mouth.

The flower-girl is in error, and leadeth the world astray, but I go not astray.

Saith Kabir, God hath mercifully preserved me from error.

The stages of man.

14

Twelve years pass away in childhood; man performeth no penance even to the age of twenty;

Until thirty he worshippeth not God; he repenteth when old age cometh upon him.

His life hath passed in talking about his property;

His arms strong as the sea have dried up.

He with his own hands constructeth a fence for a tank that hath dried up and a hedge for a reaped field.

When the thief cometh, he quickly taketh what the foot hath preserved as his own.

When the feet, head, and hands begin to totter,

And water floweth copiously from the eyes;

When words come indistinctly from the tongue,

Dost thou then, sir, hope to perform religious *works?*

If God be merciful and thou love Him, thou shalt obtain His name as thy profit.

By the favour of the guru thou shalt obtain the wealth of God[24],

Which shall go with thee as thou departest.

Saith Kabir, hear, O ye good people, ye shall not take other wealth with you;

When the Supreme God's summons cometh, ye shall depart leaving your wealth and homes.

The inequality of life due to man's own acts and not to God's caprice.

15

To one man God hath given silks and satins and a niwar bed[25],

Others have not even a ragged coat or straw in their houses *to lie on.*

Indulge not in envy and bickering, O my soul,

Do good deeds and gain *their reward.*

Out of the same earth the potter mouldeth *vessels,* but painteth different designs on them;

Into one vessel is put strings of pearls, and into another *filth.*

God gave the miser wealth to keep, *but* the blockhead calleth it his own.

When Death's mace toucheth his head, it shall be decided in a moment *whose wealth it is.*

God's slave is the highest saints he obeyeth God's order and obtaineth happiness.

He accepteth as true what pleaseth God, and God's will he treasureth in his heart.

Saith Kabir, hear, O good people, *to call things one's* own is untrue;

Death, breaking the cage, taketh away the bird[26]; its wires and strings[27] are then relaxed.

The following is a remonstrance to a Qazi who desired that Kabir should perform the usual Muhammadan fasts and ceremonies :--

16

I am God's poor slave, royal state is pleasing to thee ;

The Supreme God, the Lord of religious, never ordained tyranny.

O Qazi, nothing is done by *mere* talk ;

It is not by fasting and repeating prayers and the creed that one goeth to heaven.

The inner veil of the temple of Makka is in man's heart, if *the truth* be known.

Just decisions should be thy prayers, knowledge of God, the inscrutable One, thy creed,

The subjugation of thine evil passions the spreading of the prayer-carpet ; then shouldest thou know what religion is.

Recognize thy Master and fear Him in thy heart ; despise and destroy thy mental pride[28].

As thou deemest thyself so deem others, then shalt thou become a partner is heaven.

Matter is one but hath assumed divers shapes ; in the midst of all recognize God.

Saith Kabir, thou hast abandoned heaven and attached thyself to hell.

The following was composed on the occasion of Kabir's visit to the house of a Jogi friend whom he found dead :--

17

Not a drop now trickleth from the citadel of thy brain-- where is the music that filled it ?

The great saint hath departed with *the name of* the supreme Brahm, the supreme God.

O father, whither hath departed the soul which dwelt with thy body,

Which revelled in divine knowledge, expounded, and preached?

Whither hath the player gone who played the drum of *thy body*[29]?

Thy tales, thy words, thy divine instruction, are no *longer* heard; all thy vital energy hath been drawn away.

Thine ears have become deaf, the vigour of thine organs hath declined;

Thy feet have failed, thy hands are relaxed, no word issueth from thy lips;

The five enemies,[30] robbers all, which wander according to their own will have grown weary;

The elephant,[31] thy mind, hath grown weary; the heart which beat by the force *of thy soul,* the wire-puller, hath grown weary;

Thou art dead; the ten *breaths* which kept thee together have escaped; thou hast left thy friends and relations.

Saith Kabir, he who meditateth on God bursteth his bonds even while alive.

Mammon under the guise of a serpent.

18

Nothing is potent against the serpent

Which deceived Brahma, Vishnu, and Shiv.

The serpent having completely subdued *the world* hath entered pure water[32].

By the guru's favour I have seen her *coming* who hath stung the three worlds, *and guarded myself against her.*

O my brethren, why call out 'Serpent, serpent'?

He who knoweth the True One hath destroyed the serpent;

No one else is free *from her attack*[33].

When the serpent is vanquished what can Death do *to man*?

This serpent is God's creature;

She is weak, what can she do?

As long, however, as she abideth *with man, his soul* shall abide in bodies[34].

By the favour of the guru Kabir hath easily escaped from her.

'Throw not pearls before swine'.

19

What *availeth it* to read the Simritis to a dog?

What to sing God's praises to an infidel?

Continue to repeat God's name;

Speak not to the infidel even by mistake.

What availeth it to give a raven *valuable* camphor to eat[35]?

What to give milk to a viper[36]?

Discrimination and understanding are obtained in the company of the saints.

By the touch of the philosopher's stone iron becometh gold.

The dog of an infidel acteth in everything as he is caused to act;

His acts are in accordance with his original destiny.

Wert thou to take nectar and water the nim-tree with it,

Saith Kabir, its natural *bitter* qualities would not depart.

Worldly greatness secures not salvation.

20

There is no trace of Rawan or his line,

Though Ceylon was his fortress and the ocean its moat.

What shall I pray for? nothing remaineth stable;

While I look on, the world passeth away.

Though Rawan had a lakh of sons and a lakh and a quarter of grandsons,

Yet at last he had neither lamp nor wick in his house.

The sun and moon used to heat his kitchen[37], the fire to wash his clothes[38].

He who through the guru's instruction putteth God's name *in his heart,*

Shall remain permanent and be released from transmigration[39].

Saith Kabir, hear, O ye people[40],

Without the name of God there is no salvation.

A mystical hymn with its interpretation.

21

Hear these wonderful things, my brethren--
First a son[41] *was born,* and afterwards his mother[42];
The guru[43] worshipped his disciple's[44];
I have seen a lion[45] herding kine[46];
A fish[47] out of water give birth upon a tree[48];
I have seen a cat[49] taking away a dog[50];
The branches *of a tree*[51] below, its roots[52] above;
And its trunk bearing fruit[53] and blossom[54];
A buffalo[55] on horseback going to graze a horse[56];
An ox[57] on his way *while* his burden[58] arrived at home *before him.*
Saith Kabir, he who understandeth this hymn,
Shall know everything on repeating God's *name.*

The soul's toil to obtain a human body shall all be lost if God be not remembered.

22

God maketh the body from seed and placeth it in the pit of fire;

For ten months He keepeth it in the mother's womb; worldly love attacheth to it on emerging.

O mortal, why attaching thyself to covetousness losest thou the jewel of thy life?

In former births thou didst not sow the seed in this world:

From childhood thou hast grown to old age; what was to be hath been.

When Death cometh and catcheth thee by the top-lock[59], why then weep?

Thou hopest for *longer* life, while he waiteth for thy *last* breath--

The world is a game, O Kabir, carefully throw the dice[60].

Kabir was invited to a marriage feast. He said his own marriage was being celebrated, and he could not go elsewhere. The following is a description of it.

23

I turned my body into a dyer's vat and then dyed my heart therein[61]; the five virtues[62] I made my marriage guests;

With God I made my marriage circumambulations[63], my soul being dyed with His *love.*

Sing, sing, ye brideswomen, the marriage song:

The sovereign God hath come to my house as my husband.

I made the bridal pavilion[64] in the lotus of my heart, and divine knowledge the recitation[65] *of my lineage;*

I obtained God as my bridegroom ; so great hath been my good fortune.

Demigods, men, saints, and the thirty-three karors of gods in their chariots came as spectators.

Saith Kabir, the one God, the divine Male, hath wed and taken me with Him.

In the following again Kabir represents himself as a wedded woman :--

24

I am plagued by my mother-in-law[66], beloved by my father-in-law[67]; I dread the *very* name of my husband's eldest brother[68].

O my friends and companions, my husband's sister[69] hath seized me, and I burn by separation from my husband's youngest brother[70].

My mind hath become insane since I have forgotten God; how can I abide?

I behold not with mine eyes Him who enjoyeth me on the couch; to whom shall I tell my sorrow?

My step-father quarrelleth *with me;* my mother is ever intoxicated[71];

As long as I remained with my elder brother[72] I was dear to my Spouse.

Saith Kabir, I have lost my life struggling with the five evil passions--

Deceitful Maya hath led captive the whole world, *but* I have obtained immunity by repeating God's name.

Mammon a thieving courtesan.

25

Wordly life is like a dream,

But, believing the world to be real, I attached myself to it, and abandoned the Supreme Treasure.

O father, I made love to the *courtesan* mammon,

And she stole from me the jewel of divine knowledge.

With its eyes open the moth becometh entangled; the insect regardeth not the flame;

So, stupid *man* attached to gold and women heedeth not Death's noose.

Reflect, abandon sin; and God will save thee.

Saith Kabir, such is the Life of the world ; He hath no equal.

Kabir has found God and put an end to his transmigration.

26

Though I have assumed many shapes, this is my last[73].

The strings and wires of the musical instrument are all worn out; I am now in the power of God's name;

I shall not have again to dance *to the tune of birth and death ;*

Nor shall my heart accompany on the drum[74].

I have taken and destroyed my bodily lust and anger; the pitcher of avarice hath burst;

Lust's raiment hath grown old, and all my doubts are dispelled.

I recognize one God in all creatures; vain wranglings *on this subject* are at an end.

Saith Kabir, when God was gracious unto me, I obtained Him, the Perfect One.

The following was addressed to a Qazi :--

27

Thou fastest to appease God, yet thou destroyest life to please thy palate[75].

Thou regardest not others as thou dost thyself; why pratest thou?

O Qazi, thy one God is in thee, but thou beholdest Him not by thought and reflection.

Mad on religion, thou heedest not, wherefore thy life is of no account.

Thy books tell thee that God is true, and that He is neither male nor female;

Thou gainest nothing by thy reading and study, O mad-man since thou regardest Him not at heart;

God is concealed in every heart; reflect on this in thy mind.

Kabir loudly proclaimeth--there is the same God for the Hindu as for the Muhammadan.

God becomes not propitious by the mere wearing of religious garbs.

28

I decorated myself to meet my *Spouse,*

But God the Life and Lord of the world met me not.

God is my husband, I am his wife;

He is big; I am little.

The wife and her husband dwell together, but to cohabit is difficult.

Blessed the woman who is pleasing to her husband;

Saith Kabir, she shall not be born again.

God under the allegory of a diamond.

29

When the soul meeteth God[76], the *once* fickle mind is easily absorbed in Him.

This diamond God filleth everything with light; I have found this by the instruction of the true guru--

The praise of God were an endless story--

When a man becometh perfect he recognizeth the Diamond.

Saith Kabir, I have seen such a Diamond as filleth the world with its light;

The concealed Diamond became manifest; when I met the guru he showed it to me.

In the following allegory Kabir refers to his early understanding as his first wife and to his conversion as his second wife :--

30

My first wife was ugly, of low caste, and bad character, evil both in her father's house and mine.

My present wife is handsome, sensible, of good character; I naturally took her to my heart.

It turned out well that my first wife departed;

May she whom I have now taken live for ever !

Saith Kabir, when the young wife came I ceased to cohabit with the old one ;

The young wife is with me now, the elder hath taken another husband.

Kabir's mother addresses him in the first four lines of the following hymn. Kabir was married to Dhania. The holy men who frequented the house called her Ramjania, or worshipper of God. But the name is also applied to courtesans dedicated to idols, and it was consequently offensive to Kabir's mother. She also complains that Kabir had devoted himself to religion and neglected his business:--

31

My daughter-in-law was called Dhania;
They have *now* given her the name of Ramjania.
These shaven fellows have ruined my family;
They have set my son uttering the name of God.
Saith Kabir, hear, O my mother,
These shaven men have done away with my caste[77].

The following is a lecture against the veiling of women. It was addressed to the second wife of Kamal, Kabir's son:--

32

Stay, stay, my daughter-in-law, veil not thy face;
At the last moment it will not avail thee the eighth of a paisa.
She who preceded thee used to veil her face;
Follow not thou in her footsteps.
The only advantage of veiling thy face is
That for five or ten days *people will say* a good daughter-in-law hath come.
Thy veil will *only* be real.
If thou sing God's praises and skip and dance *in His service.*
Saith Kabir, O daughter-in-law, thou shalt be victorious[78]
When thou passest thy life in singing God's praises.

Kabir's wife Loi refused to prepare a meal for a holy visitor, upon which Kabir manifested his displeasure. The following hymn except the last two lines is Loi's pleading for forgiveness:

33

Better would it be *to be cut in twain* with the saw than that thou shouldst turn thy back on me.

Hear my entreaty and embrace me;

I am a sacrifice unto thee; turn thy face towards me, my beloved.

Why killest thou me by turning thy back on me?

Even though thou cut my body I will not turn it away *from thee*[79];

My body may perish, but I will not cease to love thee.

There hath been no quarrel between thee and me;

Thou art the same good husband and I the same wife *as before*.

Saith Kabir, hear, O Loi,

I shall believe in thee no longer.

The following was Kabir's reply to a Brahman who had advised him to bathe in the sacred rivers of the Hindus.

34

He who is foul within will not go to heaven by bathing at a place of pilgrimage:

Nothing is gained by pleasing men[80]; God is not a simpleton.

Worship the Lord, the only God;

Serving the guru is the true ablution.

If salvation be obtained by bathing in water, the frogs which are continually bathing *will obtain it*;

But as the frogs so the pilgrims; they shall be born again and again.

If a hardened sinner die in Banaras, he cannot escape hell.

If a saint of God die in Haramba[81], he saveth a whole multitude.

Where there is neither day nor night, Veds nor Shastars, there dwelleth the Formless One.

Saith Kabir, meditate on Him, ye foolish denizens of the world.

Notes and References

1. Also translated--He is not without fear and hath erred.
2. This line is also translated--The guru's words make no impression on him, he thinketh his own ideas best, he hath no love for God and no hate for Maya.
3. Literally--the rising and the setting of the sun. This phrase is also translated--when the feeling of joy and sorrow is dispelled.

4. Kabir means that the soul is the reflection of God, and blends with Him when the vessel of the body is broken.
5. So that impurities in the wood may not remain.
6. One for their bread and another for their lentils. Some strict Hindus suppose that a fireplace once used is unclean.
7. Maya or worldly love.
8. Every one treats me well and cherishes me.
9. I serve him who controls me.
10. It is only the saint who can control her.
11. The river *Jamna* is a place of pilgrimage. It is supposed that death cannot molest those who bathe in it.
12. An eminent confectioner of Kabir's time.
13. Some begin with 'The son of a barren woman went to make the animals mentioned the marriage procession, put whole is narrative form.
14. The seventy-two chambers of the body and the brain.
15. The oil and wick mean life and breath.
16. When thou diest.
17. Meditate upon divine knowledge.
18. Rapid churning is believed to spoil butter.
19. *Nat,* literally--the acrobat.
20. When desires are at an end, man obtains deliverance.
21. Why dost Thou not pardon my sins?
22. This apparently is not the river which flows by Lakhnau (Luck now).
23. *Lapasi and kasar* are both made from clarified butter, flour, and sugar, but the former is made liquid by the addition of water. Thus are both Oriental puddings.
24. God's name.
25. A niwar bed is one whose bottom is of broad cotton tape instead of the grass rope used by the poorer classes.
26. That is, the soul.
27. Also translated--The cups for the bird's food and water, that is, man leaves his possessions including his food and drink behind him.
28. Also translated--Despise thy lust and pride.
29. Where is now the life of thy body?

30. The five evil passions.
31. The mind is likened to an elephant for it heedlessly pursues pleasures as the male elephant the female.
32. Has found access even to the holy.
33. Also translated--There is no other creature so vile as she.
34. He shall suffer transmigration.
35. He will still rejoice in filth.
36. It will only become the more venomous after nourishment.
37. That is, to cook his food.
38. So potent was he over the heavenly bodies and the elements, that he subjugated them to his private purposes.
39. Literally--and go nowhere.
40. Loi. This word means people, but it was also the name of Kabir's wife.
41. Purity.
42. Maya
43. Soul.
44. Heart or mind.
45. Conscience.
46. The organs of action and perception.
47. Understanding.
48. To the company of the saints.
49. Contentment.
50. Greed.
51. Worldly desires.
52. Meditation on God.
53. Salvation.
54. Worship.
55. Endurance.
56. Fickleness.
57. Laziness.
58. Good works.
59. A lock of hair left unshaven on the top of a Hindu's head.
60. Also translated--Make recollection of God thy throw of the dice.

61. Kabir represents himself as a bride and God the bridegroom. It is usual on occasions of marriage for people to have their clothes dyed.
62. The word *panchon* is also translated the elect.
63. The Hindu bridegroom and bride circumambulate fire, in some places seven times and in other places four times, on the occasion of a marriage.
64. Four posts are erected to denote the mind, understanding, thought and pride. The posts support a cloth covering, beneath which the very youthful Indian brides and bridegrooms are married.
65. Uchar now called *gotrachar*, a panegyric on the families of the bride and bridegroom intoned by the ministering Brahmans. The word is also translated--the repetition of the Vedic sloks for marriage.
66. Maya.
67. God.
68. The god of death.
69. Evil thought.
70. Discrimination.
71. Step-father here means the body, and the mother is selfishness. *Bap sawaka* is also translated--my former heart, that is, when I was unregenerate.
72. God's love.Some understand contentment; others, divine knowledge.
73. I have had many births, but I shall not be born again.
74. At a nach, or Oriental dance, the performers are the musicians, the female singers and dancers, and the drummers.
75. On the first day after the lent of Ramzan, the Muhammadans offer a sacrifice to God. Here Kabir hints that the sacrifice is made to please their palaces, not to please God.
76. Literally--when a diamond pierceth a diamond. There are several interpretations of this line.
77. That is, I am no longer known as a weaver, but a worshipper of God.
78. Thou shalt obtain salvation.
79. Also translated--I will not wince.
80. That is, by deferring to custom.
81. Previously called Magahar.

GUJARI

The following was addressed to a Brahman who Kabir supposed would be turned into an ox for his idleness and gluttony. The Hindus believe that they who live on others' wealth without any exertion on their own parts will become oxen, in which condition they will have to labour and suffer for their idleness in human lives.

1

With four legs, two horns, and a dumb mouth, how wilt thou sing *God's* praises ?

Standing or lying down the stick will fall on thee; then where wilt thou hide thy head ?

Without God thou shalt become somebody[1] else's bullock'

Thy nose shall be torn, thy shoulders maimed, and thou shalt eat worthless straw;

All day shalt thou wander in the forest, but even then thy belly shall not be satisfied.

Thou didst not listen to the advice of holy men, and thou shalt suffer for thine omissions.

Overwhelmed with great supersition thou shalt endure hardship, and wander in many births.

Thou has lost thy precious life by forgetting God; when wilt thou *again* have such an opportunity ?

Thou shalt turn and revolve like an oilmen's bullock[2] *round his press,* and restless shalt thou pass the night.

Saith Kabir, for not having repeated God's name thou shalt smite thy head and repent.

Kabir's mother was distressed at his conduct in relinquishing his trade and adopting a religious life. The following is a conversation between the mother and son on the subject.

2

Kabir's mother sobbeth and weepth—
O God, how shall these children live ?3
Kabir hath given up all his weaving,
And hath inscribed God's name on his body.
Kabir replieth—
While the thread was passing through the bobbon

I forgot my Beloved God.4
My understanding is mean, my caste is that of weaver;
I have gained the name of God as my profit.
Saith Kabir, hear, O my mother,
The one God will provide for us and them.

Notes and References

1. Thou shalt be lent to somebody who will treat thee badly, and not as he would treat his own.
2. Also translated—Like a monkey after red seeds.
3. How shall Kabir's children be maintained ?
4. Kabir means that even that was too long a time for him to abstain from repeating God's name, and so he gave up weaving.

SORATH

All are lost without devotion.

1

The Hindus kill themselves worshipping idols, the Musalmans make prostrations;

The former are burned, the latter buried; but neither sect knoweth anything of Thee, *O God.*

O my soul, the world is stark blind;

On all sides Death's noose is thrown, *but men see it not.*

Poets kill themselves reciting verses; the Kaparis kill themselves going to Kedarnath;

Jogis kill themselves wearing matted hair; but they know nothing of Thee, *O God.*

Kings kill themselves amassing wealth and burying masses of gold;

Pandits kill themselves reading the Veds, and women in gazing on their beauty--

Without the name of God all these are lost; think and ponder upon this, O man.

Without the name of God who hath obtained salvation? Kabir giveth his admonition.

The body is frail, yet it attaches itself to worldly things which desert it.

2

When the body is burnt, it becometh ashes; when it is not burnt, a host of worms eat it up.

A soft clay vessel *will break* when water is put into it--such is the nature of the body.

Why, O brother, goest thou about puffing and blowing thyself out?

How hast thou forgotten the ten months thou didst remain inverted in the womb?

As the bee collecteth honey with great zest, so the fool collecteth wealth.

When a man is dead, they say 'Take him away ! take him away !

'Why allow a ghost to remain'?

His wedded wife accompanieth him to the door, and after that his male friends.

All the *other* members of his family go as far as the cremation-ground; the soul departeth alone.

Saith Kabir, hear, O mortals, they who have entangled themselves with the deceitful world,

Are seized by Death, and *fall into* the pit like the parrot deceived by the trap.

None may escape physical death; but it brings salvation to the holy.

3

Man hearing all the instructions of the Veds and the Purans, desireth to perform religious ceremonies *to over-come death.*

Death hath seized all people, *even* the wise; the pandits *too* depart without hope.

O man, thou hast not succeeded in thy sole object[1]

Since thou hast not worshipped the supreme God.

Men have gone to the forests, practised jog, performed austerities, and lived on the tubers and roots they picked up.

The Nadis[2] the readers of the Veds, the Ekshabdis, and the Monis[3] are all enrolled in Death's register.

Loving service[4] entereth not into *man's* heart; he pampereth his body and giveth it *to Death;*

He hypocritically *singeth* hymns, but what can he obtain from God?

Death hath fallen on the whole world; in his *register* the sceptical theologian is recorded.

Saith Kabir, they who know *God's* love and devotion to God are pure[5].

The holy are completely saturated with God.

4

With both mine eyes I look.
But I behold nothing save God;
Mine eyes gaze affectionately *on Him;*
There is now no other subject mentioned.
My doubts have departed, my fear hath fled
Since I applied my mind to God's name:
When the Actor beateth the drum,
Everybody cometh to *see* the show[6]
When the Actor collecteth the stage properties[7],
He abideth alone in His happiness.
Doubts are not dispelled by the use of words;
Everybody continueth to talk.
God filleth the heart of him.
To whom through the guru's instruction He hath revealed Himself.
When the guru bestoweth even a little kindness,
Bodies and minds are all absorbed in God.
Saith Kabir, I am dyed with the dye *of God,*
And have found the munificent Life of the world.

Man under the allegory of a milkmaid is won by the guru from neglect of God.

5

The words of the sacred texts are *as* seas of milk;
For that ocean let the guru be the churning-staff.
Be thou the churner of that milk;
Why shouldst thou be despoiled of thy butter?
O damsel, why makest thou not God thy husband?
He is the life of the world and the support of the soul.
The strait collar[8] is on thy neck and chains on thy feet
God hath sent thee wandering from birth to birth.
Thou heedest not even yet, O damsel;
Thou art the wretched victim of Death.
It is God who acteth and causeth men to act;

What power hath the poor handmaiden?
The damsel whom God awaketh
Attendeth to the duties He assigneth her.
O damsel, where hast thou obtained that wisdom
By which thou hast erased the line of doubt?
Kabir feeleth great delight,
And by his guru's favour his mind is happy.

In reply to an inquiry Kabir describes the happiness he obtained from humility and devotion.

6

When He without whom one cannot live
Is found, man's toil is productive.
Men call it a good thing to live for ever.
But there is no life without death[9].
Where divine knowledge is discussed what more remaineth to be said[10]
As we look on, the things *of this world* pass away;
As men rub and mix saffron and sandal, *so man's soul is blended with God.*
And thus seeth the world without *bodily* eyes[11].
Abandonment of the world as a father hath begotten *divine knowledge* as a son.
Though placed in an unsubstantial city[12].
I a beggar have found the Giver.
He hath given me so *much* that I cannot eat it;
I cannot leave off eating[13] or finish it;
And I have ceased to go to strangers.
The elect who know life to be death,
Have obtained a mountain of happiness.
Kabir hath obtained that wealth,
And effaced his pride on meeting God.

The lamp of holiness, not the Veds and Purans, lights up man's heart.

7

What availeth reading, what studying,
What hearing the Veds and Purans?
What avail reading and listening

If divine knowledge be not obtained?
The repeatest not the name of God, O ignorant man;
Every moment of what thinkest thou?
A lamp[14] is required in this darkness
To find the One Incomprehensible Thing[15].
The lamp hath lit up my heart,
And I have found the Incomprehensible Thing.
Saith Kabir, I now recognize Him;
And when I recognize Him my mind is happy.
People do not believe that my mind is happy;
But even if they do not, of what consequence is it?

The following was addressed to a hypocritical Brahman who advised Kabir to bathe at Hindu places of pilgrimage.

8

In thy heart is deception, in thy mouth religion;
False man, why churnest thou water?
What advantage is it to bathe the body
If there be filth in the heart?
If the gourd be washed at the sixty-eight places of pilgrimage.
Even then its bitterness will not depart.
Thus Saith Kabir deliberately--
Causes me to cross over the terrible ocean, O God.

Men should not practise deceit for the advantage of relations.

9

With great deceit man acquireth other men's wealth,
And taketh it and lavisheth it on his son and wife.
O my man, practise not deception even by mistake;
At the last moment it is thine own soul that shall have to render an account.
Every moment the body wasteth away and old age warneth thee;
Then no one will pour water into thy hands,
Saith Kabir, thou shalt have no *friend* then;
Why not repeat God's name in thy heart betimes?

The guru has shown man how to protect himself from ferocious animals, to which the evil passions are compared.

10

O saints, my wandering mind hath obtained rest.
I reckon that I have obtained my deserts.
The guru hath shown me the passage
Through which wild animals surreptitiously enter.
I have closed the gates thereof,
And spontaneous music playeth for me.
The pitcher of my heart was filled with the water of *sin;*
When I upturned it, the water was spilled [16].
Saith Kabir, the man of *God* knoweth this
And knowing it, his mind is happy.

Kabir once felt hungry and rebelled against God.

11

A hungry man cannot perform service;
Take back this rosary of Thine.
I *only* ask for the dust of the saints' feet,
Since I owe not any man[17].
O God, how shall I fare if I am shamed before Thee?
If Thou give me not *of Thine own accord,* I will beg for it.
I beg for two sers of flour,
A quarter of a ser of clarified butter and salt;
I beg for half a ser of dal
Which will feed me twice a day.
I beg for a bed with four legs to it,
A pillow and a mattress;
I beg for a quilt over me,
And then thy slave will cheerfully serve Thee.
I have never been covetous;
Thy name alone becometh me[18].
Saith Kabir, my soul is happy;
And when my soul is happy, then I recognize God.

Notes and Reference

1. To save thyself in this human birth.
2. Jogis who go about playing a small pipe.
3. Men vowed to perpetual silence.

4. Service such as that performed by Narad, the famous rikhi.
5. The Persian word *khulas,* freed or delivered, was here originally written, but the tenth Guru altered its spelling to the Arabic *khalis,* pure.
6. When God creates the world, men appear.
7. When God draws the world within Himself.
8. Connected by a chain with the feet and hindering the recumb posture.
9. Without effacing oneself.
10. Also translated—*If man effect himself not,* what use discussing divine knowledge ?
11. Also translated—Men grind and mix saffron and sandal and *waste them by applying them to idols;*
    The world appeareth to have no eyes.
12. The body.
13. So dear is God's name to me.
14. Divine knowledge.
15. God.
16. This metaphor has often occurred. The hearts of mean generally are said to be inverted. The holy have theirs effect.
17. I am not under an obligation to any one.
18. That is, I only ask for these things that I may be able to repeat Thy name.

The Gods of the Hindus are ignorant of the Creator.

DHANASARI

1

Beings like Brahma's *four* sons, Shiv,
And Sheshnag know not Thy secret.
Through association with the saints God dwelleth in the heart.
Beings like Hanuman and Garuda,
Indar and Brahma, know not, O God, Thine attributes.
The four Veds, the Simritis, and the Purans,

Vishnu, and Lakshmi know them not.
Saith Kabir, he who toucheth God's feet and seeketh His shelter,
Shall not wander *in transmigration.*

Life gradually draws to a close; man should practise devotion betimes.

2

Pahars are made up of gharis, days of pahars; life draweth to a close; the body pineth away;

Death wandereth about like a poacher *in quest* of game ; say what shall man do *to escape*?

The *last* day approacheth;

Mother, father, brother, son, wife--say whose are they[1]?

As long as the light of *life* remaineth in man's body, the brute knoweth not himself.

He is anxious to obtain a long life, but he seeth not *Death who is at hand*[2].

Saith Kabir, hear, O mortal dismiss thy mental doubts.

Repeat only the one Name, O mortal, and seek the asylum of the one *God.*

Salvation depends on the state of man's heart not on the place of his death.

3

What is strange to him who knoweth something of the love and service of God?

As water when blended with water separateth not again, so the weaver[3] hath blended with God.

O men of God, I am out of my senses--

If Kabir leave his body at Banaras, what obligation is he under to God[4]?

Saith Kabir, hear, O people, let no one make a mistake;

What *difference is there between* Banaras and the barren Magahar, if God be in the heart?

Kabir requires nothing but God's name.

4

It is through insufficient devotion men go
To the heavens of Indra and Shiv are born again.

What shall I pray for? nothing is stable.
Keep God's name in thy heart;
Fame, power, wealth, and greatness
Help no one at the last moment.
Say who hath derived any happiness
From son, wife, or wealth.
Saith Kabir, nothing else availeth me;
The name of God is *sufficient* wealth for my heart.

Remember and love God.

5

Remember God, remember God, remember God, my brethren !
Without remembering God's name the majority of men shall be lost.
Wife, son, body, house, and wealth confer happiness;
But none of these shall be thine when the time of death arriveth.
Ajamal, the elephant, and the courtesan committed sinful acts;
Yet they were saved by repeating God's name.
My brethren, you have wandered in the wombs of pigs and dogs, and yet you are not ashamed.
Why forsake the ambrosia of God's name and eat poison?
Abandon doubt regarding acts which are prescribed as well as those which are forbidden, and take God's name.
The slave Kabir saith, by the favour of the guru love God.

Notes and References

1. Literally--does any one belong to any one?
2. Also translated--He is anxious to live longer though his eyes see not.
3. *Julaho.* There is a pun on this word. It means a weaver, and elsewhere it is applied to the soul.
4. Because all people who die at Banaras must be saved, according to Hindu belief.

SUHI

Kabir calls on a worldly man to render an account of his life.

1

Having been born what hast thou done?

Thou hast never repeated God's name.
Thou wilt not repeat His name; of what thinkest thou?
What *preparation* art thou making for death, O luckless one?
Though through woe and weal thou hast brought up thy family,
At the time of death thou shalt bear thy troubles alone.
When Death seizeth thee by the neck, thou shalt utter loud cries.
Saith Kabir, why did I not remember of *God* before?

The condition of one who fears God.

2

My woman's *heart* palpitateth and trembleth;
I know not how my Spouse will treat me.
The night hath passed away ; let not the days also pass.
The *black* flies have gone; the *white* cranes have now taken their place[2].
As water will not remain in a frail vessel[3].
So the soul departeth when the body hath faded.
I adorn myself like a young virgin,
But how can I enjoy dalliance without my Spouse?
My arm is pained from driving away the crows.
Saith Kabir, this tale is at an end[4].

A dialogue between the soul and the messengers of Death. He who feels God's love needs have no apprehension.

3

Thy stewardship being ended, thou must give thine account,
When the cruel messengers of Death come to take thee.
They will ask thee what thou hast earned, and where thou hast squandered it;
They will say to thee, 'Come quickly, thou art summoned to court;
'The warrant of God's court hath come for thee'.
Thou shalt implore them, *and say, ' I have to collect* some outstandings in the village,
'And I shall adjust my accounts to-night;
'I will also pay you something for your expenses[5],
'At dawn we shall pray at an inn *on the road*[6]'
Blest, blest is he and fortunate is his lot,
Who feeleth God's love by association with the saints.

That man shall ever be happy in this world and the next;

He hath won the priceless *prize* of human birth.

He who while awake *to the world* is asleep *to God*[7] hath lost that birth;

The property and wealth he hath accumulated shall become another's.

Saith Kabir, that man hath gone astray,

Who forgetting the Bridegroom hath mixed himself up with *things of* clay.

When avarice only departs with life and there is no thought of God, human birth is in vain.

4

The eyes grow weary of seeing, the ears grow weary of hearing, *this* fair body groweth weary.

When old age urgeth thee, all thy senses grow weary; *the desire for* wealth alone wearieth not.

O foolish man, thou hast not obtained divine knowledge and meditation;

Thou hast lost thy *human* birth in vain.

O mortal, serve God as long as there is breath in thy body;

Even though thy body perish, let not thy love for Him perish; dwell thou at His feet.

He in whose heart God hath implanted His Word hath ceased to thirst.

Let the comprehension of God's will be thy game of chaupar, and the conquest of thy heart the throwing of the dice.

They who know and worship God shall not perish.

Saith Kabir, they who know how to throw such dice shall never lose their game.

Kabir has triumphed over his evil passions, his senses, and death itself.

5

There are five kings of one fortress; the whole five ask for revenue[8]--

I have not tilled land belonging to any of them; it would be hard on me to pay *a tax* for nothing.

O God's people, the village accountant[9] continually worried me,

But I raised my arms aloft, complained to my guru, and he saved me.

Nine surveyors[10] and ten judges[11] go on *tour*, and will not allow the agriculturists[12] to live;

They measure not with a full tape, and they take many bribes.

The one Being who is contained in the seventy-two chambers of the body hath written off my account;

I have searched Dharmraj's office, *and find* I owe him not an atom.

Let no one revile the saints ; the saints and God are one.

Saith Kabir, I have obtained that Guru whose name is Bibeko[13].

Notes and References

1. That is, my youth has passed, let not my old age also pass in vain.
2. My dark hair has changed to grey.
3. A vessel made of clay not hardened by fire.
4. That is, life is at an end.
5. As a bribe to the messengers of Death to allow the soul time to answer the warrant.
6. That is, give me time to-day, and we shall be well on our journey early tomorrow morning.
7. Also translated--He who after being awakened falleth asleep.
8. *Hala* from *hal*, a plough--so much revenue levied on every plough. The five evil passions claim their shares.
9. Here meant for death.
10. The nine gates of the body.
11. The organs of action and perception.
12. Virtues or good qualities.
13. *Bibeko*, God who makes one (*ek*) out of two (*bib*), who joins the soul of man with Himself.

Death triumphs over all except God's sincere worshippers.

BILAWAL

1

The world is like a show; none may remain here;

Proceed the straight way, otherwise thou shalt be severely buffeted.

Children, the old and the young, O my brethren, shall all be taken away by Death.

God hath made poor man like a mouse; Death like a cat eateth him up;

He payeth no regard to rich or poor;

He destroyeth kings equally with their subjects--so mighty is Death!

They who please God *become* His worshippers, and theirs is a special case;

They neither come nor go[1] they never die; God is with them.

Know in your hearts that by forsaking son, wife, wealth, and property *which are perishable,*

Saith Kabir, you shall meet the Lord; hear this, O ye saints.

Kabir is frenzied with devotion.

2

I am not skilled in book knowledge, nor do I understand controversy;

I have grown mad reciting and hearing God's praises.

O father, I am mad; the whole world is sane; I am mad;

I am ruined; let not others be ruined *likewise;*

I have not grown mad of mine own will; God hath made me mad--

The true guru hath dispelled my doubts--

I am ruined, and have lost my intellect;

Let nobody be led astray in doubts like mine.

He who knoweth not himself is mad;

When one knoweth himself he knoweth the one God.

He who is not intoxicated *with divine love* in this human birth shall never be so.

Saith Kabir, I am dyed with the dye of God[2].

Kabir's self-abasement.

3

Though man leave his home for the forest region and gather tubers to live on,

His sinful and evil mind even then abandoneth not misdeeds.

How shall I be saved? how cross over the great terrible ocean?

Preserve me, preserve me, O God; I Thy slave *have come to* Thine asylum.

The desire to gratify my evil passions forsaketh me not;

Though I make many efforts to guard myself against them, I am entangled in them again and again.

My life hath passed--youth and old age--no good have I done;

This priceless human life attached itself to a kauri and became like it.

Saith Kabir, O my God, Thou art contained in everything;

There is none so merciful as Thou, none so sinful as I.

The superiority of God's saint.

5

There is no king equal to God;

All the kings of this world are only for four days, they make false display[3].

Why should the slave of Him who overshadoweth the three worlds waver[4].

Who can lay hands on him when one cannot even speak with due respect before him?

O thoughtless and foolish mind of mine, think *upon God,* and the unbeaten music of ecstasy shall play for thee.

Saith Kabir, all my doubts and uncertainties are at an end; *God* hath favoured me as He did Dhru and Prahlad.

Kabir depreciates himself.

6

Preserve me, O God, though I have offended Thee.

I have not practised humility, the duties of my religion, repetition of Thy name, or worship; I am proud, I *wear* my turban on the side of my head.

Believing this body immortal I have pampered the frail and perishable vessel;

I have forgotten Him who made and favoured me, and I have attached myself to strangers.

I am Thy house-breaker and not Thy saint; I fall at Thy feet for protection--

Saith Kabir, hear this supplication; send me not intelligence of death[5].

An appeal to God.

7

O God, I stand wearied at Thy court;

Who but Thee careth for me? open Thy door and show Thyself unto me.

Thou art my wealth, O Master; Thou art generous;

Thou art lavish ; I hear with mine ears Thy great praise.

Of whom shall I beg? I see every one poor ; from Thee alone I obtain salvation.

Thou didst confer endless favour on Jaidev, Namdev, and the Brahman Sudama.

Saith Kabir, Thou art all powerful, Thou art generous, Thou bestowest the four blessings without delay.

The following was addressed to a Jogi :--

8

Thou dependest on a club, earnings, and patched coat;

In error thou wanderest in a *Jogi's* garb.

Put away thy devotional attitudes and thy suspension of breath;

Abandon deception, and ever worship God, O fool.

The *wealth* thou beggest for, the three worlds have enjoyed[6].

Saith Kabir, God is the *only* Jogi in the world[7].

Kabir mourns his lukewarmness and condemns all worldly things.

9

O Sovereign of the world, Lord of the earth, mammon hath caused me to forget Thy feet.

Even a little affection for Thee is not felt by Thy slave; what shall Thy poor slave do?

Curse on *this* body, curse on *this* wealth, curse on *these* worldly things, a double curse on this perishable intellect and understanding !

O man, firmly restrain this worldly love ; if thou subjugate it, thou shalt be saved[8].

What availeth agriclture? what commerce? false is worldly pride.

Saith Kabir, *they who practise such things* are ultimately ruined, and death cometh to them at last.

The soul's dependence is on God, not on the perishable body.

10

The body is a lake in which a peerless lotus[9] bloometh ;

The Supreme Being who hath neither outline nor form, the Primal Light, *is within it.*

O my soul, worship *that* God, abandon doubt ; God is the life of the world.

The *soul* is not seen either coming or going, as *is the body.*

Where the *body* is born, there it perisheth[10] like the leaves of the water lily.

They who knowing the world to be transitory abandon it, are happy in the contemplation of God.

Saith Kabir, worship God in thy heart.

During life Kabir was absorbed in God as the sound of a bronze vessel is absorbed in it when broken.

11

Since my attention is fixed on God, I no longer suspect that I shall suffer transmigration[11];

Even in life I am absorbed in the Infinite; the guru's instruction hath awakened me.

The sound which is produced from bronze blendeth again with it;

When the bronze is broken, O Pandit, where will the sound be?

At the union of the three breaths[12] *in the brain* I have seen Him who is awake in every heart,

And now such understanding hath entered my heart that I have abandoned *the world.*

When I knew myself, my light was blended with *God's* light--

Saith Kabir, I now know *God* and my mind is satisfied.

The holy man will not waver but be everywhere happy.

12

O God, why should that man waver in whose heart abide Thy lotus feet ?

Believe that all happiness and the nine treasures are his who tranquilly repeateth God's praises.

When God openeth the hard knot[13], man shall be wise enough to behold Him in everything.

He who ever avoideth worldly love and weigheth his heart in the scale of *meditation,*

Shall be happy wherever he goeth, O Lord, and worldly love shall not sway him.

Saith Kabir, my heart is happy since it hath been absorbed in God's love.

Notes and References

1. They do not suffer transmigration.
2. I am imbued with God's love.
3. Also translated--They make a false claim to greatness.
4. That is, allow his mind to wander from God.
5. Holy men are not led off in triumph by Death; they become insensibly blended with God.
6. That is, it is the leavings of the three worlds.
7. Also translated--He who is united with God is the real Jogi.
8. Also translated--Thou shalt be released from thine entanglements.
9. The heart.
10. That is, the body is resolved into the elements whence it sprang.
11. Literally--my doubts regarding birth and death have departed.
12. Of the left and right nostrils and their junction. *Trikuli sandhi* also includes *gyata,* the knower ; *gyan,* the means of knowledge; and *geya,* the subject of knowledge. Devout men endeavour to unite all three.
13. The distance between God and the soul.

An inquirer asked Kabir with whom one should converse. The following was his reply:—

GAUND

1

When thou meetest a saint, have some conversation with him;
When thou meetest a man who is not a saint, remain silent.
Kabir was asked again--
O father, if I speak what shall I speak about?
For instance, 'Continue to repeat God's name'.
They who talk to saints confer advantage on others;
They who talk to fools talk in vain.
By incessant talking *with them* sin increaseth;
If I speak not to them, what harm can the wretches do me[1]?

Saith Kabir, an empty vessel soundeth;
When it is full it never giveth forth a sound.

Man's dead body is much more worthless than that of a beast, and consequently an object of contempt.

2

When a man dieth he is of no use;
When a beast dieth he is of ten uses.
What do I know regarding my fate;
What do I know, O sir?
Man's bones burn like a heap of fire-wood;
His hair burneth like a bundle of grass.
Saith Kabir, man only awaketh
When the club of Death toucheth his head.

God is everywhere, even in the acts which attach to the soul.

3

God abideth in the heaven above, in the earth beneath, and in every direction.

The Supreme Being is ever the root of joy; the body may perish, but God shall not.

I am anxious to *know*.

Whence the soul cometh and whither it goeth.

Five elements combined form the body; out of what were the elements formed?

Thou sayest that the soul is bound by its acts; who gave life to the acts?

The body is contained in God, God in the body; He is uninterruptedly in all things.

Saith Kabir, I will not abandon God's name, come what may.

The soul described by negatives.

4

Somebody asked Kabir :--
What is that whose limit hath never been found,
Which dwelleth within the temple of the body?
Kabir replied--It is neither man nor demigod;
It is not a Jati or a *worshipper* of Shiv;

It is not a Jogi or an Audhut;
It hath no mother, nor is it any one's son ;
It is not a householder or an anchoret ;
It is not a king or a beggar ;
It hath neither a body nor a drop of blood ;
It is not a Brahman or a Khatri ;
It is not an ascetic or a shaikh ;
It is not born, nor is it observed to die ;
Whoever weepeth for its death
Shall lose his honour[2]
By the favour of the guru, I have found the steep way ;
Birth and death have both been erased for me.
Saith Kabir, this *soul* is a part of God.
As ink cannot be erased from paper[3]

Kabir's wife thus addressed him on the neglect of his trade and his attentions to saints.

5

Thy threads are broken, thy size is at an end,
Thy reeds shine over the door,
Thy poor brush hath gone to pieces--
May death light on this shaven fellow's head !
This shaven fellow hath lost all his property.
I am persecuted by those *fakirs* coming and going[4].
Kabir now never speaketh of his beam or his shuttle;
His mind is only concerned with the name of God.
His daughter and sons have nothing to eat;
Men with shaven heads are crammed night and day;
One or two are in the house and one or two on the way.
We have only a pallet *on the ground* ; they get a bed to *sleep on*.
They rub their heads *with satisfaction* and *carry* books in their waist-bands ;
We get parched pulse, they bread *to eat*.
The shaven-heads and my shaven-headed *husband* have become all one.
Kabir replieth--These shaven-heads are the support of the drowning.
Hear, O blind misguided Loi,
Kabir hath taken the protection of these shaven-heads.

When man dies, mammon, who is described, weeps not for him.

6

When the husband dieth, his wife weepeth not[5].
She findeth another protector;
And when that protector also dieth,
Hell awaiteth him *though* he have enjoyed pleasures here.
One woman[6] alone is dear to the world ;
She is the wife of all sentient beings.
With a necklace on her neck she looketh beautiful;
She pleaseth the world, but is *hateful* as poison to the holy.
Adorning herself she either sitteth like an abandoned woman.
Or the wretch wandereth about accursed of the saints.
When the saints flee from her, she pursueth them;
But, by the favour of the guru, she feareth punishment.
She is the body and soul of the infidel;
Her dreadful witch's eye falleth on me.
When the merciful holy guru met me,
I became well acquainted with her secrets[7].
Saith Kabir, I have now turned her out,
And she hath attached herself to the skirt of the world.

A further description of mammon.

7

The guest cometh and departeth hungry
From the house which hath no wealth.
The guest loseth patience,
And the host is blamed because he hath not means *to entertain him*.
Hail to the woman who hath turned the heads
Of very holy men and penitents high and low !
She is a miser's daughter ;
Rejecting God's worshippers she sleepeth with everybody,
At last standing at the saints' door,
She saith, 'I have sought your protection, save me !'
The woman is very beautiful ;
Her ornaments tinkle on her feet ;
As long as man is alive she attacheth herself to him ;
When he dieth she quickly departeth without waiting for her shoes.

The woman hath conquered the three worlds;
She hath made the eighteen Purans and the places of pilgrimage love her ;
She hath pierced *the hearts* of Brahma, Vishnu, and Shiv,
And infatuated great kings and sovereigns.
There are no bounds to the woman ;
She is in collusion with the five evil passions.
Where the vessels of the five evil passions burst,
Saith Kabir, I was delivered thence by the favour of the guru.

Without a guru man must fall and perish.

8

If the rafters be taken from a house, the roof will fall ;
So without *God's* name how can man be saved ?
As water will not remain without a vessel,
So without a religious guide man shall go to hell.
Burn him who thinketh not on God,
But whose mind is ever absorbed in the field of his body.
As without a ploughman land cannot be tilled,
As without a thread jewels cannot be strung,
And as without a loop clothes cannot be fastened,
So without a holy guide man shall go to hell.
As a child cannot be born without a father and mother.
As clothes cannot be washed without water,
As one cannot ride without an equipage,
As without music there cannot be dancing,
So without a guru *man cannot reach God's* court.
As the bad woman leaving her husband looketh for another, *thus eager should man be to* obtain a *guru.*
Saith Kabir, do one thing--
Become holy and thou shalt not die again.

The following hymn was a reply to some one who had addressed vile abuse to Kabir and called him a pander, a dancer, a street-walker, and a thief :--

9

Is he a pander[8] who chasteneth his heart ?
He who chasteneth his heart shall escape from death.

The pander who thoroughly chasteneth his heart, and applieth to it the touch-stone *of love,*

Shall obtain complete deliverance.

Whom do you call a pander, O people?

In everything that is spoken discrimination *should be used.*

Is he a dancer who danceth with his mind,

Who is not satisfied with falsehood, who is pleased with truth,

And who beateth time *wtih* his heart in the presence *of God* ?

God, whose mind is pure, preserveth such a dancer[9] /

Is he a street-walker who sweepeth the market-place[10],

And lighteth up the five wicks[11] ?

I accept as my guru that street-walker

Who embraceth the service of the lord of the nine continents[12].

Is he a thief who is not envious,

Who uttereth God's name and curbeth his senses ?

Saith Kabir, blessings on my divine guru,

Who possesseth all such qualities and who is very handsome and clever.

The following is an encomium on the staff of life :--

10

Hail, O God, hail, O divine guru !

Hail to the corn by which the hearts of the hungry rejoice !

Hail to that saint who realizeth this !

He shall meet God.

Corn cometh from the Primal Being--

Repeat God's name with the relish of corn.

Praise His name, praise His corn;

With water pleasant is its taste.

He who abstaineth from corn[13].

Shall lose his *honour* in the three worlds[14].

She[15]who abandoneth corn and practiseth hypocrisy,

Is neither a wife nor a widow[16].

They who publicly boast that they live on milk,

Secretly eat a whole five sers of corn.

Without corn no one is happy ;

Abandon corn and you shall not meet God.

Saith Kabir, such is what I think ;

Blessings on that corn by which man loveth *his* God !

Notes and References

1. Also translated--If I talk not to *saints*, how can I practise discrimination.
2. Shall only excite contempt.
3. Also translated--His praise cannot be erased from paper ; that is, His praise is continually written and shall be permanent.
4. This and the two proceeding lines are also translated--

   Death hath lighted on these shaven fellow's heads.

   They have caused us to lose all our property.

   There is no end to their coming or going.
5. When man dieth, his wealth does not weep for him.
6. Maya, wealth. She never becomes a widow, hence the title *suhagan*.
7. And was thus the better able to guard against her.
8. *Kutan* as a noun is a pander and as a verb to beat or chasten. There is a play on the word in the original. It was applied to Kabir, because when his daughter was visiting him, he allowed a strange man shelter in his house.
9. Also translated--God steadieth the mind of such a dancer.
10. That is, cleanses his heart.
11. Illumines his five senses. This is also translated--Who admonisheth his five evil passions.
12. Also translated--Who knoweth the nine forms of devotion to God.
13. As some ascetics do.
14. Because he practises hypocrisy.
15. The feminine gender, as usual, for man in general.
16. Is neither a worldly person nor an anchoret.

The following was addressed to a Jogi who endeavoured to induce Kabir to drink wine.

RAMKALI

1

Make thy body the vat, the guru's instruction thy molasses;

Cut up avarice, lust, wrath, pride, and envy as thy kikar bark ; thus mix thy yeast.

Is there any saint, in whose heart composure and happiness dwell, to whom I may offer my devotion and penance as commission *for procuring me such wine* ?

I will give my soul and body for one drop of the wine which that vat produceth.

I have made the fourteen worlds my furnace, and heated it with the fire of divine knowledge[1];

I have sealed the still with the gentle sound of *God's name*, and plastered it with what yieldeth mental happiness.

Pilgrimage, fasting, daily religious ceremonies, purifications, and austerities at *eclipses* of the sun and moon I would pledge *for that wine.*

Make meditation thy cup, God's ambrosial name the pure juice, and drink that elixir ;

From such a still a very pure trickling stream ever issueth, and the soul is delighted therewith.

Saith Kabir, all other wines are insipid ; this is the true elixir.

On the same subject.

2

Make divine knowledge thy molasses, meditation thy bassia flowers, and the fear of God in thy heart thy furnace;

The drinker who is absorbed in God by means of the breath of the sukhmana imbibeth *such wine.*

O Jogi, my mind is intoxicated--

When that wine ascendeth to the brain man relisheth no other[2]; there is then light in the three worlds.

Joining God and the soul I have prepared a furnace and drunk the excellent elixir ;

I have burnt lust and wrath as firewood, and escape from worldliness.

The light of divine knowledge appeared to me when I met my true guru and obtained understanding.

The slave Kabir is intoxicated with that wine, and will never abstain therefrom[3].

Kabir was likened to a Kotwal for his severity to the wicked, and to a dog for his barking. He accepted both imputations.

3

I honour the saints and I punish the wicked ; this is my court-house[4].

I shampoo Thy feet, *O God,* day and night ; I turn my hair into a chauri and wave it over, Thee.

I am the dog at Thy court ;

I bark in front of it[5] putting forward my snout.

In a former birth I was Thy servant ; *that position* I cannot now resign.

The gentle order of Thy court was branded on my forehead[6].

They who bear such brand fight bravely in battle; they who bear it not flee away.

He who is holy knoweth how to serve God, and God putteth him into His treasury[7].

In the house *of the body* is the chamber *of the heart, which becometh* the most precious chamber of all *when filled* with meditation *on God.*

The guru hath granted *God's name,* the Real Thing, to Kabir, *saying,* 'Take it and guard it';

Kabir hath offered it to the world, but only he who was so destined receiveth it--

Abiding is the married state of her who hath found the immortal elixir.

The Brahman trusts not to God but to the Veds and the Gayatri, and hence he shall be lost.

4

Why shouldst thou, O Brahman, forget Him from whose mouth the Veds and the Gayatri issued?

Why shouldst not thou, O Pandit, utter the name of God, whose feet every one toucheth?

O my Brahman, why not repeat God's name ?

If thou utter not His name, O Pandit, thou shalt be cast into hell.

Thou *callest* thyself exalted, yet thou eatest in the houses of the low, and fillest thy belly by the exaction of alms[8].

On the fourteenth and fifteenth days of the half month thou devisest tales and beggest, but even with a lamp in thy hand thou shalt fall into the pit.

Thou art a Brahman, I am a weaver of Banaras ; how can I be a match for thee ?

By repeating the name of God I have been saved, while thou, O Pandit, shalt be lost by trusting to the Veds.

A mystic hymn in which God is represented under the allegory of a tree.

5

There is one tree[9] it hath endless branches and shoots; its blossoms[10] and leaves[11] are filled with nectar[12].

This *world* is a garden[13] of ambrosia ; God who is perfect hath created it.

The few holy men in whose hearts the light of God shineth,

Know the story of my beloved sovereign God.

One bumble-bee[14] intoxicated with the juice of the flowers hath fixed his mind within the twelve petals of the lotus of the heart ;

He then raising his breath to the lotus of sixteen petals in his brain gaineth the ecstatic fruit thereof[15].

Another tree[16] was produced in the silent vacuum; it dried up the waters of the earth[17].

Saith Kabir, I am a servant of those who have seen that tree[18].

The following was addressed to a Jogi :--

6

Make silence thine earings, mercy thy wallet, and meditation thy cup;

Stitch thy body for thy patched coat, and make the Name thy support.

O Jogi, practise such Jog

That thou mayest while enjoying *the world* perform thy devotion, penance, and austerities under the guru's instruction.

Make the knowledge *of God* the ashes thou smearest on thy body[19], and meditation thy horn;

Abandoning the world, roam in the city of the body, and play thy heart as a kinguri;

Plant the five virtues in thy heart so that thy contemplation may be undisturbed by the world.

Saith Kabir, hear, O saints, make honesty and mercy your garden.

Kabir in a fit of introspection and self-abasement addressed himself.

7

For what object wast thou born in the world, and what advantage hast thou gained from thy *human* birth ?

Thou hast not applied thy mind even for a moment to God, the Fulfiller of desires, the Vessel to take thee across the terrible ocean.

O God, such sinners are we,

That we have never performed service for that Lord who gave us our souls and bodies.

The passion to possess others' wealth, children, and wives, and to slander and caluminate others hath not forsaken us.

We suffer transmigration again and again ; this law is not broken.

I have not wandered even for a moment to where the conversation of the saints of God is held.

Libertines, thieves, panders, and drunkards--with them have I ever consorted.

My possessions are lust, wrath, covetousness, pride, and envy.

Mercy, honesty, and service to the guru *have* not *come to me even* in my dreams.

O God, compassionate to the poor, merciful, dear to the saints, Remover of fear,

Prayeth Kabir, preserve Thine afflicted slave, O God, and I will perform Thy service.

Remember God and do Him homage.

8

Remember in thy heart the Being,
By whose remembrance thou shalt obtain the gate of deliverance,
Go to heaven, and *return not to this* world.
Play the trumpets in the house of the Fearless One,
And the unbeaten strain shall ever fully resound for thee.
Without remembering Him deliverance can never be obtained.
Heartily bow before the Being,
By remembering whom none may refuse thee;
Who conferreth salvation by which great loads *of sin* drop off,
And thy transmigration is at an end.
Remember Him through whom thou enjoyest thyself.
And an everburning[20] lamp shall be placed within thee--
The lamp[21] which rendereth the world immortal,
And expelleth the poison of lust and wrath.
Twine and wear on thy neck the rosary
Of Him by remembering whom Thy salvation shall be obtained.
Wear that rosary, doff it not,
And by the favour of the guru thou shalt be saved.
Remember the Beloved day and night,
And thou shalt have no regard for men;
Thou shalt sleep at home in silken bed-clothes.

And thy heart shall be gladdened by a pleasant couch.
Ever remember God in thy heart and sing *His praises.*
By remembering Him thy troubles shall depart,
And Maya affect thee not.
From the true guru learn how to remember God;
Remember Him every day and night.
Standing or sitting, at every expiration and inspiration,
Waking or sleeping, enjoy the sweets of remembering *Him;*
By remembering God thou shalt be united with Him[22].
Make the remembrance of God's name thy support;
By remembering Him no weight of sin shall oppress thee.
Neither wrought nor spoken incantations can prevail with Him[23];
Saith Kabir, who hath no limit.

The condition of him who has put his passions under subjection.

9

He who hath captivated the captivators[24],
Shall obtain deliverance, and the guru shall put out the fire of his passions[25].
When I had thoroughly examined my heart,
I made my ablutions within it.
To dwell in God, the Lord of life, is the best thing;
There is then no death, or birth, or decay.
Turning away from mammon I restrained my mind,
And I entered the region of God[26].
I have pierced the serpent's way[27].
And assuredly met God.
Worldly love and mammon no more affect me;
The sun hath restrained the moon[28].
When I completely stopped my breath,
The lute played spontaneously.
The preacher hath communicated this instruction ;
The hearer hath heard and treasured it in his heart.
He who acteth according to it shall be saved,
Saith Kabir verily.

God is a luminous diamond whose light fills creation.

10

The moon and sun are both forms of light;
God the unequalled pervadeth their light.
O wise man meditate on God
In whose light creation is contained.
Beholding God, the Diamond, I prostrate myself before Him.
Saith Kabir, He is bright and *yet* invisible.

Some Hindus asked Kabir to give them instruction, upon which he composed the following :--

11

O world, be alert and wakeful ; even while awake you are being robbed, my brethren.

Even while the Veds, who are alert sentinels, look on, Death will take you away.

The fool, the blockhead, and the pagan think that the nim is a mango, and the mango a nim[29].

That a ripe plantain-tree[30] is but a prickly bush, and that the fruit of the coco-nut[31] is like the ripe fruit of the simmal.

God is the sugar which hath been spilled in the dust; it cannot be picked up by the elephant.

Saith Kabir, renounce family, caste, and lineage, become an ant, and thou canst pick up and eat *the sugar.*

Notes and References

1. I have taken the light of divine knowledge to guide me.
2. Also translated--Those who are intoxicated with *celestial* wine never taste *earthly* wine.
3. Also translated--that wine whose intoxication shall never subside.
4. The Kotwal in modern times is a police-officer, but in the time of Kabir the Kotwal was a magistrate and police-officer combined.
5. That is, I pray to Thee.
6. That is, I was branded as Thy slave in a former birth.
7. Because he is a genuine and not a counterfeit coin.
8. Literally--by obstinate acts, by threatening suicide, & C.
9. God.
10. Saints.

11. The rest of sentient beings.
12. God's name.
13. In which the branches and shoots have been planted.
14. The searcher for God.
15. There is supposed to be a lotus with twelve petals in the heart. Kabir means that his mind as a bumble-bee has entered that lotus. There is also supposed to be another lotus in the brain which has sixteen petals, and to this again his mind ascends.

    Others suppose that the numbers twelve and sixteen in the above lines mean the repetition of *Oam* similar number of times.
16. This tree is divine knowledge which has its seat in the brain.
17. It removed man's earthly desires.
18. In this hymn tree is also said to mean the universe, the branches and shoots are the planets and stars, the flowers are the saints, the leaves the rest of sentient beings.
19. Jogis smear ashes on their naked bodies as clothing or protection against the elements.
20. Literally--a lamp not fed with oil.
21. Divine knowledge.
22. Also translated--Thou shalt obtain good fortune.
23. God is only moved by our remembering Him and repeating His name with devotion.
24. He who has put his passions under subjection.
25. These two lines are also translated--

    They who are attached to worldly things fall into the net of Death,

    While they whose avarice the guru extinguisheth are delivered.
26. *Gagan*--literally, the firmament--is a word applied by Jogis to the brain or tenth gate of the body where God dwells.
27. A supposed passage for air through the spinal marrow to the brain.
28. The brain retains the breath, and a state of exaltation supervenes.
29. They think good evil and evil good. The fruit of the nim is bitter, or the mango sweet.
30. God's name.
31. Association with saints.

A remonstrance to a Brahman for offering animal sacrifice to an idol.

MARU

1

O Pandit, what folly meditatest thou ?

Thou shalt be ruined with all thy family for not having repeated God's *name,* O luckless man.

What availeth thee to read the Veds and the Purans?

It is like loading a donkey with sandal *whose perfume he valueth not.*

Thou knowest not how *to repeat God's* name ; how shalt thou be saved?

Thou takest life and deemest it religious ; tell me, my brother, what thou callest irreligious.

Thou makest thyself out an excellent muni ; whom callest thou a butcher ?

Mentally blind thou knowest not thyself[1];

What shalt thou cause others to know?

Thou sellest knowledge for money, thy life passeth in vain.

Narad and Vyas declare--and thou mayest go and ask Sukdev also--

Saith Kabir, *too,* by uttering the name of God ye shall be delivered; otherwise ye shall perish, my brethren.

It is the condition of the heart, not man's garb or place of residence, which produces happiness.

2

Unless you remove evil from your hearts, how shall you find *God* by dwelling in the forest ?

They who deem their own homes equal to the forest are perfect *among* men.

You shall obtain true happiness.

If you lovingly repeat *the name of* the Life *of the world.*

What avail *wearing* matted hair, smearing yourselves with ashes, and dwelling in caves ?

He who hath conquered his own heart hath conquered the world, because he is free from the deadly sins.

All people use eye-wash, but there is a difference in their blandishments.

The eyes to which the surma of divine knowledge is applied, are acceptable *to God.*

Saith Kabir, I now know *God* ; the guru hath explained divine knowledge *to me* ;

I have met God who dwelleth in the heart ; my mind shall now on more wander.

The following was addressed to a Jogi whom Kabir found begging and boasting that he had obtained all spiritual wealth and perfection :--

3

What hath he who hath obtained spiritual wealth and supernatural power to do with any one?

What shall I say regarding thy language ? I am much ashamed to speak to thee.

He who hath obtained God.

Wandereth not from door to door.

This false world greatly burneth *for wealth* in the hope of using it for a few days.

Whosoever drinketh God's water shall not be thirsty again ;

He who knoweth *God* by the favour of the guru abandoneth all worldly desires.

When the heart is withdrawn *from the world,* the True One appeareth everywhere.

The name of God saveth him who hath tasted its savour.

Saith Kabir, I have become gold, my doubts have fled, and I have crossed the ocean.

It was made a reproach to Kabir that he being a weaver dared preach to men of high caste. Upon this he preached equality of all men.

4

As the bubbles of the river are accounted water and blend with the water of the ocean,

So the man who looketh on all with an equal eye, shall become pure and blend with the Infinite.

Why should I return *to this world* ?

Transmigration taketh place by God's order ; he who obeyeth it shall blend with Him.

When this fabric of five elements perisheth, my wandering shall be at an end.

Forswearing sects, I look on all as equal and meditate on the one Name.

I devote myself to and perform the duties which God assigned me.

If God bestow mercy on me, I shall be absorbed in Him under the instruction of my guru.

He who in life is in death, and who from death[2] returneth to life shall not be born again.

Saith Kabir, he who is permeated with the Name fixeth his love on God.

Kabir in a vision beheld God and rushed to embrace Him, but was repulsed. The following was composed on the occasion:--

5

If Thou repulse me, then show me *the way* of deliverance ;

One God in many forms, Thou art contained in everything ; why dost Thou now illude me ?

O God, whither dost Thou take me for salvation ?

I ask Thee where Thou wilt give me salvation and of what degree[3] *seeing that* by Thy favour I have already obtained it ?

I called Thee my *future* saviour until I knew the reality[4];

I have now become pure in heart, saith Kabir, and my mind is happy.

Kabir is said to have uttered the following to a man whom he found committing an act of immorality.

6

Rawan had to leave the golden fortress and strongholds which he had made--

O man, why actest thou as it pleaseth thyself ?

When Death cometh and catcheth thee by th hair, *only* God's name will save thee.

Death and life are the work of God ; this deceitful world is only an entanglement ;

Saith Kabir, they who have the elixir of God in their hearts shall ultimately be saved.

The body likened to a village, the soul to its headman, and the senses to its agriculturists.

7

The body is a village ; the soul placed therein is its headman ; five husbandmen dwell in it--

The senses--eyes, nose, ear, tongue, and touch--which obey not my orders.

O father, I shall no longer dwell in this village ;

The accountants called Chitr and Gupt ask for an account of every moment of mine,

So when Dharmraj calleth for my account, there will be a heavy balance against me.

The five husbandmen will then have all fled, and the bailiffs will arrest the soul.

Saith Kabir, hear, O holy men, settle your accounts on the field[5] ;

Pardon for this once thy slave, so that he may not *have* to return to this terrible ocean.

A Bairagi who had come from Dwaraka told Kabir he had seen God there, and he asked him to go there too, and he would also see God. Upon this the following colloquy occurred.

8

O Bairagi, no one hath seen the Fearless One ;

Can the Fearless One be obtained without fearing Him Certainly not[6].

O Bairagi, if *man* were to see the Lord present, he would feel fear ;

He who obeyeth God's order is without fear-- 'Certainly'

O Bairagi, though all people are imbued with hypocrisy.

Practise it not thou before God--'Certainly not'.

O Bairagi, *men* set not covetousness aside ;

Egoism hath destroyed the body-- 'Certainly'.

O Bairagi, the fire of care hath burnt the body,

But thou *shalt escape from it* if thou deaden thy feelings 'Certainly'.

Without a true guru there can be no contempt of world, O Bairagi,

Even through everybody desire it--'Certainly'.

O Bairagi, if it be God's will, thou shalt meet the true guru,

And shalt easily obtain God--'Certainly'.

Saith Kabir, O Bairagi, *address* one prayer *to God,*

To take thee over the terrible ocean--'Certainly'.

Krishan was one day going to visit Duryodhan, but he heard that Duryodhan was then holding court. Krishan, in order to avoid the regal ceremonial and entertainments connected therewith, remained the night with Vidur. Next day when Krishan and Duryodhan met, the latter upbraided him in a friendly manner for not having gone straight to him. The following is Krishan's reply :--

9

O king, who would go to thee ?

I have seen such affection on Vidur's *part* that the poor man pleaseth me.

Beholding thine elephants, thou hast been lost in error and hast not recognized God.

I consider Vidur's water as nectar in comparison with thy milk.

I got vegetables *without condiment,* but to me they were equal to *khir,* and the night passed in Vidur's singing *God's* praises.

Kabir's God is joyous and happy, and payeth no attention to anybody's caste.

Shloks

The following two sloks in the Rag Maru are attributed to Kabir. The battle referred to is perhaps intended to represent man's struggle with his evil passions. These are the only lines in the Granth Sahib relating to war.

When the drums sound aloud, the conspicuous *warriors* fall wounded[7];

The brave have entered the battle-field ; now is the time for combat.

Recognize him as a hero who fighteth for the love of his religion ;

He may die cut in pieces, but will never desert the battle-field.

The following was a sharp remonstrance addressed to some men of high rank.

10

You have forgotten your religion, O madmen ; you have forgotten your religion.

You fill your bellies, you sleep like beasts, you have lost your human births ;

You have never associated with saints, but have adopted false occupations ;

You wander like dogs, pigs, and ravens ;
You deem yourselves great and others small[8] ;
I have seen you going to hell in thought, word, and deed
The lustful, the wrathful, the deceitful, the dissemblers[9], and the idlers,
Pass their time in doing evil and never remember God.
Saith Kabir, fools, blockheads, and pagans reflect not ;
They know not God's name ; how shall they be saved ?

Men should remember God and not be led astray by worldly pleasures.

11

Remember God *or* thou shalt repent it ;

O sinful soul, thou practisest avarice, but thou shalt depart to-day or to-morrow.

Though thine attachment to avarice and being led astray by mammon, thou hast wasted thy life.

Be not proud of thy wealth and youth; they dissolve like paper.

When Death cometh and seizeth thee by the hair and knocketh thee down, on that day shalt thou be powerless.

Thou hast not remembered God, or worshipped Him, or shown mercy to His creatures, therefore shalt thou be smitten on the mouth.

When Dharmraj asketh for thine account, what face shalt thou show him ?

Saith Kabir, hear, ye good men, ye shall be saved in the company of the holy.

Notes and References

1. That is, God who is in thee.
2. Being dead toward God.
3. There are four degrees of salvation—*saloh,*heaven, *samip,* being near God; *sarup,* assuming God's form; *sayuj,* being absorbed in God.
4. That Thou hadst already saved me.
5. That is, while alive. The metaphor is derived from the pra which prevailed before British rule of taking payments in Creditors' and debtors' accounts were settled on the harvest field.

6. *Wana hanbai*. In the Malwa dialect *hanbai* means yes.
7. Also translated—(a) Aim is taken, and wounds are inflicted; (b) When the guru's drum soundeth, the disciple, at whom it is aimed, is wounded.
8. Literally—you deem yourselves vowels and others consonants.
9. Literally—actors.

The condition of him who has obtained salvation during life.

KEDARA

1

They who abandon praise as well as blame, who reject honour as well as dishonour.

Who consider iron and gold the same, are the image of God--

Few, *O Lord*, are Thy servants !

They who abandon lust, wrath, covetousness, and worldly love behold God's feet.

What are called the qualities of impulse, ignorance, and goodness are all contained in Thy Maya.

Only they who understand the fourth degree, have obtained the supreme position ;

They never entertain love for pilgrimages, fasting, or for the religious ceremonies, purifications, and austerities of *the superstitious*.

By meditating on God, avarice, worldly love, and doubt depart ;

The darkness of the mansion in which the lamp *of divine knowledge* burneth is dispelled ;

Its owner abideth completely fearless, and his doubts have fled ; saith Kabir, I am his slave[1].

The saint deals in holiness and is thus emancipated during life.

2

Some deal in bronze and copper, others in cloves and betel-nut ;

The saints deal in God's name ; that is my merchandise.

O dealers in the name of God,

The priceless diamond hath come to hand, and worldly thoughts have fled.

They whom the True One attached to truth, remain attached to it ; truth is their occupation.

They dispatched a load of the true thing, and it reached *God* the storekeeper.

God is Himself the gem, the jewel, and the precious stone; He is Himself the jeweller ;

He is in every direction immovable ;

He setteth *everything* in motion ;

He is permanent dealer.

O man, make thy heart the ox, meditation the road, fill thy sack with divine knowledge, and load it *on the ox* ;

Saith Kabir, hear, O saints, my goods have arrived at their destination.

The following was addressed to a Jogi who fortified himself for his austerities by potations of wine.

3

O ignorant and stupid brawler[2], reverse thy breath and direct it *to thy brain* ;

Then turn thy brain into a furnace, draw the nectareous stream, and thou shalt become *divinely* intoxicated.

O brother, call upon God for assistance.

O saints, ever drink this wine so difficult to obtain, and your thirst shall easily be quenched.

In the fear of God is love ; he who knoweth this shall obtain God's elixir, my brother.

Ambrosia is in every heart : *God* giveth it to whomsoever He pleaseth.

There is one city[3] ; it hath nine gates ;

Restrain thy wandering *mind from issuing by them.*

After the exercise of the ira, pingla, and sukhmana, the tenth gate openeth and the mind becometh intoxicated.

When *the soul obtaineth* the fully fearless dignity, suffering is at an end, saith Kabir deliberately.

Turning from the way of *the world* I have obtained this wine, a cup of which causeth *divine* intoxication.

Religious instruction addressed to a dissolute fop.

4

Thou who art saturated with lust, wrath, and covetousness, knowest not the way of the One God.

Thine eyes are burst, thou seest nothing, thou art rowned *even* without water.

Why walkest thou so foppishly ?

Thou art a compound of bones, skin, and filth, and saturated with evil odour.

Thou repeatest not God's name ; in what doubts hast thou gone astray ? Death is not far from thee.

Whatever efforts thou makest to preserve thy body, shall it last when *thy term of* life is complete ?

Nothing resulteth from thine efforts ; what can any mortal do ?

If it be God's will, man shall meet a true guru and repeat the One name.

Thou livest in a house of sand and puffest out thy body, O simpleton.

Saith Kabir, they, however clever, who remember not God are lost.

The following was addressed to the same person.

5

Crooked they turban[4], crooked thy gait[5], thou beginnest to eat betel[6];

Thou hast naught to do with the love and service of God ; *thou sayest* 'I have business in court'.

Thou hast forgotten God in thy pride ;

Ever gazing on thy gold and thy very beautiful women thou deemest them permanent ;

The life passeth away in covetousness, falsehood, sin, and great arrogance.

Saith Kabir, Death will attack thee at last, O fool.

Kabir reminds a worldly person of his death.

6

Having beaten thy drum for four days, thou shalt depart.

With all thine earnings, thy ready money, and thy buried treasures, thou shalt take nothing with thee.

Thy dear wife will sit and weep in the portico ; thy mother *will go* as far as the gate with thee ;

All thy friends and relations will accopany thee to the burning-ground ; *but* thy soul shall depart alone.

Thou shalt not again behold thy sons, thy wealth, thy towns, and thy cities.

Saith Kabir, why remember not God ? thy life is passing in vain.

Notes and References

1. Also translated—The slave Kabir saith.

2. *Kalivar*—also translated as if written *kalal,* a wine-seller, then a drunkard.
3. The body.
4. Thou wearest they turban on the side of thy head like a fop.
5. Thou walkest foppishly.
6. So as to give a rosy colour to thy lips.

God's name is Kabir's sold property.

BHAIRO

1

The name of God is my wealth ;
I cannot tie it in a knol, or sell it for my livelihood.
The name is my field, the Name is my garden;
I Thy slave, *O God.* perform Thy service and *seek* Thy protection.
Thy name is my wealth, Thy name my capital ;
I know none but Thee.
Thy name is my kindred, Thy name my brethren.
Thy name my associates, who will assist me at the last moment.
Saith Kabir, I am a slave to him.
Whom God keepeth in the world, but *who is* indifferent to it

The following was addressed to a rich man who had offered Kabir money :--

2

Naked thou camest and naked shalt thou depart ;
None shall remain--*not even* kings or rulers.
I have the sovereign God as my nine treasures ;
Thou hast the love of property, women, and wealth ;
But they did not come with thee, nor shall they go with thee.
What availeth thee to have elephants tied at thy gate ?
The fortress of Ceylon was made of gold,
But what did the fool Rawan take with him ?
Saith Kabir, meditate some good acts :
The gambler shall depart with empty hands.

God alone is pure.

3

Impure is Brahma, impure is Indar ;
Impure is the sun and impure the moon.
This world is defiled with impurity ;
Pure is God alone who hatah neither end nor limit.
Impure are the gods of the worlds ;
Impure are nights, days, and months *devoted to idolatry.*
Impure are pearls, impure are diamonds.
Impure are wind, fire, and water ;
Impure are Shiv, Shankar, and Mahesh[1] ;
Impure are Sidhs, Sadhiks, and *those who* wear religious garbs ;
Impure are Jogis, and Jangams with their matted hair ;
Impure is the body with the soul--
Saith Kabir, only those who know God,
Are pure and acceptable.

The following was addressed to a hypocritical Muhammadan priest who had advised Kabir to make a pilgrimage to Makka.

4

Make thy mind thy Kaaba, thy body its enclosing temple, Conscience[2] its prime teacher ;
Then, O priest, call men to pray to that mosque
Which hath ten gates.
Sacrifice[3] wrath, doubt, and malice ;
Make patience thine utterance of the five prayers.
The Hindus and the Musalmans have the same Lord ;
What can the Mulla, what can the Shaikh do *for man* ?
Saith Kabir, I have become mad ;
Stealing my mind away *from the world* I have become blended with God.

Some one represented to Kabir that he was completely spoiled by his religious exercises. The following was his reply:--

5

When a stream is lost in the Ganges,
It becometh as the Ganges itself ;
Kabir is similarly lost *in God* by invoking Him ;

I have become as the True One and need not go elsewhere.
The perfume of the sandal is communicated to other trees ;
They then become as the sandal itself.
When the philosopher's stone is applied to copper,
It becometh gold ;
So Kabir having met the saints,
Hath become as God.

The following was addressed to some Brahmans who had attributed Kabir's contempt for their religious ceremonies to madness.

6

You *wear* tilaks on your foreheads, *carry* rosaraies in your hands, and *put on sectarial* dresses :

People think that God is a plaything--
If I am mad, *O God,* I am still Thine.
How can people know my secret[4] ?
I gather no leaves[5] and I worship no idol ;
Without devotion to God *other* worship is fruitless.
I worship the True Guru, and ever and ever propitiate Him ;
For such service I shall obtain happiness in His court.
People say Kabir is mad,
But *only* God knoweth Kabir's secret.

Kabir renounces both the Hindu and the Muhammadan priests.

7

Turning away *from the world* I have forgotten both caste and lineage ;

My weaving is *now* in the infinite silence[6].
I have now no quarrel *with any one* ;
I have given up both the Pandits and the Mullas.
I weave clothes and I wear them myself ;
Where *I see* no pride[7] there I sing God's *praises.*
What the Pandits and the Mullas prescribed for me.
I have received no *advantage* from, and have abandoned.
My heart being pure[8] I have seen the Lord ;

Kabir having searched and searched himself, hath found God within him.

Kabir when reproached with his poverty replied :--

8

Nobody respecteth the poor man ;
He may make hundreds of thousands of efforts, but no one will heed him.
If a poor man go to a rich man,
The latter, though opposite him, will turn his back.
If a rich man go to a poor man,
The latter respecteth, *yea*, inviteth him ;
Yet the poor man and the rich man are brothers :--
God design cannot be set aside.
Saith Kabir, it is he who is poor,
In whose heart the Name abideth not.

Worship God betimes.

9

When man serveth the guru and worshippeth God,
It is only then he really hath a human body[9].
Even the demigods[10] long for this body ;
Therefore having obtained it,
Worship God ; forget Him not ;
That is the advantage of human birth.
Before the disease of old age hath come upon thee,
Before Death hath seized thy body,
Before thy voice hath grown weak,
O man, worship God.
If thou worship Him not now, when wilt thou, my brother ?
When the end cometh thou canst not do so.
Whatever thou doest, it is best to do now ;
Otherwise thou shalt not be saved, and shalt afterwards repent.
He is worshipper whom God applieth to His worship ;
It is he who shall obtain the pure God.
The doors of *his understanding* shall open to him by meeting the guru,
And he shall not return again by the way of the womb.
This is thine opportunity, this thy time;
Look into thy heart and reflect *on this* .
Saith Kabir, *O man,* whether thou win or lose,

I have many times called out to thee.

In the following Kabir appears to mean that God resides in the brain.

10

The best knowledge abideth in the city of Shiv[11] ;
Having obtained it there, meditate *upon God*[12].
And thou shalt know this world and the next.
Why should I kill myself performing works of pride ?
My attention is fixed on the special place--*the brain* ;
The name of the Sovereign God is my divine knowledge,
He who hath closed his sphineter and[13]
Hath placed the moon above the sun[14].
At the western gate the sun is hot[15]
The breath then riseth to the brain from the spine.
The western gate is closed by a rock[16]
There is a window[17] over that rock.
Over the window is the tenth gate--
Saith Kabir, *He who dwelleth there* hath neither end nor limit.

Kabir gives his ideas of what a Mulla, a Qazi, and a superior of Jogis ought to be.

11

He is a Mulla who struggleth with his heart,
Who by the instruction of the guru contendeth with Death,
And crusheth Death's pride.
Salutation ever to that Mulla !
God is present ; why describe Him as distant ?
If thou restrain *thy* pugnacity, thou shalt obtain the Beautiful One.
He is a Qazi who pondereth on his body,
Who burneth it with divine fire,
And alloweth not his seed to drop even in his dreams–
For such a Qazi there is no old age or death–
He is an emperor[18] who *knoweth how* to draw up his two breaths[19],
Who recalleth his mind when it goeth abroad, who collecteth the army *of breaths*[20] in his brain--
Such a one is an emperor, and hath an umbrella over his head.
The Jogis cry out 'Gorakh, Gorakh';

The Hindus repeat 'Ram, Ram';
The Musalmans have Khuda,
But Kabir's God is the All-pervading.

The following hymn, which is a homily against idolatry, is said to have been composed by the fifth Guru from a theme of Kabir.

12

Vain is his devotion,
Who saith a stone is God.
Idle shall be his labour
Who falleth at the feet of a stone.
My God always speaketh[21];
He bestoweth gifts on all living things.
He who is blind knoweth not God who is within him ;
He is led away by superstition, and entangleth others.
A stone speaketh not, nor bestoweth gifts ;
Vain are the ceremonies *of idolaters* and fruitless their service.
Say what advantage can be gained
By anointing a corpse with sandal.
If any one roll a corpse in the dirt,
What harm can it do the corpse ?
Saith Kabir, I proclaim with a loud voice--
Understand me, ye infidels and pagans ;
The love of other *gods* hath destroyed many homes,
The saints of God are ever happy.

The universal influence of Maya and the means of counteracting it.

13

The fishes in the water are led by Maya[22];
The moths round the lamp are influenced by Maya ;
Through Maya the elephant feeleth lust ;
Creeping things and bumble-bees[23] perish through Maya--
My brethren, Maya is so bewitching
That she illudeth all living beings--
Birds and beasts are imbued with Maya ;
She causeth great hardship to the honey-bees[24];

Horses and camels are saturated with Maya ;
The eighty-four Sidhs are the sport of Maya ;
The six Jatis are the slaves of Maya ;
So are the nine Naths, the sun, and the moon ;
Penitents and the supreme Rikhis are lulled by Maya ;
In the power of Maya are Death and his five messengers[25];
Dogs and jackals are imbued with Maya ;
So are the monkeys, leopards, lions,
Cats, sheep, and foxes ;
Trees and tubers are subject to Maya ;
The demigods are saturated with Maya ;
So are the ocean, the firmament, and the earth.
Saith Kabir, he who hath a belly is *subject* to Maya ;
But man shall be freed *from her influence* when he hath found a saint.

Let man fix his attention on God and not on worldly things.

14

As long as man speaketh of things as his own,
So long not one of his affairs shall prosper.
When he ceaseth to speak of things as his own,
Then God shall come and adjust his affairs.
To that end, O man, ponder on divine knowledge.
Why rememberest thou not God, the Destroyer of misery ?
As long as lions inhabit the forest,
So long shall the forest not flourish[26]
When the jackal eateth the lion[27]
The whole forest bursteth out in bloom.
They who think themselves victorious are lost ; *and they who think themselves* defeated are saved[28] ;
By the favour of the guru they cross over.
The slave Kabir admonisheth all men.
To fix their attention on God alone.

A brief description of God's court to which Kabir craves admittance.

15

Who will introduce poor me to Him
Who hath seven thousand commanders,

A lakh and a quarter of prophets,
Eighty-eight karors of men called Shaikhs,
And fifty-six karors of servants to amuse Him ?
His court is afar off ; who can reach His private chamber ?
He hath thirty-three karors of play-houses ;
Eighty four lakhs of beings wander *in them*[29].
He showed some favour to father Adam,
And put him into paradise for a long time.
The faces of those whose hearts are not right are pale, and their utterance *is confounded* ;
They forsake their books and work evil.
They who attribute blame *to God* and are angry with Him,
Shall obtain the fruit of their acts.
Thou art the giver, *O Lord* ; I ever beg of *Thee* ;
If Thou refuse me, I am ruined[30].
The slave Kabir is in Thy sanctuary.
Keep me, O Merciful One, near Thee.

Kabir desires not heaven but absorption in God.

16

Everybody saith he is going thither[31]
I know not where heaven is.
They who know not the secrets of their own hearts
Glibly talk of heaven;
As long as man desireth heaven,
He shall not dwell at God's feet.
I know not where heaven's gate is,
Nor its moat, nor its plastered fortress.
Saith Kabir, what *more* can I now say.
Than that the society of saints is heaven ?

Kabir tells how he subdued his evil passions.

17

How shall I subdue this beautiful fortress[32], my brother,
Which hath double walls[33] and triple moats[34],
Whose entrenchments are the five *subtle elements,* the twenty-five *categories,*[35] worldly love, pride, jealousy, and very powerful Maya ?
I who am poor cannot obtain strength to *take that fortress* ; what shall I do, O God ?

Lust is its folding doors, woe and weal its gate-keepers, demerits and merits its gates ;

Anger, which is very quarrelsome, its commander ; and the heart its rebel king.

The *defenders* had dainties for their coats of mail, egoism for their helmets and evil understanding for the bows they drew ;

Covetousness, which dwelleth in *the quiver* of the heart, became their arrows ; thus the fortress was impregnable ;

But I made *divine* love the fuse, meditation the howitzer, and divine knowledge the shells ;

I gently lit the fuse with the fire of God's *name*, and captured *the fortress* with one shot.

I began to fight assisted by truth and contentment, and battered both its doors ;

By the favour of the congregation of the saints and of the guru I made its king a prisoner.

By dint of remembering God I, a coward, have cut the noose of Death.

The slave Kabir hath scaled the fortress, and secured an imperishable empire.

The following refers to another persecution of Kabir :--

18

The Ganges is a deity deep and profound ;
I, Kabir, was made to stand in it with chains on my feet.
My spirits fell not ; why should my body fear ?
My mind was absorbed in God's lotus feet ;
My chains were broken by the ripples of the Ganges,
And I found myself seated on a deer-skin.
Saith Kabir, I had no friend or companion
But God the Protector both by water and land.

Notes and References

1. Three names of Shiv.The Hindu say that there are eleven Shivs.
2. Literally--thy speaker.
3. *Mismil* a corruption of the Arabic *bismillah,* in the name of God, an expression used by Musalmans when slaughtering animals.
4. That is, the cause of my madness.
5. To offer to idols.
6. In the realms of God.

7. That is, in the society of the saints.
8. Also translated--being freed from the world.
9. That is, it is only then his human birth is profitable.
10. The demigods are proud, and do not praise God. They can only obtain deliverance by being born in human bodies.
11. The brain or tenth gate.
12. This and the preceding line are also translated--Men of the highest intellect raise their breath to the brain ;

    Do thou meeting them contemplate God.
13. So that all the breath of the body may go to the brain. This act is done mechanically by resting the anus on the heel.
14. This verse is explained--He has set knowledge with its tiny light above universal ignorance.
15. When the breath rises to the top of the spine.
16. A piece of flesh which the Jogis suppose to be at the top of the spinal column.
17. This is a second obstacle to the passage of the breath.
18. Sultan--By this word is here meant a superior of Jogis.
19. Who knows how to exercise the ira and pingla. Also translated--who shoots two arrows--knowledge and contempt of the world.
20. The body is supposed to have ten breaths, all of which the Jogis believe they can collect the brain.
21. He is not silent like an idol.
22. Their sense of taste, their palates.
23. The lotus closes on them at night.
24. In their anxiety to store honey.
25. The five evil passions.
26. The other animals of the forest will be unhappy.
27. When divine knowledge destroys pride.
28. This verse is also translated--They who are overcome by their evil passions are lost, and they who conquer them are saved.
29. Also translated--wander as His jesters.
30. The gyanis translate--a stain shall attach to Thee. The line is also translated--if I reply, I shall be at fault.

31. To heaven.
32. The body.
33. The two walls are doubt and wrong-headedness.
34. The three moats are the three qualities.
35. The twenty-five categories of the Sankhya philosophy. See Monier William's *Indian Wisdom* and the Introduction to Cockburn Thompson's *Bhagawat Gita*. An enumeration of the categories here would not assist the Sikh student.

God and his residence.

ASHTAPADI

1

God constructed an inaccessible fortress[1] for His residence,
Which He illumined with His light.
The lightning playeth and pleasure reigneth
Where the youthful[2] Lord God reposeth.
If the soul love God's name,
Man shall be released from old age and death, and his doubts shall flee away.
He whose mind loveth *to consider* whether a man's caste is high or low.
Chanteth the hymn of egoism.
The sound of the unbeaten music is heard.
Where the Lord God reposeth.
He who fashioned continents and different countries,
The three worlds, the three *gods,* and the three qualities,
Though styled inaccessible and invisible, dwelleth within the heart.
None can find the limit or the secret of the Sustainer of the earth ;
He shineth in the plantain blossom and in the sunshine,
And hath taken His dwelling in the pollen of the lotus.
God's spell is within the twelve petals of the heart
Where the holy Lord of Lakshmi reposeth.
The great *God* reacheth from the lower to the upper regions of the firmament ;
He illumineth the silent realm,
Where there is neither sun nor moon.
He was in the beginning ; He is without stain and happy.
Know that he pervadeth the body *as well* as the universe ;

He batheth in Mansarowar[3] ;
His pass-word is 'Soham' (I am He) ;
He is not subject to merits or demerits,
Nor concerned with caste, with sunshine, or with shade ;
He is only found in the guru's asylum.

He who fixeth his attention on Him removeth it not, becometh released from transmigration,
And absorbed in the Infinite.
He who knoweth God in his heart
And repeateth His name, becometh as He.
Saith Kabir, that mortal shall be saved.
Who fixeth in his heart *God's* light and spell.

God, God's servants, and God's court.

2

Millions of suns shine for Him ;
He hath millions of Shivs and Kailases[4] ;
Millions of Durgas shampoo *His limbs* ;
Million of Brahmas recite the Veds for Him--
If I beg, *let me beg* only of God ;
I have naught to do with any other god--
Millions of moons form His lamps ;
Thirty-three demigods cook His food ;
The nine planets[5] *multiplied* millions of times stand *on duty* in his court ;
Millions of Dharmrajas are His porters ;
Millions of winds from the four cardinal points fan Him ;
Millions of Sheshnags lay His bed ;
Millions of oceans are His water-carriers ;
The eighteen million loads *of vegetables* are His hair.
Millions of store-keepers fill His store-houses ;
Millions of Lakshmis decorate Him--
He removeth many millions of demerits and merits--
Millions of Indars wait on Him ;
The fifty-six millions of *clouds are* His messengers ;
He is celebrated and unrivalled in every land.
With His tresses loose and with terrible *aspect* He moveth--
God playeth in millions of ways--
There are millions of feasts at His court ;

Millions of celestial singers hail Him ;
Millions of sciences all describe His attributes,
But even then they cannot find His end.
In His hair are millions of Bawans,
And *Rams* who out generalled Rawan's army,
And Krishans who humbled the pride of Duryodhan,
Greatly extolled by a thousand million Purans.
Millions of Cupids cannot compete with Him *in beauty*--
He stealeth away the inmost heart.
Saith Kabir, hear me, O God,
Grant me the fearless dignity, the gift I crave.

Notes and References

1. The tenth gate or brain.
2. Some translate this the minute or invisible.
3. In the lake of the heart.
4. A peak in the Himalayas where the Ganges is supposed to rise.
5. These are--Suraj Chand, Mangal, Budh, Brihaspati, Shukkar, Sanichar, Rahu and Ketu. The days of the week are named, in India, after the first seven.

The following was written under the grateful influence of early spring in the north of India.

BASANT

1

The earth bloometh, the firmament rejoiceth ;
Every heart is gladdened by God's light.
The Lord God rejoiceth in endless ways ;
Whithersoever I look, there is He contained.
The four Veds rejoice in worldliness ;
So do the Simritis with the books of the Musalmans.
Shiv practising Jog rejoiceth--
Kabir's Lord bloometh equally in all things.

Kabir accepts as saints Shukdev, Akrur, Hanuman, and Shiv, famous for their continence, and rejects the hypocritical Brahmans, Jogis, Sanyasis, and Penitents of his time.

2

The Pandits grow proud reciting the Purans,
The Jogis in practising Jog,
The Sanyasis in saying there is no one like themselves;
The Penitents even in their different penances
Are all intoxicated with pride ; none of them is awake.
The thieves[1] who rob houses are *already* with them.
Shukhdev and Akrur[2] are awake ;
Hanuman with the tail is awake ;
Shiv is awake and worshippeth *God's* feet ;
In this Kal age Namdev and Jaidev *are awake*[3].
There are several forms of waking and sleeping:--
He who is awake under the guru's instruction is the best.
The most important duty of this body,
Saith Kabir, is to repeat God's name.

To obtain salvation without a guru would be impossible.

3

Hath a wife ever given birth to her husband ?
Hath a boy ever dandled his father ?
Hath a woman without breasts ever suckled ?
See, O people, the peculiarity of this Kal age--
Hath a son ever taken his mother in marriage ?
Can a man without feet ever leap ?
Can a man without a mouth burst into laughter ?
Without sleep can man repose ?
Can one churn milk without a churn ?
Can a cow without an udder give milk ?
Can one accomplish a long journey without a road ?
So the way cannot be found without a true guru,
Kabir saith, and admonisheth *all men*.

God saves his saints as He did Prahlad.

4

Prahlad was sent to school for instruction ;
He took several boys with him as his class-fellows.
He said to his teacher :-- 'Why teach me worldly entanglements ?
'*Rather* write on my tablet *the name of* God.

I will not, sir, abandon the name of God ;
'I have no concern with any other instruction'.
His tutor's sons, Sanda and Marka[4], went and reported *the matter to Prahlad's father.*
He sent for Prahlad, *telling them* to run quickly to him ;
Then he addressed him :-- 'Abandon the habit of repeating God's name ;
'I will let thee goat once if thou obey my words'.
Prahlad replied, 'Why dost thou continually annoy me ?
'I should be a sinner were I to abandon the one God
'Who made the water, the dry land, the hills, and the mountains.
'Throw me into the fire or kill me if it please thee'.
His father became angry and drawing his sword *said,*
'Show me that Preserver of thine'.
Upon this God expanding came forth from a pillar,
And killed Harnakhas by tearing him with His nails.
It was the Supreme Being, the God of gods, *who appeared.*
For the sake of His saint He became *incarnate* as the man-lion.
Saith Kabir, He whose limit cannot be seen.
Saved Prahlad several times[5].

Kabir prays to be protected from lust.

5

Within this body and mind is the thief Cupid,
Who hath stolen my jewel of divine knowledge.
I have no patron, O God, to whom I may make my complaint.
Whom hath *Cupid* not ruined ? Who am I *that I should escape* ?
O God, this terrible pain cannot be endured ;
What power hath my fickle mind *against Cupid* ?
Sanak Sanandan, *the sons of Brahma,* Shiv, Shukdev,
Vishnu, Brahma, and others know *his power.*
The poets, the Jogis, the wearers of matted hair,
Passed their lives guarding themselves against him.
Thou, O God, art unfathomable ; I cannot find Thy depth.
O God, Lord of the poor, to whom *else* may I tell my woes ?
Let the pain of birth and death subside, *and grant me* continence.
Kabir singeth the praises of the Ocean of happiness.

The body under the allegory of a merchant.

6

There is one head of the firm and five traders[6]
Who take with them spurious *wares* on twenty-five oxen[7].
There are ten bags[8] and nine poles[9] *to lift them* ;
The body is bound by seventy-two ropes.
I have nothing to do with that commerce.
By which my capital is lessened, and my interest ever increased.
I have trafficked by joining the seven threads[10] ;
I have joined with them *good* acts and *God's* love.
The three tax-gatherers[11] wrangle *for their share* ;
But I a trader put them aside and departed.
The capital of the five traders is lost, their trade is ruined,
And the oxen disperse in every direction.
Saith Kabir, O man, thy business shall prosper,
And thy doubts depart when thou art absorbed in God.

A Brahman had censured Kabir for not having paid due attention to caste rules in eating. The following was his reply :--

7

Thy mother was impure, thy father was also impure, and impure is the fruit they have borne.

The unlucky people came impure, they departed and died impure.

Tell me, O Pandit, what place is pure
Where I may sit and take my food.

My tongue is impure, what it saith is impure, the ears and eyes are all impure.

The impurity of the senses departeth not, O thou who art burning with Brahmanical wrath.

Fire is also impure, water is impure, and impure the place where thou sittest and cookest it.

With an impure ladle it is served up, and impure are those who sit and eat it.

Impure thy cow-dung, impure thy cooking-square, and impure the lines which mark it out.

Saith Kabir, that man is pure who hath obtained true knowledge.

Kabir's wife had ground corn and gone out without collecting the flour. Kabir being left alone in the house paid more attention to his devotion than to his housekeeping. A dog came and began to lick the flour on the hand-mill. The following was addressed to the intruding animal :--

8

Thy stride is like that of a cow ;
The hair over thy tail is shiny.
Search for and eat anything in this house ;
Go not to another's house,
Lick the hand-mill, eat the flour ;
Whether takest thou the towel [12] of the hand-mill ?
Thou gazest very intently on this safe ;
Take care that the stick fall not on thy back[13].
Saith Kabir, thou hast fared well ;
Take care that no one throw a brick or a clod at thee[14].

Notes and References

1. The evil passions.
2. An uncle of Krishan.
3. The persons mentioned did not allow worldly matters to interrupt their devotions.
4. Brahma's son was Bhrigu, Bhrigu's son was Shukkar, Shukkar's sons were Sanda and Marka.
5. His life had been often in danger before from the bigotry and violence of his father, and the present occurrence was but the culmination of many acts of paternal cruelty.
6. The head of the firm is man, the five traders the five senses.
7. The spurious wares are worldly things.
8. Generally understood to be the ten breaths of the body.
9. The nine gates of the body.
10. *Bairag*, contempt of the world ; *bibek*, discrimination ; *khai sampat*, the six acquisitions ; *moksh ichha*, desire of deliverance ; *shrawan* hearing God's name ; *manan*, obeying God's will, *nididhyasan*, profound and continued meditation.

    The six sampats or acquisitions are--*Sam*, restraint of the mind ; *dam*, restraint of the senses ; *uparati*, the preservation of the heart from love and hate ; *taliksha*, endurance of pain ; *shradha*, faith ; *samadhanta*, attention to the guru's instruction. Others by the seven threads, understand the five organs of perception, the mind, and the understanding.

11. The three qualities.
12. A cloth to collect the flour as it falls from the hand-mill.
13. That is, run away before my wife or my son returns ; you shall meet with a different reception from them.
14. This hymn is also applied allegorically to man.

Kabir endeavours to recall man to a sense of his insignificance.

SARANG

1

Why, O man, art thou proud of a small matter ?

With a store of only ten *mans* of corn and four double *paise* in thy pocket thou swaggerest along.

Even if thou obtain greatness, yea, a hundred villagers, and have an income of two lakhs of rupees,

Thy authority shall only last for four days like the green leaves of the forest.

No one hath brought wealth with him, and no one shall take it away.

Greater sovereigns than even Rawan departed in a moment ;

God's saints who worship Him and repeat His name *abide* for ever.

They to whom God is merciful meet the society of the saints.

Neither mother, father, wife, son, nor wealth shall go with thee at the last moment.

Saith Kabir, worship God, O fool, *or* thy life shall pass away in vain.

God's omnipotence.

2

O God, I know not the measure of Thy regal authority ;

I am the handmaiden of Thy saints.

They who go laughing return weeping, and they who go weeping return laughing ;

What is inhabited becometh deserted, and what is deserted becometh inhabited.

God turneth water into dry land, dry land. He turneth into wells, and wells into mountains ;

He can raise man from earth to heaven, and when he hath ascended to heaven dash him down.

He can turn a beggar into a king, and a king into a beggar.

He can turn an idiot into a pandit, and a pandit into an idiot.

He can turn a woman into a man, and a man into a woman.

Saith Kabir, God is beloved of the saints ; I am a sacrifice unto Him.

Man should rely on God and practise humility.

3

Without God what succour hath man?

The love of parents, brethren, sons, and wife is all fleeting.

Construct a raft for the other world ; what reliance can be placed on wealth ?

What confidence can be reposed in this vessel, if it be chinked in the slightest[1] ?

Thou shalt obtain the fruit of all religion and good works if thou desire to become the dust of everybody's feet.

Saith Kabir, hear, O saints, the mind is like the flying bird of the forest.

Notes and References

1. If it receive even the slightest external pressure.

Kabir's bliss in feeling that he is saved--

PRABHATI

1

My dread of transmigration is at an end
Since God displayed His love for me.
The light hath dawned, the darkness is dispelled ;
I have obtained the jewel God by meditation on Him.
When *He conferreth* happiness sorrow fleeth away ;
The jewel of my heart is absorbed in God's love.
Whatever occurreth is according to Thy will, *O God* ;
He who understandeth this shall be easily absorbed *in Thee*.
Saith Kabir, all my sins have been blotted out,
And my soul is absorbed in the Life of the world.

God is not confined as regards place to the mosque or the temple, or as regards time to any month or day.

2

If God dwell only in the mosque, to whom belongeth the rest of the country ?

They who are called Hindus *say* that God dwelleth in an idol : I see not the truth in either sect.

O God, whether Allah or Ram, I live by Thy name,

O Lord, show kindness unto me.

Hari dwelleth in the south: Allah hath His place in the west.

Search in thy heart, search in thy heart of hearts ; there is His place and abode.

The Brahmans *yearly* perform twenty-four *fastings* on the eleventh *day of the dark and light halves of the lunar month* ; the Musalmans fast in the month of Ramzan.

The latter put aside eleven months of the year, *and say* that the Treasure is in one alone.

What availeth the Hindus to bathe at *Jagannath* in Urisa (Orissa), what *the Musalmans* to bow their heads in a mosque ?

With deception in their hearts they repeat prayers ; what availeth them to go on a pilgrimage to Makka ?

The men and women Thou hast created, *O God,* are all in Thy form.

Kabir is a child of Ram and Allah, and accepteth all gurus and pirs.

Saith Kabir, hear, O men and women, seek the sanctuary of the one God ;

O mortals, only repeat God's name, and then shall you be assuredly saved.

In Kabir's presence a Brahman and a Muhammadan priest were reviling each others' sacred books. The Muhammadan expatiated on the merits of sacrifice.

3

Say not that the Hindu and Musalman books are false false is he who reflecteth not on them.

If you say that the one God is in everything, then why kill fowls ?

O priest, say *is this* God's justice ?

Thy mental doubts forsake thee not ;

Thou seizest and bringest living things, and takest their lives, but thou *merely* killest *their bodies of* clay.

Their souls return to the Indestructible ; say what has thou killed.

What avail thy purifications, thy rinsings of the mouth and thy prostrations in the mosque ?

If thou pray with deception in thy heart, what availeth thee thy pilgrimage to Makka ?

Thou art impure; thou knowest not the Pure One; thou knowest not His secrets.

Saith Kabir, thou hast missed heaven, and art satisfied with hell.

Kabir offered to God the following oblation in stead of incense, light, and the other accessories of Hindu worship.

4

Hear[1] me, God of gods, Supreme Lord, primal and omnipresent, *I offer my* vespers unto Thee.

The Sidhs *even* in *deep* meditation have not discovered.Thy limits but they continue to cling to Thine asylum.

Accept this oblation[2], O bright Spirit ; worship the True Guru, my brethren.

Brahma standeth and readeth the Veds, but the Unseen is seen not by him[3].

With divine knowledge as mine oil and Thy name my wick I have made a lamp to illumine my body.

I have lit *the lamp* with the light of the Lord of the world ; he who knoweth *how to do this* knoweth the Omniscient[4].

The unbeaten sounds of God who dwelleth with man, are my five musical instruments.

O Thou Formless and Undisturbed. Thy slave Kabir hath made. Thee this oblation[5].

Notes and References

1. Sun, also translated--as an epithet of God--without desires.
2. Of flowers, incense, light, &c.
3. That is, God does not heed him.
4. Also translated--The wise man knoweth how to do this. If *sujhe* were read for *bujhe* the two words would be translated--The Omniscient would become manifest.
5. This hymn is included in the Arati of the Sikhs.

KABIR'S SHLOKAS

1

Kabir, my rosary is my tongue, on which I repeat God's name ;
In every age it bringeth peace and comfort to all *God's* servants.

2

Kabir, everybody laugheth at my caste ;
I am a sacrifice to this caste in which I repeat the Creator's name.

3

Kabir, why waverest thou? Why lettest thou thy mind vacillate ?
God is the Lord of all happiness : quaff the essence of His name.

4

Kabir, if golden earrings were to be made and rubies set in them.
They would appear like burnt reeds if God's name were not in the *wearer's* heart[1].

5

Kabir, there are few who while alive are dead[2].
And who fearlessly sing God's praises ; whithersoever I look there is He *to save me.*

6

Kabir on the day I am dead there shall be rejoicing after me[3];
I shall *then* have met my God, and my friends will worship Him *instead of weeping.*

7

Kabir, I am the worst of men ; except myself everybody is good ;
He who holdeth the same opinion is my friend.

8

Kabir, *worldly* love came to me in various disguises.
But my guru preserved me ; *worldly love then* made me obeisance and *departed.*

9

Kabir, destroy that *Maya* whose death shall make thee happy ;
Every one shall *then* say it is well ; no one shall *deem it* ill.

10

Kabir, when the nights are dark, thieves arise ;
They run about with nooses *for men* ; know that they are accursed of God.

11

Kabir, the sandal-tree is good even though surrounded by the dhak-tree[4];

If the latter be near the sandal-tree, it will also become fragrant as sandal.

12

Kabir, the bamboo is drowned in its pride[5] ; may nobody be drowned so !

It may grow near the sandal, but it is never perfumed by it[6].

13

Kabir, man hath lost his faith through mammon, *but* mammon will not accompany him ;

He hath carelessly struck his foot with an axe by his own hand.

The following is said to have been written in reply to some one who had invited Kabir to attend a religious fair :--

14

Kabir, wherever I wandered I saw spectacles everywhere ;

Without the saint who loveth God, *the world* is in my opinion a desert.

15

Kabir, the hut of the saints is comfortable ; the village of the false is a furnace.

May fire prey upon that mansion where the name of God is not !

16

Kabir, why weep when a saint dieth, *since* he is merely going home?

Weep *rather* for the poor infidel who is sold at every shop[7]

17

Kabir, the infidel is like a dinner of garlic ;

One may sit in the corner and eat it, *but its smell* becometh manifest at last.

18

Kabir, the body[8] is a churn, the breath *of life* its churning-staff ;

The saints eat the butter, the world drinketh the butter-milk.

19

Kabir, the body is the churn, the breath *of life* the stream of iced water[9] ;

He who hath churned shall eat the *butter* and *so shall* his helpmates also.

20

Kabir, Maya is a thief who breaketh into and robbeth the shop[10] ;
One man, Kabir, who hath chased her in every direction[11] she shall not rob[12]

21

Kabir, they who make many friends are not happy in this world ;
But they who keep their minds fixed on the one God ever enjoy happiness.

22

Kabir, while the world feareth death, my heart is pleased therewith;
Since it is only by death supreme bliss is obtained.

23

Kabir when thou obtainest the jewel of God's *name* keep it to thyself[13],
For there is no bazaar *to sell it in*, no connoisseur, no purchaser, no price *for it*.

24

Kabir, love him who *hath made* God his master ;
Learned men, kings, lords of the soil--of what avail is *love for them*?

25

Kabir, by loving the one God all other love departeth,
Whether thou wearest long hair, or shavest thy head clean[14].

26

Kabir, the world is a chamber of soot ; blind are they who enter it, *and they become defiled*.
I am a sacrifice to those who have entered it, and come forth *clean*.

27

Kabir, this body shall depart ; if possible detain[15] it ;
They who had hundreds of thousands and millions departed barefooted.

28

Kabir, this body shall depart ; put it on some road
On which it may either hold converse with saints, or sing God's praises.

29

Kabir, everybody dieth in his turn, but no one even knoweth how to die ;

When thou diest, so die that thou shall not have to die again[16].

30

Kabir, it is difficult to obtain human birth; it cometh not again and again ;

As the ripe fruit of the forest, when it falleth to the ground returneth not to the *parent*-branch.

Somebody came to visit Kabir, and asked him if Kabir (great) was his name. The following, addressed to God, was his reply :--

31

It is Thou, *O God,* who art Kabir (*great*), and whose name is Kabir (*great*) ;

Man shall only obtain the jewel of the Lord when he despiseth his body.

32

Kabir, utter not idle complaints *against God* ; nothing shall result from what thou sayest ;

No one can set aside what the merciful One doeth.

33

Kabir, nobody who is counterfeit can withstand God's touchstone;

Only he who in life is dead can bear its ordeal.

34

Kabir, men wear gaudy robes, and eat betel leaves and betel nut ;

But without the name of the one God they shall be bound and taken to the city of Death.

35

Kabir, my boat is old, and leaketh in a thousand chinks ;

Boats very lightly laden cross over, but those with *heavy* cargoes[17] founder.

36

Kabir, *man's* bones burn like firewood, his hair burneth like grass;

Kabir is sad on seeing everybody burning[18].

37

Kabir, be not proud of thy bones wrapped up in skin ;

They who rode excellent horses, *and* under umbrellas, were at last buried in the earth.

38

Kabir, be not proud on seeing thy lofty dwellings ;

To-day or to-morrow thou shall lie *beneath* the earth, and the grass shall grow over thee.

39

Kabir, be not proud, let none laugh at the poor ;

Now thy bark is on the sea ; who knoweth what shall happen[19]

40

Kabir, be not proud on seeing thy beautiful body ;

Thou shalt leave it to-day or to-morrow as a serpent its slough.

41

Kabir, if thou must plunder, then plunder, but let thy plunder be the name of God ;

Otherwise thou shalt afterwards repent *when* life hath left thy body.

42

Kabir, few[20] have been born who have applied the fire of *divine knowledge* to their bodies.

Who have burnt the five evil passions, and with *the same* continued to love God.

43

Is there any one who will sell me his son ; any one who will sell me his daughter[21]

Is there any one who will go into partnership with Kabir, and deal in God's *name* with him ?

44

Kabir, I remind thee, O man--and entertain no doubt on the subject--

Thou canst not exchange the pleasures thou hast already enjoyed for even a morsel of coarse sugar[22]

45

Kabir, I *first* thought that learning was good, *then* that the Jog *philosophy* was better than learning ;

But *now* I shall never forsake the service of God, even though men revile me for it.

46

Kabir, how can the wretched people who have no divine knowledge in their hearts, revile me[23] ?

Kabir having abandoned every occupation continueth to repeat God's name.

47

Kabir, the wanderer's skirt hath caught fire on all sides[24] ;

The tattered garment hath been burnt and reduced to charcoal, but the flame hath not touched the waist-string[25]

48

Kabir, the tattered garment hath been burnt and reduced to charcoal, the skull hath burst into atoms ;

The poor Jogi hath had his day, and dust only remaineth where he sat.

49

Kabir, man is like a fish in a little water ; the angler casteth in his net;

Man shall not escape in this little pond ; he ought to think of returning to the Ocean[26]

50

Kabir, leave not the Ocean, though it be very brackish[27].

If thou search for shelter in every pond[28] no one shall call thee good.

51

Kabir, they who had no guru were wafted away ; there was no one to stop them--

Practise meekness and humility[29] come what may.

52

Kabir, the bitch of God's saints is good, but the mother of the infidel is bad ;

The former ever heareth the Lord's name and praises, the latter goeth to commit sin.

53

Kabir, man is like a lean stag ; this world is a lake surrounded by verdure ;

There are hundreds of thousands of hunters and but one life--how long can it escape[30].

54

Kabir, if thou make thine abode on the bank of the Ganges, thou mayest drink pure water ;

But thou shalt not obtain salvation without devotion to God ; the great departed have said this[31].

55

Kabir, me whose mind is pure as Ganges water,
God followeth and addresseth, 'Kabir ! Kabir ! [32].

56

Kabir, turmeric is yellow and lime white ;
When both colours are blended, the beloved God is met[33].

57

Kabir, turmeric then loseth its yellowness, and not a trace of *the whiteness* of lime remaineth ;

I am a sacrifice to that love by which tribe and caste and lineage are effaced.

58

Kabir, the door of salvation is narrow, *the breadth* of the tenth of a grain of mustard;

The mind is *as large as an* elephant,[34] how can it pass through ?

59

Kabir, if I meet a true guru and he kindly favour me,

The door of salvation shall be *made* wide, and I can easily pass through.

Kabir's hut once fell, and people asked him to repair it; the following was his reply :--

60

Kabir, I have no hut or shed; I have no house or village;
I have no caste or name that God should ask who this man is.

61

Kabir, I desire to die, *but* when I die let it be at God's gate,
So that God may ask, 'Who is this lying at My door ?'

62

Kabir, I did not do this, nor will I do it again, nor am I physically able to do it;

How do I know that God may have done ? *Yet* it was all Kabir.[35]

63

Kabir, the skin of my body shall be shoes for his feet
From whose mouth in his muttering dream issueth God's name.

64

Kabir, we are puppets of clay, but bear the name of men ;
Though guests for only four days, we occupy very great space.

65

Kabir, I have converted myself into henna and thoroughly ground myself,

But, even so, God never inquired about me and never allowed me to touch His feet.

66

Kabir, the door from which no visitor is repelled
How shall I leave, since such a door there is ?

67

Kabir, I was drowning, but the wave of good qualities quickly *washed me ashore* and saved me ;

When I saw the bark was rotten, I leapt from it at once.

68

Kabir, the saint is not pleasing to the sinner ; the latter cannot bear the worship of God ;

The fly avoideth the sandal, and goeth where there is an evil odour.

69

Kabir, the physician is dead, the patient is dead, the whole world is dead in *spiritual* ignorance ;

One person alone, Kabir, for whom none shall weep is not dead.

70

Kabir, man meditateth not on God ; such great sin attacheth to him;

The body is a wooden pot ; it cannot be put on the fire a second time[36].

71

Kabir, it so happened to me that God did what was pleasing to my mind[37] ;

Why fear death when thou hast taken the red lead[38] in thy hand ?

72

Kabir, as one sucketh sugar-cane, so ought one to strive most earnestly[39] for virtue ;

None calleth that man good who is without virtue.

73

Kabir, *the body is like* an ear then pot filled with water ; it will burst to-day or to-morrow ;

If thou remember not thy great *God,* thou shalt be plundered half-way[40].

74

Kabir, I am God's dog ' Moti[41] is my name ;

There is a string[42] on my neck ; where I am pulled there I go.

75

Kabir, why displayest thou to men thy wooden rosary ?

If thou remember not God in thy heart, what availeth this rosary ?

76

Kabir, separation from God, like a serpent which yieldeth to no charm, dwelleth in the heart ;

He who is separated from God shall not live, or if he do, he shall become insane[43].

77

Kabir, the philosopher's stone and sandal have one good property *in common* ;

By the touch of the former iron becometh the best *metal*[44]; *by the touch of the latter* inodorous wood is *perfumed.*

78

Kabir, Death's club is bad ; it cannot be endured ;

I have met a holy man[45] and he hath attached me to his skirt.

79

Kabir, the physician, saith, 'I am the only good physician ; *all* medicines are in my power' ;

This thing *life* is God's property,He taketh it when He pleaseth.

80

Kabir, take and beat thy drum for ten days[46] ;

This world is like the meeting on a river-boat *of persons* who shall never meet again[47].

81

Kabir, were I to make the seven oceans my ink, the trees of the forest my pens,

And the earth my paper, I should not *succeed* in writing God's praises.

82

Kabir, what harm can my weaver caste do me since God dwelleth in my heart ?

God hath embraced Kabir, and released him from all his entanglements.

83

Kabir, there are few willing to burn their own houses[48].

Destroy their five children[49] and concentrate their love on God.

84

Kabir, there are few who will set fire to their own bodies[50] ;

Fools understand not though Kabir continueth to shout to them.

85

Kabir, the sati mounted on the pyre crieth out 'Hear my friends on this cremation-ground ;

As people have all departed so do we at last.

86

Kabir, the mind is a bird which flieth and flieth in every direction ;

Man is rewarded according to the company he keepeth.

87

Kabir, the position thou wast seeking thou hast found ;

Thou hast changed into God whom thou thoughtest was different.

88

Kabir, I am dying of evil company like the plaintain near the wild caper ;

The latter waveth and the former is pierced *by its thorns,* so avoid the apostate.

89

Kabir, men[51] affect to travel with the burden of other men's sins on their heads ;

Why fear they not the burden *of their own* since the road in front *of them* is difficult to travel ?

90

Kabir, a standing forest tree[52] which is burning calleth out--

'May I not fall into the power of the smith[53] who would burn me again *in his forge*[54].

One day Kabir was sitting on the bank of the Ganges. He saw a hunter who had shot a deer. The deer had two young ones in her womb. Both these died. The buck then came, and was also shot by the hunter. The latter went to pick up the animal and was mortally bitten by a snake. The hunter's wife then came and died through grief, or because the snake bit her too. Thus died four males and two females.

91

Kabir, on the death of one two died ; on the death of two, four ;

On the death of four, six died--four males and two females[55].

92

Kabir hath seen and searched the world, but found no *abiding* place anywhere ;

Why doth he, who hath not thought of God's name, lose himself in other *speculations* ?

93

Kabir, associate with the saint ; he will save thee at last;

Associate not with the infidel ; his company will be thy ruin.

94

Kabir, knowing that God is everywhere diffused in the world[56] I have remembered Him in this life ;

They who have thought not of God's name, have been born in vain.

95

Kabir, hope in God ; all other hope is hopeless ;

They who are bereft of God's name shall admit *its power* when they fall into hell.

96

Kabir hath made many disciples and followers, but hath not made God his friend ;

He set out to meet God, but his heart failed him half-way.

97

Kabir, what shall poor man do if God assist him not?

Whatever branch I put my foot on bendeth *beneath me.*

98

Kabir, sand shall fall into the mouths of those *who practise not* what they preach to others ;

They watch others property, while their own fields are beign eaten up.

99

Kabir, associate with holy men even though thou eat only barley bran ;

What will be, will be ; associate not with the apostate *even though he give thee better fare.*

100

Kabir, by association with the saints the love of *God* doubleth day by day :

The infidel is like a black blanket ; he becometh not white by washing.

101

Kabir, thou hast not shaved thy heart ; why shave thy hair ?

Man's sins are the work of his heart ; shaving the head is out of place.

102

Kabir, forsake not God ; if thy body and wealth must go, let them go.

They whose hearts are devoted to God's lotus feet, shall be absorbed in His name.

103

Kabir, the strings of the instrument we play upon are all broken[57] ;

What can the poor instrument do when the player[58] hath departed?

104

Kabir, shave the mother of that guru from whom doubt departeth not ;

He is drowned himself in the four Veds and he drowneth his disciples therein.

105

Kabir, man concealeth all the sins he committeth ;

But at last they are all disclosed when Dharmraj maketh his inquiry.

106

Kabir, ceasing to remember God thou hast reared a numerous family ;

Thou continuest to practise thine avocations though thy brethren and relations are no more[59].

107

Kabir, the woman who ceasing to remember God goes to a wake at night[60] *to practise witchcraft,*

Shall be born against as a serpent, and eat her own off-spring[61]

108

Kabir, the woman who ceasing to remember God fasteth in honour of Hoi[62],

Shall be born again as a donkey and carry a weight of four mans[63].

109

Kabir, very great skill is *required* to utter God's *name* in the heart;

If the *acrobat* who performeth on the high pole fall, he cannot survive[64].

110

Kabir, blest is his mouth who uttereth God's *name* ;

His *whole* village shall be blest, *to say nothing of* the poor *creature* himself.

111

Kabir, the family is fortunate in which a slave of God is born ;

The family in which a slave of God is not born shall be *fruitless* as the *dhak*-tree.

112

Kabir *hath seen* hundreds of thousands of horses, elephants, and carriages, and banners wave as thick as clouds--

Begging, when the days pass in remembering God, is better than *all* this state.

113

Kabir, I have traversed the whole world with my drum on my shoulder ;

I have seen and carefully examined[65] everything and *I find* no one hath a friend.

114

Kabir, pearls were scattered on the road ; a blind man came that way *and saw them not* ;

Without the light of the Lord of the world everybody like the blind man passeth the pearls by.

It is said that Kamal, Kabir's son, met a rich leper who was going in despair to drown himself in the Ganges. Kamal bagged him to desist and promised to cure him. Kamal took up some Ganges water in the palm of his hand, breathed on it, repeated the name of God, and then threw the water on the leper. The latter was instantaneously cured. He rewarded Kamal with a large gift of money. In the following couplet Kabir censures his son for having accepted it :--

115

Kabir's family was ruined when his son Kamal was born ;
Ceasing to remember God he brought home wealth.

116

Kabir, go to meet a holy man but take no one with thee[66] ;
Do not go back ; go on, come what may.

117

Blind not thyself, O Kabir, with the rope[67] by which the world is bound ;

As salt is lost in flour, so shall this gold-like body *disappear.*

118

Kabir, the soul shall fly away and the body be buried ; man knoweth not *when his time shall come*[68].

Yet even now he will not let covetousness escape from his eyes.

119

Kabir, may I behold Thee, *O God,* with mine eyes, hear Thy name with mine ears,

Utter Thy name with my tongue, and put Thy lotus feet within my heart !

120

Kabir hath escaped from heaven and hell by the favour of the true guru ;

I bask for ever and ever[69] in the joy of God's lotus feet.

121

Kabir, say how can I guess the joy of God's lotus feet;

Their beauty cannot be described ; it can only be realized when seen.

122

Kabir, even if I see them, to whom shall I describe them ? no one would be satisfied *with my words* ;

God is His own parallel ; I dwell in the delight of singing His praises.

123

Kabir, the kulang pecketh *its food* and at the same time remembereth *its young* ; it pecketh, and pecketh, and pecketh and remembereth *its young* ;

As its young are dear to the kulang, so is worldly love to the mind.

124

Kabir, the sky is overcast with clouds ; lakes and tanks are filled with rain-water ;

Yet what shall be the condition of those who *choose* to remain thirsty as the chatrik[70] ?

125

Kabir, the sheldrake which at night is separated from her mate, meeteth him in the morning ;

But the man who is separated from God meeteth Him again neither in the morning nor in the evening.

126

Kabir, O shell, remain in the ocean ; if thou leave it,

Thou shalt have to scream at sunrise at every temple[71].

127

Kabir, what dost thou, O man, by sleeping ? arise and weep through fear *of hell and its* torments :

How can he whose dwelling is in the grave sleep in peace[72] ?

128

Kabir, what dost thou by sleeping ? why not arise and repeat God's *name*?

One day thou shalt sleep stretched out at full length *in the grave*.

129

Kabir, what dost thou by sleeping ? awake, arise ;

Attach thyself to Him from whom thou art separated.

130

Kabir, leave not the way of holy men, walk on their road ;

Purify thyself by the sight of them, and repeat God's name on meeting them.

131

Kabir, associate not with the infidel ; flee far away *from him* ;

If thou touch a black pot, some filth shall attach to thee.

132

Kabir, thou hast not thought of God, and old age hath come upon thee ;

When the door of thy house is on fire, what can be taken out and saved ?

133

Kabir, the work which the Creator did was accomplished *once for all.*

There is no God *but Him,* the one Creator.

134

Kabir, when the fruit *trees* begin to bear fruit, and the mango beginneth to ripen,

The fruit reacheth its owner if meantime the crows[73] have not eaten it.

135

Kabir, men purchase and worship an idol, and obstinately go on pilgrimages ;

Like actors they imitate one another, but they only err and lose their way.

136

Kabir, men have turned a stone into God ; everybody worshippeth it ;

They who abide in this belief are drowned in the sable stream.

137

Kabir, books[74] form a prison, the doors of which are the writing thereon :

Stones[75] have drowned the world ; pandits have pillaged the road.

138

Kabir, do now the work of to-morrow ; and if thou do it now, do it at once ;

Nothing can be done hereafter when Death standeth over thy head.

139

Kabir, I have seen such and such a person polished like wax[76].

He appeareth quick and very virtuous, but he is without understanding and unholy.

140

Kabir, Death will not disgrace mine understanding[77].

Since I have repeated the name of the Cherisher who created him.

141

Kabir, *God* is as musk ; all His saints are as the bumble-bees *around it* :

The more Kabir's service, the more God dwelleth *in his heart.*

142

Kabir, man falleth into the clutches of family ; God is left in the background :

Dharmraj's myrmidons fall on man in the midst of his pomp.

143

Kabir, better than an infidel is a pig[78] which keepeth the village clean;

When the poor infidel dieth, nobody will mention him.

144

Kabir, men have amassed hundreds of thousands and millions, kauri by kauri ;

But when departing they got nothing ; *even* their waist-cloths are taken from them.

145

Kabir, were one to be a follower of Vishnu and wear a beautiful[79] necklace, what would it avail him ?

He may be externally gold twelve times purified, but within he is only stuffed with wax.

146

Kabir, become the broken stones of the road ; lay aside thine intellectual pride ;

If such a servant there be, he shall meet God.

147

Kabir, *but* what would it avail to be the broken stones ? they would hurt the traveller's feet ;

O God, Thy servant should be as the dust of the earth[80].

148

Kabir, *but* what would it avail to be dust which flieth and falleth on men's bodies ?

The servant of God ought to be like water which *cleanseth* all the limbs[81].

149

Kabir, *but* what would it avail to be water ? it becometh cold or hot *according to the season* ;

Every servant of God ought to be *perfect* like God Himself.

150

Flags wave on the tops of lofty mansions *full* of gold and of women--

Better than all are the bread of alms[82] and singing God's praises in the company of His saints.

151

Kabir, the wilderness where God is worshipped is better than a city;

The place without the beloved God is in my opinion as the city of Death.

152

At the ferry of Sahajsun where the Ganges and the Jamna meet[83]

Kabir hath built a hut where saints and men *of God* seek the way.

153

Kabir, were man to continue to the end *loving God*[84] as he was born.

Millions of precious stones, to say nothing one poor diamond, would not be equal to him.

154

Kabir, I have seen a strange thing--a diamond was sold in a shop ;

In the absence of a purchaser *who knew its worth,* it went for a kauri[85].

155

Kabir, where there is divine knowledge there is virtue ; where there is falsehood there is sin ;

Where there is covetousness there is death ; where there is forgiveness there is God Himself.

156

Kabir, what availeth it to abandon worldly love if pride be not *also* abandoned ?

Munis and their spiritual superiors perished by pride ; their pride ate them all up.

157

Kabir, a true guru met me and shot one word at me ;

When it struck me I fell to the earth ; there was a hole made in my heart.

158

Kabir, what can the true guru do if his disciples be at fault ?

Not one *word* of his impresseth the *spiritually* blind : it is like blowing into a bamboo.

159

Kabir, the lady of a monarch who possesseth horses, elephants, and carriages in abundance,

Is not equal to the female water-carrier of a saint of God.

160

Q. O Kabir, why revilest thou the king's lady ? Why honourest thou God's handmaiden ?

A. The former parteth her hair with evil intentions ; the latter remembereth God's name.

161

Kabir, I propped myself up with *God's name,* and steadied myself; the true guru gave me courage :

I purchased large diamonds on the bank of lake Mansarowar.

162

Kabir, God is the diamond, God's servant the jeweller who hath taken *the gem* and set up a shop *for it* ;

As soon as an assayer is found, the price of the diamond shall be *ascertained.*

163

Kabir, as thou rememberest God when occasion requireth, so remember Him always ;

Make thine abode in the immortal city ; God will restore the wealth thou hast lost.

164

Kabir, for worship two beings are necessary, one the saint, and the other God--

God who bestoweth salvation, and the saint who causeth us to repeat His name.

165

Kabir, crowds followed the pandits by the way they went ;

The one road to God by which Kabir hath been ascending is difficult.

166

Kabir, man acteth out of regard for his family and thus dieth from worldly troubles ;

Who hath family pride when he is placed on the cremation ground?

167

Kabir, O wretched people, ye shall be ruined through your great regard for *the opinion of others* ;

Know that the fate of your neighbours shall also be yours.

168

Kabir, good is the meal of alms made of different kinds[86] of corn ;

I have no claim on any one *for it* ; great is the country and great its government[87].

169

Kabir, heart-burning ariseth from claims ; he who hath no claim is without anxiety ;

He who hath no claim deemeth Indar poor in *comparison with himself.*

170

Kabir, the lake is filled to the brim, yet few can drink the water[88] ;

With great good fortune hast thou found it ; drink it in handfuls, Kabir.

171

Kabir, as the stars pass away in the morning, so doth this body pass away ;

But the two letters of God's name pass not away ; Kabir holdeth them fast.

172

Kabir, the house of wood is on fire on all sides[89] ;
The pandits perish in the fire while the illiterate escape.

173

Kabir, dispel doubts, leave the books of the *pandits* ;
Having searched the Sanskrit books fix thy thoughts on God's feet.

174

Kabir, saints abandon not their saintship, even though they meet millions who are not saints :

Even though sandal be entwined with serpents, it loseth not its coolness[90].

175

Kabir, the mind becometh cool when it hath obtained the knowledge of God :

The fire which burneth the world is as water of God's servant[91].

176

This world is the Creator's play ; hardly any one understandeth this;
The Master Himself or the slave at His court[92] understandeth it.

177

Kabir, it is well for me that I felt the fear *of God* and forgot all else;
From hail I melted into water, and flowing on I blended with the Ocean[93].

178

Kabir, *God* having collected dust made bodies like a *physician's* powders--

Spectacles for four days, but after all they are only dust.

179

Kabir, all bodies are as the rising and setting of the sun and moon[94];
But if they meet not God and the guru, they all turn into dust again.

180

Where the Fearless One is, there is no fear of others ; where there is fear, there God is not :

Kabir speaketh *thus* deliberately ; O saints, give me willing ear.

181

Kabir, they who know naught pass their time in the sleep of peace:

While they who think they know have their fill of trouble.

182

Kabir they who are subdued *by worldly love* utter many cries, but different, the cry of the pir[95] :

Kabir who was struck on a vulnerable spot[96] fell where he stood.

183

Kabir slight is the stroke of a lance ; though struck by it man may breathe *for a time* ;

But he who can endure the stroke of the Word is a guru[97] and I am his slave.

184

Kabir, why, O mulla, ascendest thou the minaret ? the Lord is not deaf :

Search within thy heart for Him for whose sake thou callest to prayer.

185

Why doth the Shaikh who is without resignation, perform a pilgrimage to the Kaaba ?

Kabir, how can God be for him whose heart is not firm *in his faith*?

186

Kabir, offer thy homage to God, by remembering whom trouble shall depart ;

The Lord will be manifest in thy heart, and the fire[98] which burneth thee shall be extinguished.

187

Kabir, to use force is tyranny though thou call it lawful ;

When thine accounts are called for at *God's* office, what shall be thy condition ?

188

Kabir, an excellent dinner is khichari[99] *seasoned* with *sufficient* salt to make it palatable ;

Who would cut his own throat by *eating* meat with his bread[100] ?

189

Kabir, know that the guru will have touched thy heart when worldly love and ambition have been effaced ;

Joy and sorrow shall not then affect thee ; thou *shalt become* God Himself[101] .

190

Kabir, there are different ways of saying Ram[102] ; there is one point to be considered :

He whom everybody calleth Ram was *only* a mountebank[103].

191

Kabir, call Him Ram who is omnipresent ; we must discriminate in mentioning *the two Rams;*

The one Ram (God) is contained in all things ; the other (Ram Chandar) is only contained in one thing, *himself*[104].

192

Kabir, in the house in which saints are not served God is not served;

That house is like a cremation-ground, and ghosts dwell therein.

193

Kabir, I have become dumb, insane, deaf,

And lame from the stroke of the true guru's arrow.

194

Kabir, the brave true guru shot an arrow *at me* ;

On its striking me I fell to the ground with a hole in my heart[105].

195

Kabir, the pure rain of heaven[106] hath fallen on barren soil ;

Know that without good association it becometh like the ashes of a furnace ;

196

But, Kabir, when the pure rain of heaven meeteth absorbing soil[107],

It cannot be removed, however much clever, men may worry themselves.

Kabir, I was going on a pilgrimage to the Kaaba, and I met God on the way ;

The Lord fell a quarrelling with me, Who ordered thee to go to that place ?

198

Kabir, I have often made the pilgrimage to the Kaaba--how many times, O Kabir ?

O my Master, what fault have I committed that Thou wilt not speak to me?

199

Kabir, when God produceth His record, what shall be the fate of him.

Who violently killeth animals and calleth it lawful ?

200

Kabir, to use violence is tyranny ; God will call for thy defence ;

When thine account is produced from His office, thou shalt be beaten on the mouth.

201

Kabir, to render thine account is easy, if thy heart be pure:

In that True Court no one shall molest thee[108].

202

Saith Kabir, O duality in earth and heven thou art very difficult to destroy[109] ;

The six religious systems and the eighty-four Sidhs are involved in doubt.

203

Kabir, whatever there is in me is not mine ; whatever there is, is Thine, *O God*.

If Thine own property be rendered unto Thee, what doth it cost me?

204

Kabir, by repeating, Thou, Thou, I have become Thou, O God ; I have not remained in myself ;

When the difference between Thee and me was removed, wherever I looked there *wast* Thou.

205

Kabir, man meditateth sin and entertaineth delusive hopes ;

None of his desires is satisfied ; he departeth in despair.

206

Kabir, he who remembereth God is happy in *this* world ;

He whom the Creator protecteth wavereth not either in this world or the next.

207

Kabir, I was being pressed like a handful of sesame when the true guru rescued me ;

He came and appeared to me by primal and ancient destiny.

208

Kabir, my days have been spent in evading *payment of my debts to God* ; interest goeth on increasing ;

I worshipped not God, nor had I my account torn up when Death arrived.

Guru Arjan has here inserted the three following couplets:--

209

Kabir, man is a barking dog which runneth after carrion[110] .

By grace I have obtained the true guru who hath delivered me.

210

Kabir, the earth belongeth to the holy, but thieves have taken possession of it ;

The earth feeleth not their weight ; to them it is clear gain[111]

211

Kabir, on account of the husk rice is beaten with a mallet ;

So when men sit in bad company, Dharmraj shall call them to account.

Here Kabir's couplets continue :--

212

O Namdev, worldly love hath bewitched *thee* , said his friend Trilochan ;

Why printest thou chintzes and thinkest not on God ?

213

Namdev replied 'Repeat God's name with thy lips. O Trilochan,

Perform all thy duties with thy hands and feet, *but let* thy heart be with God'.

Guru Arjan again interposes :--

214

O Kabir, no one hath any concern with me nor I with any one ;
I am contained in Him who hath created this world.
Kabir's instructions are resumed :--

215

Kabir, when flour hath fallen into the mud, none of is saved ;
It is that which is chewed while being ground this availeth[112].

216

Kabir, man knoweth everything and yet he knowingly committeth sin ;

What advantage is it to a man to have a lamp in his hand if he fall into a well ?

217

Kabir, my love is for the Friend; foolish people *try* to dissuade me;

How can it be proper to break with Him to whom belong my life and soul ?

218

Kabir, why killest thou thyself on account of houses, and mansions, and their decoration,

When three and a half cubits, or at most three and three quarters, shall be thy lot ?

219

Kabir, if *God* do not what I desire, what availeth my desiring it ;
God doeth what He Himself desireth, not what I desire.

The following couplet of Guru Amar Das, is here found :--

220

God produceth anxiety in man, and also freeth him therefrom ;
Nanak, praise Him who taketh care of all.

A couplet of Guru Arjan here follows :--

221

Kabir, man thinketh not of God ; he goeth astray through greed ;
He dieth committing sin, and his life is at an end in a moment.

Here Kabir's couplets continue :--

222

Kabir, the body is a frail vessel of only frail metal :

If thou wish to make it permanent, worship God, otherwise it will perish.

223

Kabir, call out the name of God ; sleep not listlessly ;

By calling out night and day *God* may sometime hear thy cries.

224

Kabir, the body is a plantain grove, the heart an elephant maddened by passion, which *breaketh it down* ;

The jewel of divine knowledge is the goad, and a rare saint the tamer[113] of the elephant.

225

Kabir, God's name is a jewel, the mouth a purse to hold it ; open it before him who can appreciate *the jewel* ;

If any purchaser be found, he may take it at a high price[114].

226

Kabir, *man* knoweth not God's name while bringing up a numerous family ;

He dieth in the midst of his worldly duties, and is not heard of in the outer *world*.

227

Kabir, in the twinkling of an eye and in a moment life passeth away;

Since the mind freeth not itself from entanglements,

Death beateth his drum, *and leadeth away his victim in triumph*.

228

Kabir, God is as a tree, abandonment of the world as its fruit ;

The saint who hath abandoned bootless discussions[115] as its shade.

229

Kabir, plant the seed of such a *tree* as shall bear perennial fruit.

Whose shade shall be cool, whose fruit shall be profuse, and on which birds[116] shall play.

230

Kabir, the Giver is a tree whose fruit is mercy *which sheddeth* favours on men ;

When the birds which it sheltereth migrate,[117] they say 'O Tree, mayest thou be fruitful !'

231

Kabir, association with saints is obtained by destiny ;

By such association the boon of salvation is obtained, and the difficult road *to God* not obstructed.

232

Kabir, even for a ghari, half a ghari, or half that again, Converse held with the saints is clear gain.

233

Kabir, the mortals who eat bhang and fish[118] and drink wine.

Shall all go to hell, whatever pilgrimages, fastings, and daily devotion they may perform.

234

Kabir, If I cast down mine eyes and take the Friend into my heart.

I enjoy every pleasure with my Beloved, and I disclose this to no one.

The fifth Guru here interposes :--

235

For the eight watches, the sixty-four *gharis* of the day, my soul looketh towards Thee, O God.

Why cast down mine eyes since I behold the Beloved in every heart?

236

Hear, my companions, either my soul dwelleth in my Beloved or my Beloved in my soul.

I know not whether my soul is in my heart, or my Beloved dwelleth in my soul.

237

Kabir, the Brahman is the guru of the world, but he is not the guru of the saints ;

He killeth himself over the perplexities of the four Veds.

238

God is as sugar scattered in the sand, but the elephant cannot pick it up ;

Saith Kabir, the guru gave this excellent advice, 'Become an ant and eat it'[119].

239

Kabir, if thou desire the Beloved, cut off thy head and make it into a ball[120] ;

While playing attain such a state of *ecstasy* that *thou shall be satisfied* with whatever happeneth thee.

240

Kabir, if thou desire the Beloved, play with a true guru.

If unripe oil-seeds be pressed, neither oil-cake nor oil will be obtained[121].

Here a couplet of Namdev is introduced :--

241

Man searching for God stumbleth like a blind man and recognizeth not the saint ;

Saith Namdev, how shalt thou obtain God without the meditation of His saints ?

The following lines of Rav Das are here inserted:--

242

He who forsaking God the diamond yearneth for other gods,
Shall go to hell, verily saith Rav Das.

243

O Kabir, if thou embrace a domestic life, act honestly ; otherwise abandon the world ;

But if any one, having abandoned the world, *again* become entangled *with it*, great indeed shall be his misfortune.

Notes and References

1. This is understood to be a satire on Indian bankers who generally wear large earnings.
2. That is, who practise humility and efface their pride.

3. Also translated--On the day my pride is dead there shall be rejoicing.

4. The *Bulea Frondosa*.

5. It holds its head high, yet it is hollow in the centre.

6. They who are hardened in their pride are not improved by association with the humble.

7. Who has to undergo transmigration.

8. *Maya* here means body, because it is the result of illusion.

9. Put into the churn in India in the hot weather to assist the churning process.

10. Who breaks into the heart, and robs it of its virtues.

11. Others translate--Kabir hath cut her up in twelve pieces.

12. Kabir chased her to arrest her, but she ran in every direction, literally, by twelve ways to avoid him, and so she cannot rob him.

13. Literally--Open not the knots of thy dress in which it is tied.

14. Some understand this line to mean--Whether thou adoptest a worldly or an ascetic life. Sanyasis or hermits shave their heads.

15. Let not thy human birth go in vain.

16. That thou shalt have no more transmigration.

17. Of sin is meant.

18. This was written after witnessing a cremation.

19. Thou mayest be brought low thyself, and men will laugh at thee.

20. In the original none, but this apparently is an exaggeration of religious enthusiasm.

21. This slok is an allegory. By son Kabir meant soul, and by daughter body. Is there any one who will devote his soul and body to God's worship ? Another explanation is the following--Is there any one who will give me his son--his heart--in exchange for my daughter, religious instruction.

22. The pleasures thou hast enjoyed are useless to thee now.

23. That is, what care I for their reviling ?

24. Death has attacked man's body.

25. The soul.

26. The little water and the little pond mean the world. The ocean is God from whom man emanated, and with whom he ought to seek refuge from the angler's net, that is, death.

27. Forsake not God's service even though it be attended with hardship.

28. If thou have recourse to the gods and goddesses of the vulgar.

29. Also translated--make humility thy religion.

30. Man is like a hungry stag let loose on the grassy margin of a lake. He revels in the rich pasture afforded him, has no time for other reflection, and consequently becomes an easy prey to Death the hunter.

31. Also translated--Saying this, Kabir departed from Banaras for Magahar.

32. Also translated--Kabir, God followeth those whose minds are pure as Ganges water, and saith that they are superior to it.

33. Turmeric and lime stand for men of different castes. Turmeric means men of low castes, lime men of high castes. High caste men were originally fair in comparison with the brown aborigines of India. When turmeric and lime are blended, a red product used for sacrificial marks on the forehead results. When holy men of different castes meet, God is obtained by their association, and their castes disappear.

34. Man is very proud.

35. This slok has already been given in the life of Kabir.

36. Human birth shall not be again obtained by those who meditate not on God.

37. God admitted me to His service.

38. That is, why fear death which is imminent and unavoidable ?

39. Literally--to weep and die in one's efforts to obtain it.

40. All the good works you have performed shall only help you halfway ; but if you have meditated on God, you shall be saved.

41. Moti—literally pearl—is a common Indian name for a favourite dog.

42. God's love.

43. The serpent shall sting him, and he shall either die or become insane.

44. Gold.

45. Ramanand.

46. Be happy while you may.

47. Compare--

    The world's a city full of straying streets,

    And death the market-place where each one meets.

48. To mortify their flesh.

49. The five evil passions as dear to men as their children.

50. To subdue their concupiscence.

51. The Brahmans.

52. The body.

53. The god of death.

54. That is, subject me to transmigration after the miseries of this life.

55. This enigmatical couplet is thus explained--On the death of spiritual ignorance, superstition and attachment to worldly things die. When these two evils die, then die lust, anger, worldly love, and covetousness. When these four deadly sins die, then die birth and death (jointly called transmigration), joy, grief, hope and desire. The first four are feminine, the last two are masculine.

56. That is, not in the temple, or the mosque, or in any other place especially set apart for religious worship.

57. The body has grown old, and its limbs have become useless.

58. Life.

59. That is, thou wilt not take warning by the fate of others.

60. After the cremation of a corpse and before the bones are collected strangers go to the burning-place at night, and practise incantations with the object of retaining the ghost of the departed so as to be serviceable to them in their worldly objects. When the relatives of the departed know of the ceremony, they do not allow it.

61. It is supposed that a female snake draws a circle round her eggs and then breaks them herself. The young snakes which can go outside the circle are allowed to depart and live, but those not so able the mother is said to eat.

62. Hoi is a representation of the goddess of small-pox. A festival is held by women in her honour in the month of Kartik, eight days before the Diwali. Unmarried woman make clay images of her with the object of obtaining their desires. These images are thrown into water after the Diwali. In the Panjab Hoi is known as Sanjhi.

63. At that time the man (maund) only weighed thirty-five pounds avoirdupois. At present it weighs eighty pounds.

64. If man, having once entered the path of devotion deflect from it, he shall find no abiding place.

65. *Thok bajana* is to clink a vessel with the middle finger to test its soundness.

66. That is, do not wait for a companion. It may also mean--take not with you a companion who may want you to change your mind, and turn back on the way.

67. Worldly love.

68. Also translated--He expresses his wishes to his relations by signs.

69. Literally--in the beginning and the end.

70. Those who accept not the teaching of holy men which is as plentiful as rain.

71. That is, O man, remain absorbed in the contemplation of God, otherwise thou shalt have to undergo many births. At Hindu temples it is a custom to blow shells in the morning to summon worshippers.

72. Unless we have repented before death.

73. If the evil passions of men do not mar their good works, they shall reach God. *Kanb* is also an insect which destroys fruit. The meaning of the slok is--Man may perform penance and many acts of worship, but all will be unavailing if there be a flaw in his devotion, if his heart be not right.

74. The writings in which idolatry and pilgrimages are prescribed.

75. Idol worship.

76. Bracelets made of white wax are worn by women. They are shown but unsubstantial.

77. That is, he will do as I request him.

78. He is the village scavenger, and is remembered when the poor infidel is forgotten.

79. Also translated--four necklaces as some followers of Vishnu wear.

80. Which is soft, and hurts not the traveller's feet.

81. When soiled by the dust.

82. *Madhukari*. This word is derived from the Sanskrit *madhukar*, the bee which extracts honey from every flower.

83. The gyanis generally translate this--In the sukhmana where the breath of the left and right nostrils meet.

84. The belief is that the foetus in the womb prays to God, but when a child is born and brought into contact with the world, his devotion fails.

85. Divine grace so priceless was spurned by the common herd, and only valued at a kauri.

86. And thus affording variety.

87. That is, the world is wide, and great is the empire of the holy. The words *dawa kahu ko nahin* are also translated--To which no one hath a claim.

88. The saints are filled with holiness, yet for accept instruction from them. The verse is also translated--The lake is full, but there is a dike in front owing to which few can drink the water. The dike means worldly love, which hinders men from having recourse to the guru.

89. That is, evil passions assail the body.

90. As poisonous serpents have no effect on sandal wood, so the evil do not corrupt the holy.

91. The evil passions which inflame mankind produce no impression on him.

92. *Diwani* may also mean divine enthusiast deemed made by the world.

93. Kabir's heart was at first cold and hard as hail. When the fire of divine love shone on it, it melted into water, which, flowing on, blended with the ocean of God.

94. Animals' bodies are born and die.

95. Also translated--Many cry out that they are struck by God's love, but the pain *they exhibit* tells a different story. The word *pir* has two meanings : (a) a priest or saint ; (b) pain.

96. That is, the heart.

97. It can only be endured by a guru.

98. Some read *nai* and translate--The fire *of thy heart* shall be extinguished by God's name.

99. Rice and *dal* boiled together.

100. Kabir was a vegetarian, and objected to the slaughter of animals.

101. Thou shalt have no consciousness of existence distinct from God.

102. Ram is the name of God throughout Kabir and the other Bhagats compositions. Sometimes Har, Hari, Gobind, and other names are used, but it is understood that the reference is always to the Supreme God, the Lord of creation.

103. Although in some of their hymns Kabir and some of the other Bhagats of the Granth Sahib appears to have believed in the Hindu incarnations, they occassionally ridiculed them.

104. Some Sikhs translate this and the preceding shloka as follows:-

Kabir, there are different ways of uttering Ram ; in this there is an important point.

People in general utter Ram one way, and the saints another way.

Kabir, utter Ram, Ram, but use discrimination in uttering it.

Some *while doing so* are engaged in their various *pursuits* while others are absorbed in the one God.

105. That is, the guru's exhortation made an impression on my heart.

106. The true guru's instruction.

107. When the guru's instruction is communicated to men capable of receiving it.

108. Literally--catch thee by the coat.

109. If *tubari* be read as one word, the translation will be--In earth and heaven there are two beggar's bowls--desire and covetousness--difficult to destroy.

110. Literally--a skeleton.

111. In this line if *bharan,* be read as one word, the translation will be The earth feeleth their weight: *O God,* remove them.

112. Human life is the time for man to work out his salvation. It is too late when the soul has departed.

113. *Khewal,* literally--the pilot who steers the elephant.

114. He may even give his life for it.

115. The saint, like a tree's shade, affords comfort to man.

116. Holy men.

117. The saints wander abroad to blazon God's goodness.

118. In Kabir's time the Banaras pandits used to partake largely of fish.

119. The humble succeed where the proud fail.

120. Such is the sacrifice that must be made to enable man to play with the saints, and share in their bliss.

121. Nothing can be obtained from a false guru's instruction.

Index

A

Abhimanyu, 47.
Adi Granth, 73-75.
Akbar, 1, 9, 241.
Amar Das, Guru, 275.
Ansuya, 34.
Arjun, 47.
Arjun Dev, Guru, 99.
Ayodhya, 32, 34, 57.

B

Bairagi, Krishan Das, 127.
Balwa, 63.
Baghela, Vir Singh, 59.
Balwinder Singh, 70.
Banaras, 5, 15, 47, 49, 50, 52, 55, 58, 61, 65, 70, 89, 97, 105.
Bandali, 63.
Bandogarh, 65.
Bangladesh, 98.
Bankhandi, Bairagi, 35.
Bengal, 113.
Bhagirathi River, 3.
Bhagwan Das, 98.
Bhaktas of Vishnu, 44.
Bhakti Movement, 101.
Bhattacharya Vidhusekhra, 113.
Bhima, 3.
Bihar, 113.
Bijli Khan, 12, 59.
Brahmadev, 1.
Brahmanism, 73.
Brahmans of Banaras, 4, 5, 31, 50, 51, 56, 78, 83, 101, 106.
Burhanpur, 19.

C

Central India, 62.
Central Provinces, 62.
Chhattisgarh District, 62.
Churaman, 66.
Churamani, 72.
Couplet of Namdev, 278.

D

Dadu Panthis, 60.
Dadu, Saint, 60.
Das Gupta, Dr. 113.
Dattatreya, 83.
Derawali, 82.
Dhania, 37.
Dharam Das, Mahant, 60, 64-66, 71.
Dhiraj, 72.
Diamond, 3.
Dwarka, 223.
Dwivedi, Hazari Prasad, Dr., 114.

F

Farid, Seikh, 99.
Female Bairagis, 64.
Fide Khan, Nawab, 62.

G

Gandhiji, 16, 116, 117.
Ganga, 3, 4, 35, 36, 260, 263.
Ganpati, 34.
Giri Raj Singh, Dr., 47.
Gorakh Nath, 83.
Gorakhpur, 57, 59, 62, 105.
Govind, 26, 29.
Govind Singh, Guru, 99.
Guru Granth Sahib, 18, 60, 224.

H

Hastanapur, 2.
Hindi Literature, 105.
Hindi Pandits, 113.
Hindi Places of Pilgrimage, 8, 194.
Hindu Sadhus, 63.
Hinduism, 16.
Hindus, 59, 78, 87, 101, 218.
Hiranyaksh, 82.

I

Indian Nationalistic Literature, 16.
Italian Cleric, 16.

J

Jabalpore, 65.
Jagannath, 62.
Jatayu, 47.
Jaydev, 10.
Jhali, Queen, 61.
Jiwa, 56.
Jugla Nand, 66.

K

Kabir Bani, 19.
Kabir Bijak, 60, 73-78, 108.
Kabir Chaura, 55, 62, 63, 70, 72.
Kabir Granthavali, 108, 113, 114.
Kabir Ki Vichardhara, 112.
Kabir's Aerostic, 157.
Kabir's Couplets, 276.
Kabir's Lunar Days, 165.
Kabir's Panthis, 61, 65, 67, 69, 70.
Kabir's Sacred Remains, 59.
Kabir's Sanctity, 50.
Kabir's Self Abasement, 202.
Kabir's Slokas, 249.
Kabir's Super Human Power, 56.
Kabir's Week Days, 168.
Kamal, 44, 45, 47, 61, 64, 184, 263.
Kashi, 8, 82.
Kashi Nagari Pracharini Sabha, 100.
Khurswal, 63.
King of Banaras, 59.
Koodarmal, 66.
Krishna, 82.
Kshatriyas, 82.
Kusha, 1.

L

Lahar Lalao, 55.
Lahartala, 7, 8.
Lahartara, 106.

Lakshmi, 7, 8.
Lava, 1.
Literature on Life and Teachings of Kabir, 108.
Lodi, Bahlol, 53.
Lodi Sikandar Khan, 12, 52, 105.

M

Maghar, 57-59, 62.
Mahaprabhu Chaitanya, 17.
Mammon, 182, 209.
Manikarnika Ghat, 3.
Math of Puri, 62.
Maths of Kabir, 62, 63.
Mathura, 60, 82.
Mela at Math, 65.
Muhammad Hidaytulla, 21, 25.
Muhammadam Math, 63.
Muslin Invaders, 73.

N

Nabhaji Bhagatmal, 23, 24.
Namdev, 10, 99.
Nanak Guru, 12-14, 17, 18, 99, 101.
Narayan, 1.
Narbada, 56.
Nathas, 107.
Niru, 5, 6, 8, 9.
Northern India, 62, 73, 105.

P

Panchanga Ghat, 28.
Philosophy of Kabir 108.
Picture of Rangidas, Mahant, 64.
Powers of Brahmins, 73.
Prahlad, 1.
Pramodh Nams, 72.
Puran Das, Baba, 99.
Puranas, 87, 193.

Q

Queen of Chittor, 61.
Quran, 87.

R

Rag Maru, 224.
Rama, 1, 26, 29, 32, 45, 76.
Rama Krishna Mission, 16.
Ramanand, 5, 7, 11, 12, 14, 17, 28-30, 56, 58, 107, 170.
Ramanuja Acharya, 17.
Ramayan, 1, 2.
Ramjaniya, 37.
Ramini Kabir, 107.
Ratan, 60.
Rav Das, Saint, 46, 278.

S

Salagram, 82.
Samadhis of Mahants, 64.
Sarjit, Pt. 55, 56.
Shaikh Tagi, 52.
Shiva, 3, 8, 106.
Shuka, 4.
Shukla, Ramchandra, Acharya, 113.
Shyam Sunder Das, Baba, 100, 112.
Sikh Gurus, 61.
Siddhas, 107.
Singh, Mohan. Dr., 11.

Sudh Nidhan, 72.
Sudras, 50.
Sukh Dass, 70.
Sukhdev, 241.
Sukrit Dhyan, 65.
Sultan Sikandar, 14.
Superiority of God, 203.
Surat Goapl, 61, 69.

T

Tagore, Rabindranath, 100.
Tata, Brahman, 56.
Teg Bahadur, Guru, 99.
Tiwari, Paras Nath, Dr., 108.
Tiwari, R.P. 108.
Tribhuvannatji, 38.
Trigunayat, Dr., 113.
Tulsidas, 2.

U

Udhav, 1.
Ugranam, 66.
Upanishads, 116.

V

Vaikunth, 33.
Vajrana Buddhists, 116.
Valmiki, 1, 2.
Vashisht, Indu, 106.
Vata-Savitri, 14.
Vedas, 87, 193, 214.
Verma, Ram Kumar, Dr., 108, 112.
Vichardas, 114.
Vishnu, 4, 7, 8, 37, 38, 45.
Vishnu Bhakta, 4.
Vishwanath, 114.
Vyas, 83.

W

Worship of Maya, 172.

Y

Yog Sadhna, 107.

❑❑❑